SACRAMENTAL THEOLOGY
for a Modern and Future World

SACRAMENTAL THEOLOGY

for a Modern and Future World

The Seven Sacraments in History and in The Christian Community

MICHAEL DEBUS

Translated by James H. Hindes

Lindisfarne Books | 2022

Lindisfarne Books
An imprint of SteinerBooks / Anthroposophic Press, Inc.
402 Union Street, No. 58, Hudson, NY 12534
steinerbooks.org

 Translated by James H. Hindes from the original German volume *Auferstehungskräfte im Schicksal. Die Sakramente der Christengemeinschaft* (Urachhaus, 2011).

Book design by Jens Jensen

Front cover image: *Ascension,* watercolor painting by Ninetta Sombart, with kind permission of Raffael-Verlag and the family, 45cm x 45cm.
Photograph © Thomas Spalinger

Library of Congress Control Number: 2021949367
ISBN: 978-1-58420-898-3 (paperback)

Printed in the United States of America

Contents

Translator's Preface

There are many books on sacramental theology—some orient themselves toward a specific denomination, while others aspire to rigorous academic objectivity. Some also serve as an introduction to a particular branch of Christianity, and although Michael Debus's book could serve that purpose well, its integration of theological developments through the centuries with a discussion of the evolution of consciousness* makes it unique. Human beings have not only thought different ideas through the millennia; the very way in which thinking takes place in the mind, our relationship to our thoughts and to ourselves, to God and the angelic hierarchies, has changed dramatically. This evolution accounts for our modern insistence on the spiritual autonomy of individuals.

Clearly, there is no place for dogmatic authority in churches today. But does that mean there is no place for churches? In 1922, forty-five young people (average age, twenty-eight) felt strongly there is a place in the modern world for corporate Christian worship. With the help of Rudolf Steiner (1861–1925), they founded The Christian Community, Movement for Religious Renewal, and went forth into the world establishing congregations with the seven sacraments in a new form. Anthroposophy, representing the

* The best succinct presentation of the evolution of consciousness, a much-misunderstood concept, is found in Owen Barfield's book *Saving the Appearances: A Study in Idolatry* (1988). A less arduous introduction would be Barfield's *History in English Words*, a depiction of words' changing meaning through time.

worldview of Rudolf Steiner, supported and, in many cases, even enabled their understanding of Christianity as they established a new priesthood. They began preaching Jesus Christ as lord and savior, performing sacraments and rituals to mediate his blessing power and to comfort and aid individuals seeking pastoral care. Since then, congregations have been established across Europe, from Russia to Ireland, from Finland to Italy and Spain. They can also be found in southern Africa, Australia, New Zealand, Japan, as well as North and South America.

From the outset it was clear that this new movement was not to be seen as an extension of the Anthroposophical Society, although it has been called a daughter movement. Although he gave essential advice on how a church with a priesthood should function in our time, The Christian Community was not founded by Rudolf Steiner. He himself used the word "inaugurate" to indicate his role, meaning to mark its beginning. The actual founding initiative came from the aforementioned forty-five men and women. Anthroposophy is concerned with acquiring knowledge of the spiritual world. The Christian Community is a church for those seeking Christ, that is, for everyone regardless of any interest in "esoteric" knowledge. Confusing the two movements would be destructive to both, insofar as anthroposophy was never meant to be a religion, and The Christian Community's task is to foster a personal, living experience of Jesus Christ.

However, in my forty-six years working as a Christian Community priest I have frequently been confronted by anthroposophists who upbraided the church for having so many Society members, as if priests' efforts to preach the Gospel were somehow aimed at anthroposophists. The facts are very different. Many people have found Christian Community services to be a place where they can worship God, where they can feel Christ's presence, which compels them to return. Eventually, they discover our book tables and libraries, with many books and pamphlets describing the Gospels, the sacraments, and altogether the meaning of life on earth. These written materials frequently rely on spiritual insights originating in anthroposophy, through which newcomers then discover Rudolf Steiner. Frequently they enthusiastically begin drinking from the cup of wisdom given to humanity through anthroposophy and decide to join the Anthroposophical Society. But they also continue attending services at the church. The most insightful concepts alone rarely supplant the actual experience of Christ. However, as Debus points out, the two support each other just as head and heart supplement one another. Of course, in an age of spiritual autonomy, no one is forced to go to church, nor to pursue spiritual knowledge; neither should anyone be criticized for seeking one or the other or both simultaneously.

The Christian churches existing in 1922 balked at the idea that any spiritual wisdom could be obtained by individuals, rather than by an authoritative ecclesiastical body. Subjective spiritual intuitions might still be experienced by mystics, but any revelation of spiritually objective facts had ended long ago. Traditional theologians of the dominant churches were offended by the very idea that it is possible for someone "to understand any part of the mind of God," that is, to see into the spiritual world. The very claim that deeper ("esoteric") knowledge was possible was not even for individuals to evaluate, for allowing such private decisions would amount to denying church authority. Rudolf Steiner's life work, his description of a path to higher knowledge, was declared anathema, and his books and lectures were put on the index of forbidden reading for Catholics. The Lutheran church declared that the new sacrament of Baptism was not even Christian, a pronouncement upheld even today.

Michael Debus's book addresses many of these questions, examining them in the context of not just sacramental theology, but theology altogether, as it has evolved together with human consciousness through time. In doing so he naturally employed many of the most esoteric sounding yet essential concepts and distinctions presented by Rudolf Steiner. There was no alternative. Although many new-age movements have broken through antiquated conceptual barriers and brought significant insights that facilitate a deeper appreciation of modern reality, none of them, to my knowledge, have satisfactorily explained (in detail!) how our physical, material world is interwoven with the spiritual world. For those seeking the spirit, just such an understanding is essential in our materialistic age. The task of a church is to mediate between heaven and earth, between spirit and matter. The spiritual worldview given by Rudolf Steiner has made it possible for many people today to find new meaning in these words that characterize this great polarity of our time, the world of the senses and the world of the spirit. Debus's book can serve as an example for how anthroposophical terminology is necessary in order to make the conceptual distinctions essential for understanding sacramental processes. Just such processes that are *both physical and spiritual* otherwise elude theological understanding.

Here follows a brief disquisition on translating this book and anthroposophy in general.

The German word for *community* is the same word used for *congregation*: *Gemeinde*. Every instance required a decision as to which English word best fit the context. Occasionally, when both meanings were intended, I chose the more encompassing word *community*. This is relevant to the actual name of our movement, *Die Christengemeinschaft*, which is translated as *The Christian Community*—although the literal translation would be *The Community of Christians*. Over the decades there has been much discussion within the church whether the translation should perhaps be more literal. This distinction has important implications for Debus's discussion of The Christian Community's relationship to other churches, found in part 1, section 1.

The German word *Kultus* with its adjectival form *kultische* are translated in academic theology as *cult* or *cultus* and *cultic*. Although the technical meaning of *cult* is "a system of religious beliefs and ritual," its modern derogatory implications, which do not adhere to the German *Kultus*, led me to translate it as *ritual* in most instances.

The word *Geist* comes up repeatedly when translating German theological texts or the work of Rudolf Steiner. It can mean *mind, intellect, wit, spirit, ghost*, etc., all of which concern the human mind. It can refer to simple mental activity or the presence of the (a) spirit, or both. There is much room for misunderstanding, especially when *Geist* is found in the compound noun *Geisteswissenschaft*, which can be translated literally as *science of the spirit* or *spiritual science*, both of which in English easily sound like oxymorons. *Science,* from the Latin, *to know,* has evolved in English to refer exclusively to laboratory sciences such as physics, chemistry, biology, etc., that is, investigations of the world of the senses. Hence, it is not necessarily self-evident for English speakers that *science* can also be applied to things of the mind, such as philosophy or theology. Yet, *Wissenschaft* also describes the mental activity carried out to acquire knowledge of anything. The standard translation of *Geisteswissenschaft* is *humanities* or *liberal arts*. But for theology or anthroposophy this is totally inadequate. Here the language itself displays most clearly Steiner's claim that actual knowledge of spiritual matters is possible. The challenge to his translators then is to convey this claim in such a way that does not lend itself to immediate dismissal.

Another headache for any translator of anthroposophical terminology is *Wesensglieder,* usually found combined with *Mensch* as *Menschlich Wesenglieder*. The most literal translation is *human being's limbs of being* or *human being's essential limbs;* second choice for a literal translation would be *human being's members of being*. The word *Glied* (English, *limb* or *member*) serves as a picture in German for the *parts, aspects, elements, components, features, sheaths, facets* or *qualities of an organic whole*. Any or all of those meanings might be appropriate. This word, not found in any German–English dictionary, was created by Rudolf Steiner to describe the four essential components of a human being: *physical body, etheric body, astral body*, and *"I,"*—i.e., *ego*. Due to the fact that not all of these bodies are material, the word *body* seems inappropriate. In medical contexts *Wesensglieder* has accurately been translated as *higher organizing processes*, which draws attention to their functions rather than their bodily nature. Sometimes the word *sheath* is used as in *human being's sheaths*. A *sheath* is a structure that closely envelops something. Each of these bodies provides a *sheath,* or *vehicle,* for the higher members.

Wesensglieder underscores Rudolf Steiner's difficulty in finding earthly words for spiritual things, which are not things but processes, activities or even gestures of spiritual beings. One could say that it is no accident that he thought and wrote in German, which allows for countless neologisms simply by combining existing words. I have resorted to a number of linguistic circumlocutions in dealing with *Wesensglieder*. Because it is usually referring to the four bodies or members of a human being I use, when possible, the words *human bodily nature*, implying all four members, bodies or sheaths.

Another perennial translation challenge is the German prefix *Ur-* (as in *Urbild*), variously translated as *archetypal image*, *archetype, primitive, prototype, pre-image,* or *prefiguration*. The basic idea contained in *Ur-* is twofold: *original*, as in first, and *proto*, as in first and thus establishing the basic dynamic for what follows. A translator must use many different words depending on context.

I have kept *The* capitalized in all references to *The Christian Community, Movement for Religious Renewal* in order to eliminate ambiguity and because it is the official name of our church.

Debus's references to Rudolf Steiner's collected works are to the German edition, the *Gesamt Ausgabe* (GA). Each volume has a number. Because English translations have only recently begun to correlate exactly to the German GA volume, finding an English edition location for his references would have been prohibitively time intensive. However, in many instances, readers seeking them will be able to track them down in English. Translations from the New Testament are mine, unless otherwise noted.

Introduction

"What Christ Jesus taught is not what is most important, but rather what he has given humanity. His resurrection is the birth of a new faculty within human nature." —Rudolf Steiner

This book is intended to contribute to the sacramental theology of The Christian Community, Movement for Religious Renewal, which was founded in 1922. Feeling unable to connect with what was handed to them from the past, its founders intended to begin something entirely new in the history of Christianity. New names also had to be created in order to avoid confusion with the past. For example, for years, many of the founders rejected the word *church,* because it seemed to point to a relic that was no longer relevant. This inner orientation toward the future is still the most important characteristic of The Christian Community, but in the meantime we can see more clearly that its understanding of its role in the world needs to be refined. The Christian Community is not only a *creation out of nothing* but is rather embedded in a certain stream within the development of Christianity, which Rudolf Steiner once referred to as the *church stream.* He also formulated the principle of continuity for spiritual streams: that a new spiritual impulse must always connect in some form with what has preceded it, if it is to become fruitful for the world. The Christian Community must be able to account for where it spiritually connects with the past, without allowing itself to be determined by the past.

With this in mind our intention is to examine the evolution of sacramental theology to find practices and concepts that can be understood as the foundation stones for a new sacramental understanding. In particular, we seek to discover where developments in human consciousness over the course of the last two millennia require an entirely new starting point.

From the new perspective that arises out of the examination of the nature of sacramentalism (parts 1 and 2), we will discuss the sacraments of The Christian Community in detail (part 3). We will be less concerned with practical congregational issues than with an understanding of the spiritual processes that come to expression in each ritual. The Sacrament of Marriage will be an exception, for with this sacrament, it seems necessary to approach the theme more intensely from its practical, concrete side. Furthermore, the chapters in that section do not follow a uniform pattern and are developed in detail unevenly, in part with longer inserts (Baptism), in part concentrating on essential, basic elements (Act of Consecration of Man). At the end we consider the whole again, but with an increased understanding of renewed sacramentalism. Those readers interested primarily in individual sacraments could also begin with part 3.

This book is intended for readers interested in the spiritual foundations of The Christian Community and its place in the history of theology. In general, a certain familiarity with the basics of anthroposophy is assumed; for example, when it comes to the various sheaths of the human bodily nature—i.e., physical body, etheric body, astral body and "I," ego or self. Furthermore, in a study such as this, it is sometimes necessary to introduce more detailed points of view derived from the anthroposophical worldview. It must be mentioned that anthroposophy as such is not, in a narrower sense, the source of The Christian Community's theology, but for many important questions, anthroposophy does offer crucial insights that help one to understand the issues better.

The present book has a history. It began in 1969 at the Priest Seminary of The Christian Community in Stuttgart, Germany, when Gottfried Husemann* commented with regret during a class that The Christian Community has until then not developed its own sacramental theology. This reflected the fact that most of the founders of The Christian Community came out of Protestantism and for this reason concerned themselves more at the beginning with a new understanding of the Gospel. Here, too, Rudolf Steiner offered a wealth of suggestions with respect to that task. Those first forays into theology have led to numerous remarkable publications in books and periodicals, even into the present time. However, efforts to better understand the sacraments have been largely limited to the fundamentals and introductory literature. Had there been more founders coming from a Catholic background, then the theological emphasis on these two areas would presumably have been otherwise—perhaps even reversed. The first seed for a theology specializing in the sacraments was planted by Rudolf Frieling† in a short essay that appeared in 1939 in the periodical *Die Christengemeinschaft*. This was not developed further, not even by Frieling himself.

The thoughts expressed here have not arisen from

* Gottfried Husemann (1900–1972) was a co-founder of The Christian Community and the first director of the priest seminary founded in 1933 in Stuttgart.

† Rudolf Frieling (1901–1986) was a co-founder of The Christian Community and beginning in 1960 its leader. The essay has since appeared as a reprint. See the bibliography.

personal studies alone; they came about through almost thirty years of teaching at The Christian Community priest seminary in Stuttgart; they are the result of dialogue with students and other teachers. They do not claim to be the final word on this topic, but rather seek to stimulate additional dialogue in this important area of theology. For this reason, I would like to thank numerous students as unnamed coauthors in the background. Then I would like to extend my gratitude to the students, colleagues and coworkers at the priest seminary in the summer semester of 2005 for making a ten-week absence possible, and to Dorothea and Michael Schmidt for a place to live on their farm in Ontario while writing this book; my gratitude goes out also to those who read and gave helpful comments on this work during its creation. Heartfelt thanks to Arnold Suckau in particular for a critical first reading of the manuscript and for the valuable theological advice he provided. Finally, I would like to thank Dr. Wolfgang Niehaus for encouraging this project from the beginning and for accompanying it through to the end as an insightful, knowledgeable reader.

PART I:
UNDERSTANDING SACRAMENTS FOR A MODERN AGE

Chapter 1

Renewed Sacraments in the Development of Christianity

Since 1922, the seven sacraments have been celebrated in a renewed form. They stand at the center of the work of The Christian Community, which was founded as a *Movement for Religious Renewal.* Because religious renewal has been a constantly recurring theme in the evolution of the Christian church it may at first appear that The Christian Community belongs in a series of reform movements reaching into the past. Especially toward the end of the Middle Ages the call for reform was growing, as internal and external conditions of the church corresponded less and less to human beings' changing consciousness and the infamous state of ecclesiastical affairs was worsening. With increasing vehemence an internal purification of the church was expected by church and civil authorities while the call for "reform of the church in head and members"* grew louder and louder. Thus began the reform councils;† through four centuries they repeatedly dealt with the same questions, but with little effect—the necessary breakthrough was not achieved. Eventually, instead of a reform of the church, the

* These words were used for the first time at the 1311/12 council of Vienna.

† Five councils held in Lateran (1123, 1139, 1179, 1215, 1512–1517), the council at Constance (1414–1418) and the council of Basel/Ferrara/Florence, beginning in 1431.

Reformation broke out, initiated by the priest-monk Martin Luther (1482–1546). At first, Luther also wanted nothing more than to reform the existing church. For this reason, wherever the Reformation took hold, it was understood that the same church buildings would be used and, at first, the same ordained *Catholic* priests would be speaking at the same altars, albeit with different words. However, to the extent that they were protected by sovereign princes, these priests took the liberty of finally beginning with longed-for reforms. In so doing they freed themselves from the authority of Rome, committing apostasy in the eyes of the Pope, whom they vehemently rejected; in the eyes of Martin Luther, the Pope was the Antichrist residing in Rome.

Thus, a process began that eventually led to unintended consequences. At first, the Reformation's goal was internal and ecclesiastical, but ultimately it nevertheless led to the foundation of another, *second* church. What had been unthinkable in the Middle Ages became a reality; earlier it was impossible to conceive of *Church* in the plural, for there was only *one* Church for all Christians.

It could be objected that the great Schism had already occurred in the eleventh century with the separation between the Eastern Orthodox Church and the Western Roman Catholic Church. Nevertheless, despite all the painful feelings connected with the event, the separation was (and still is) not understood to have created two Churches, but rather a separation within the one Church. The priests in the Eastern Church stand in the same recognized line of apostolic succession as the priests in the Western Church; their performance of the sacraments is still valid in the eyes of the Roman Catholic Church. The understanding that it is a separation within the one church allows full Communion with Orthodox churches.* It is thus only through the Reformation that a second church arose, one in which the foundational facts of the Catholic Church have been nullified.† However, entirely in keeping with the consciousness that belongs in the Middle Ages, the Catholic Church's understanding is that a second church cannot even exist. Consequently, Protestants stand outside the one Church, and full Communion with that church is not possible. In any case, the Protestant Baptism *can* be recognized, because *in an emergency* Baptism can be performed without any connection to the ordained priesthood.

As the reformers based everything entirely on the Bible as the *word of God,* sermons acquired unprecedented significance in Christianity, used as both proclamation and edification within a church service. This was completely in keeping with a new state of human consciousness on the threshold of the modern age when people increasingly began to feel the need to form their own judgments, particularly in religious matters. Of course, this conscious awareness of one's own spiritual autonomy is still entirely appropriate for today, but this meant that Protestantism lost the Mass; additionally, most ritual elements have disappeared from church services.‡

* According to Catholic church law the possibility exists of a limited sacramental fellowship for the following sacraments: Eucharist (Lord's Supper with Communion), Confession and Anointing of the sick.

† The basic change is seen in the fact that there is no longer any ordained, consecrated priesthood. Protestant ministers are not found in the line of apostolic succession. Of the seven sacraments from the church in the Middle Ages Luther retained only Baptism and the Lord's Supper, because he could find grounds for them alone in the Bible. His doctrine of the Eucharist rejects the idea that bread and wine are actually transformed into the body and blood of Christ, the Transubstantiation.

‡ To be sure, there are several areas of Protestantism in the twentieth century that do again include liturgical elements. See, for example,

Furthermore, the understanding of sacraments prevailing until then in the (Catholic) Church was abandoned.

Given this historical background, we can ask ourselves how The Christian Community sees itself in the stream of Christian development. From the beginning, its stated mission, the renewal of the religious life, was not intended as an internal renewal of any Church (nor as a reform), even though several of its most influential founders were Protestant theologians. Friedrich Rittelmeyer even held a leading position within the Lutheran church. The idea of a "Third Church" (from Schelling*) played a certain role for the founders. This Third Church was understood to be a future-oriented synthesis of Catholicism and Protestantism, much like the Johannine church that followed the Petrine and Pauline forms of Christendom.† Johannes Werner Klein was the one in whom this ideal first came to life.‡ Yet a correct understanding of The Christian Community does not confirm this picture: it certainly does not wish to be any kind of Third Church, at least not in the same way as the Catholic and Evangelical Lutheran Church in Germany. For many priests in The Christian Community the word *church* even had a

---

Walter Birnbaum, *Das Kultusproblem und die liturgischen Bewegungen des 20. Jahrhunderts*; and Wilhelm Stählin, *Berneuchen antwortet.*

* Cf. Goebel, *Schelling: Künder einer neuen Epoche des Christentums*, pp. 118ff.

† Eberhard Kurras, *Christus-Erfahrungen: Petrus–Paulus–Johannes.*

‡ Already in 1919, he wrote in a letter: "The ideal that stands before me is the institution of a great, spirit-bearing, Christian Church for all the people. You know my reverence for the Catholic ritual as the protector of true, great mysteries.... But as a man I stand before the fact that the Catholic Church has failed, like every other.... It rules through authority, enlivened with the power of the mysteries.... We demand the achievements of Protestantism for everyone: spiritual freedom and freedom of conscience.... A new church can be built only upon anthroposophic ground" (Gädek, *Die Gründer der Christengemeinschaft*, p. 89).

negative connotation for a very long time—they preferred to refer to The Christian Community not as a church, but as a movement (for religious renewal), despite their creed clearly naming the Church as a crucial fact in its eleventh sentence: "Communities whose members feel the Christ within themselves may feel united in a Church to which all belong who are aware of the health-bringing power of the Christ." These words can illuminate what is meant by the word *church*, for although this new kind of church is something very different from an earthly based medieval church, it nevertheless has no plural. It is *the one Church* that *all true Christians* belong to. Insofar as there are undoubtedly many different congregations and communities "whose members feel Christ within themselves," The Christian Community recognizes communities—not Churches—that confess Christianity. Furthermore, there could hardly be any reason for The Christian Community to judge other communities with respect to their Christianity, for what makes a community Christian is the actual people who "feel the Christ within themselves."* For this reason, baptisms performed in other faith communities are not generally judged by The Christian Community with respect to their validity, nor in terms of how Christian they might be. At most, such a judgment might be thinkable with regard to individuals—that is, whether or not someone is a *true* Christian—but such a state of soul is so intimate that it falls outside the scope of any external evaluation and would be for God alone to judge.

* Translator's note: The German name of The Christian Community is *Die Christengemeinschaft*. As a compound noun its two parts are nouns, not adjectives. The most accurate translation would therefore be *The Community of Christians*. In 1928, when the movement came to the English-speaking world, it was decided that a simpler appellation would be more appropriate. Hence, the word *Christian* became an adjective.

Ultimately, when it comes to communities that confess Christianity, the question arises: Was the path to a relationship with Christ Jesus cultivated within such communities appropriate for our time? In other words: Is there a concrete relationship to the spiritual world (not just theoretical and abstract) beyond the world of senses, and is there complete freedom of conscience and freedom of thought in the realm of religion? Simply put: Is there a concrete experience of "God in spirit,"* and does absolute religious freedom exist? The Christian Community exists only because there are people who seek a path to Christ appropriate for this time in Earth's history.

When we speak here of *renewed sacraments,* we do not mean that something already existing has been reformed, for it is not the case that the Roman Catholic or Orthodox sacraments have somehow been revised by The Christian Community. It also cannot be said that The Christian Community grew out of or is derived from any existing church. To say it directly and simply, The Christian Community has come forth from the revelation of Christ in our time. Christ's revelation did not end with his appearance 2,000 years ago, as formulated once again by the Catholic Church in 1965 at the second Vatican Council (1962–1965)† but continues from age to age. Patristic age Christianity had a different form from that of the Reformation and reached yet another stage in the twentieth century. Today we call his progressive movement through time the *second coming.*

* John 4:23.

† "The Christian dispensation, therefore, as the new and definitive covenant, will never pass away and we now await no further new public revelation before the glorious manifestation of our Lord Jesus Christ." *Dogmatic Constitution on Divine Revelation*, chap. 1, article 4. Nov. 18, 1965.

It is the source of true renewal in Christianity, out of which the *one* Christian Church can be established today. It is also the source of ritual forms appropriate for the modern age as well as the origin of the succession of a priesthood at work on the earth. The renewed seven-fold nature of the sacraments also originates from this source. Powerful spiritual assistance was necessary in order for The Christian Community to come into being; namely, it required a man who had fully conscious access to this spiritual source, someone perhaps comparable to Moses who received the Levitical rituals from Yahweh on Mount Sinai. In that same way, Rudolf Steiner was the crucial midwife for the birth of The Christian Community.

The essential elements of the rituals of The Christian Community, their words and gestures, were not created by human beings—e.g., by a committee of theologians—but rather they originated from Christ's revelation, mediated by a human being. With respect to their Christian content, for The Christian Community they have the same order of priority as the New Testament, which also originated through Christ's revelation. The Christian Community acknowledges no other source of revelation. This statement seems necessary because the assumption, or even sometimes the assertion, is often expressed (above all by theologians from other Christian streams) that The Christian Community has anthroposophy as a second and possibly more important source of revelation above and beyond the New Testament. This is not true. Altogether, anthroposophy is, by its very nature, a (spiritual) science; that means entirely grounded in human reason. Of course, this assumes that the human capacity for knowledge can be expanded beyond the kind of thinking bound to the world of the senses. In this case, anthroposophy is not simply given as a revelation but rather must be worked for, through thought. It is not what the Brockhaus dictionary defines as *revelation*: "…a revealing, leading back to God, of a previously 'hidden' religious reality, which human beings experience as existentially important for their lives and cannot be understood or established by means of human reason." For this reason also, Rudolf Steiner rejected any doctrinal authority for anthroposophy: nothing should be "received because of faith in authority."* Those who find no access to understanding specific anthroposophic ideas can let the matter rest. This, of course, also applies to priests of The Christian Community. But it must also be said that it is precisely through the anthroposophical worldview that many people are able to find the traditional contents of Christianity (e.g., Trinity, Baptism, Eucharist, Resurrection) to be understandable for the first time. Of course, understanding something does not finalize anything. This is also true for the contents of the New Testament. In this sense, for the vast majority of priests in The Christian Community, anthroposophy plays a crucial role in carrying out their profession. *It is a help in understanding, not a source of revelation.*

However, the text of the rituals presents an entirely different matter. The words in the rituals are indeed given as revelation, just as the New Testament is given. These words have an integral authority within them that is perceptible for those who live with their meaning over time. Whether, or to what extent, they also understand the words is a question of religious maturity as well as actual experience living with the

* CW 254 (*CW* = The Collected Works of Rudolf Steiner), lecture of Oct. 18, 1915. Cf. "Cited Titles from The Collected Works of Rudolf Steiner" in this book.

rituals. It is a growth process that never ends. For this reason, the freedom possessed by every priest in The Christian Community to teach the truth as they see fit (especially with respect to anthroposophy) finds a limit with the words of the rituals. Even the wording of the rituals, which might not be understood by a priest, cannot be challenged without at the same time putting him- or herself into question. An essential step that must be taken during preparation for Ordination in The Christian Community entails attaining certainty that one will never intend to consciously change the words of rituals.

What is not true for anthroposophy does apply to the rituals of The Christian Community. As a second source of revelation, they are on equal footing with the New Testament. This also means that the relationship between *liturgy and theology is exactly the opposite* of that found in the Catholic Church, where liturgy can only attest to what is certain in faith. For the Catholic Church theology has primacy over liturgy, as is stated in *Munificentissimus Deus,* the Papal Bull of Pope Pius XII from 1950: *Since the liturgy of the church does not create Catholic faith, but rather presupposes it, and religious practices come forth from this faith as fruit from a tree....* (This is the same Bull in which Mary's bodily assumption into heaven also became official dogma.) Here liturgy arises from theological insight. New liturgical forms can result from the decisions arrived at in a Council. Thus, major changes were made in the liturgical realm as a result of the second Vatican Council. These include the creation of an entirely new ritual for the Baptism of children, which replaced the 2,000-year-old custom of using the adult Baptism ritual for children. This change would have been unthinkable in The Christian Community, where the forms and texts of rituals cannot be created—nor even changed—based on theological insights.

Interestingly, the illusion that it is possible to create ritual based on theology played a problematic role in the founding of The Christian Community. After Johannes Werner Klein was the first to ask Rudolf Steiner a question concerning the possibility of religious renewal in February of 1920, he received this answer: *If you carry out what you have in mind here—and the forms for it can be found—then that would signify something monumental for humankind.* Klein was thinking of Schelling's third church, which he had envisioned as going beyond both Catholicism and Protestantism. Steiner's response had been to offer help. However, Klein misunderstood and created a plan for future years: Klein thought he should end his studies at the University, begin a study of all the cults and rituals of humankind, proclaim anthroposophy, create an organization, create new rituals. At Easter 1921, Klein realized his mistake. The foundation of The Christian Community had thereby been delayed by a year or more. Meanwhile a circle of founders began to form and began collaborating with Rudolf Steiner, which eventually led to the spiritual revelation of new ritual forms.

The Christian Community did not grow out of anthroposophy; neither are its rituals simply anthroposophical texts, nor did they come into existence because of one man's philosophy. They arose through the mediation of Rudolf Steiner out of the revelation of Christ. In the words of Rudolf Steiner, they were "provided through anthroposophy."* He wanted

* CW 260a, Dornach 1987, p. 397.

to convey that the rituals originated not in his own personal philosophy but in an objective fount of spiritual reality. Fundamental theological insights can be achieved through working with such ritual texts in the life of a congregation. This is the reverse of the Catholic understanding.*

This brings us to our starting point: the texts of the rituals themselves. Our method for seeking an understanding of the renewed sacraments will begin with the cultus itself.† Additionally, anthroposophy provides crucial insights and perspectives. Ultimately, we will address the question of exactly where The Christian Community fits into the history of Christianity. Even though its origin is not found in any of the existing churches, nevertheless it belongs in the ecclesiastical stream of Christianity‡ and builds upon existing sacramental theology. This is especially true for Catholic theology until the Council of Trent (1545–1563). We can disregard what emerges afterward, "for post trentine theology has contributed nothing essential to fructify sacramental theology."§ New developments in Catholic theology in the twentieth century are indeed of interest on many issues (e.g., theology of the mysteries) and worth engaging by The

* It should be noted that within Catholic theology there are other views that see liturgy as a "Factum Ecclesiae" (Pius IX), that is, as a force sufficient to establish dogmas. They refer to a statement by Pope Coelestin I (432): *"Legem credenda statuat lex orandis"* (May the law of prayer determine the law of faith). Pope Pius IX quoted this principle as a precedent when in 1854 he declared the dogma of Mary's immaculate conception. Otherwise this view is not generally accepted in Catholic theology.

† The texts of these rituals have been published as part of the complete edition of Rudolf Steiner's works. The theological courses are CW 343, 344, and 345.

‡ CW 343, Oct. 4, 1921

§ Finkenzeller, in *Lexikon für Theologie und Kirche*. p. 224. The Council of Trent (*Concilium Tridentinum*) held between 1545 and 1563 in Trent (Trento, in northern Italy) issued 17 dogmatic decrees covering disputed aspects of the Catholic Church.

Christian Community. However, those developments have not served as foundation blocks in the narrow sense, for the movement has begun its own theological tradition.

Chapter 2
Rituals and Sacraments

2.1 Rituals in The Christian Community

There are eleven ritual texts that are celebrated as congregational festivals.*

1. Baptism. It is primarily intended as a children's Baptism and can be performed until Confirmation and, as a rule, not afterward.
2. Confirmation. Performed in the time between Easter and Ascension for fourteen-year-olds. Baptism is a precondition.†
3. The Act of Consecration of Man (The Eucharist or Mass). Communion is intended for individuals fourteen years and older, i.e., for those of Confirmation age or older.
4. Sacramental Consultation. It assumes the spiritual autonomy of men and women today.
5. The Last Anointing. This sacrament is performed when the death process is manifest.
6. Ordination of Priests. This sacrament can be performed on men and women alike (since the founding in 1922). Celibacy is not a requirement.

* Cf. E. Fischer, J. Lenz, Chr. Rau, H.-W. Schroeder.

† The Baptism rituals of other Christian Churches are generally recognized as valid.

7. Sacrament of Marriage is performed for the union of a man and woman.
8. The Sunday Service for Children is held for children of school age until Confirmation and, as a rule, occurs on Sundays.
9. The Christmas Service for Children is held for children up to Confirmation age and takes place yearly, as a rule, on December 25.
10. The Funeral Service for Children. This is held for children up to Confirmation age (burial or cremation).
11. Funeral Service. For adults after Confirmation age. There are two parts: the first is a blessing performed at home, or in a chapel for family and closest friends. The second is public with the coffin closed. These two services are often performed in sequence together.

The first seven rituals are sacraments in the narrow sense, the last four are not regarded as sacraments. Why not? And what makes a ritual a sacrament? To begin with, sacraments as *healing medicine* are connected with the *convalescence* made necessary by incarnation. This means a healing of *the sickness of sin,* which is always related to an incarnated human being. Hence, sacraments are for living, incarnated human beings. The two last listed rituals are, for this reason, not stand-alone sacraments because they are not held for living people. But why aren't the Sunday Service for Children and the Christmas Service for Children sacraments? One perspective on this question: the spiritual substance entrusted to The Christian Community is in essence the substance of the seven sacraments. Furthermore, each of the sacraments has a *radius of application* within which other rituals can be found. In this sense the Funeral Service for Children belongs to the Baptism, while the Sunday Service for Children and the Christmas Service belong to Confirmation, and the Funeral Service is covered by the Last Anointing. In this way, we can include in the total organism of the sacraments those rituals that are not sacraments in the narrower sense. Because they belong to specific sacraments, they acquire a sacramental character.*

The sacramental substance of The Christian Community contains in essence nothing other than the entirety of the *seven Sacraments*. Additional rituals possessing special relationships to particular sacraments also belong to this substance. Thus, the rituals can be summarized in the sevenfold nature of the sacraments:

1. Baptism *and Funeral for Children*
2. Confirmation *and Sunday Service/Christmas Service for Children*
3. Act of Consecration of Man (aka the Eucharist, or Mass)
4. Sacramental Consultation
5. Last Anointing *and Funeral Service*

---

* Before the foundation of The Christian Community the Sunday Service for Children and the Christmas Service for Children had already been given by Rudolf Steiner to the teachers of Independent Religious Instruction at the first Waldorf School in Stuttgart, Germany. (At the request of parents an independent religious instruction curriculum had been instituted at the Waldorf School for children whose parents did not belong to the two dominant denominations [Lutheran and Catholic] at that time. Such parents were called "dissidents.") Thus, the texts of these rituals were identical. They were, however, celebrated by teachers only within the context of the Waldorf School. Emil Bock had a conversation with Rudolf Steiner in which he inquired if there was a difference when these rituals were held within the context of The Christian Community. Afterward Bock recorded Steiner's response in his (unpublished) notebook: From the beginning it was clear that these rituals, simply through the fact that they are celebrated by priests wearing vestments within our church setting, would have to become an integral part of our sacramentalism.

6. Ordination of Priests
7. Sacrament of Marriage

When a child dies before Confirmation, the Funeral Service for Children does justice to such a special destiny. The child has left earth already without having attained full earthly maturity, which is why the ritual form is not the same as for adults. We could say that Baptism passes over into the Funeral for Children, which is related to it in its trinitarian structure and in the substances used (water and ash). In content and form the funeral is related to the Baptism.

Confirmation is prepared for seven years through the Sunday Service for Children and the Christmas Service. Here, too, there exists a clear relationship in form and content between Confirmation (especially its first part) and these two rituals.

The Last Anointing and the funeral service are united by the threshold of death. The Last Anointing leads the person to this threshold while the Funeral Service continues the path on the far side of the threshold.

2.2 SACRAMENTS IN THE CATHOLIC, ORTHODOX, AND PROTESTANT CHURCHES

Seven sacraments are also celebrated in the Catholic Church. The following formulation was recorded in 1547 at the Council of Trent (against the Reformation): "Who says that the sacraments of the new covenant are not all instituted by Christ Jesus, our Lord, or are more or less than seven, namely Baptism, Confirmation, Eucharist, Penance, Last Anointing, Ordination, and Marriage, or that one of these seven is not actually and really a sacrament, he shall be expelled." The sevenfold nature of the sacraments in the church has been generally acknowledged since the end of the twelfth century.*

Baptism is performed on children and adults.

Confirmation has been performed on individuals of various ages in the course of history. It is performed by bishops. The age for Confirmation (10 or 12 years) was set as the time after First Communion by Pope Pius X (1903–1914). There have been recent proposals to extend the age for Confirmation into the teen years.

Beginning with First Communion, individuals can partake of the *Eucharist (Communion with Mass)*. The age of First Communion was established in 1215 (Fourth Lateran Council) as "the year of discrimination," which was determined to be somewhere between seven and twelve. In 1910 Pius X established age seven as the norm.

Penance (*Confession*) prepares a person for Communion. Questions have arisen concerning confessions taken from children at too early an age. In defense of existing protocols in 1971, Catholic bishops were once again called upon not to deviate from "the current practice" of leading children to Confession before their First Communion, which is usually during their seventh year. †

The Last Anointing has been so named since the twelfth century. It is for "Christians, who have been afflicted by a life-threatening illness and who have attained the age of reason." Those headed for certain death—e.g., those condemned to death or soldiers in life-threatening situations—cannot receive the Last Anointing, whereas it is advisable

* The sevenfoldedness of the sacraments first appeared in a church document in 1208 in the confession of faith of Pope Innocent III against the Waldensians.

† Johann Auer and Joseph Ratzinger, *Kleine Katholische Dogmatik*, vol. 7, p. 375.

for those whose illness has reached a point where death is inevitable. "Such people are equipped with the sacrament of Confirmation for tasks that demand of them that they be exposed to life-threatening situations in the fullness of life, or that demand that they surrender themselves to certain death—with a corresponding moral attitude, be it the courage of martyrs or faithfulness to fatherland or a sacrifice to save one's neighbor or to fulfill atonement."*

Ordination of priests (which can be performed only on men who are unmarried) and Marriage are considered "civil office sacraments" because they are not necessarily a part of a human biography, but rather give those who receive them a particular position in civil society. (This was especially true in the past when all marriages involved civil authorities who were often representatives of the church hierarchy, either as priests or occupying higher offices.)

Aside from the sacraments themselves there is a wealth of rituals, which are referred to as *sacramentals*. We will discuss them in the next section.

Seven sacraments are also celebrated in the orthodox churches of the East. Despite their separation from the Roman Catholic Church in the eleventh century, two hundred years later they adopted the concept of sevenfoldedness for the sacraments from the Western church. They did this even though the liturgical practice of the Eastern churches is far less amenable to such differentiation.† There the sacra-

* Schmaus, *Katholische Dogmatik*, vol. III/2, p. 419.

† Their language speaks of "holy deeds" and thereby includes not only sacraments, but also various consecrations and blessings. At the union Council of Lyons in 1274, one of the failed union councils attempting to reconcile the Eastern and Western churches, the Orthodox churches accepted the *"Professio fide,"* the sevenfoldedness of the sacraments. But the teaching office of the church pronounced its stand on the sevenfoldedness of the sacraments first in the "Orthodoxos Homologia"

ments are called *mysteries*. The seven mysteries are:

Baptism—Chrismation (*Confirmation with anointing*)—*Eucharist*. These three sacraments appear at the beginning of life as a single celebration. The small child receives with Baptism also Chrismation and Communion (usually in liquid form, i.e., wine only). Additional mysteries are: *Ordination* (it can only be performed on men; a married man can be ordained after marriage but an unmarried man is forbidden to marry), *Marriage, Penance, and Anointing of the Sick*, which is performed on the sick and is not to be considered a sacrament in the sphere of death. However, sevenfoldedness plays a much smaller role in the awareness and theology of the orthodox churches than in the West. Indeed, at the end of the nineteenth century it was put into question by Eastern theologians. The Russian hieromonk Tarasij stated in 1903, "The practice of the entire Eastern Church has never traveled the narrow path of official theology and has ascribed great effectiveness to other holy rituals and prayers.... The limitation of the number of mysteries and their definitions are completely arbitrary and deceptive; they arise directly out of Latin Scholasticism and its legal, juristic ways."*

Protestant churches speak of only two sacraments: Baptism and the Eucharist. According to Martin Luther there is a justification for only these two in the New Testament. Proclaiming the Word is equally justified, if not superior to these two symbolic actions. Luther wrote, "Words are a divine vow, promise and testament. The signs are sacraments,

---

(*Confession orthodoxa*) of Petrus Mogila. All the participants at a synod in 1642 in Jassy agreed with Mogila's statement. Since then all Eastern Patriarchs have followed suit. It is counted as one of the "symbolic books" of orthodoxy and is, as such, a normative rule of faith.

* Quoted in Hotz, *Sakramente im Wechselspiel zwischen Ost und West*, p. 274f.

that is, holy signs. Now, since much more is riding on testament than on sacrament so much more depends upon words than on signs. For there may be no signs but we nevertheless can have words even without sacraments but we cannot become blessed without testament."[*] Sacraments lose even more significance when compared to the Word, according to Calvin and Zwingli. Zwingli even had difficulty with the word *sacrament* itself, because it seemed to suggest to him a significance that should not be attributed to Baptism, or even to the Eucharist. He wrote, "I very much wish that the Germans had never adopted the word 'Sacrament' into their language, unless they had adopted it into a German that could not be misunderstood."[†]

A synopsis of Catholic, Orthodox and Protestant conceptions of the sacraments shows that the sevenfoldedness of the sacraments is firmly anchored only in Catholic theology where it was dogmatically asserted at the Council of Trent. Even here however, in recent years notable theologians have produced formulations that ascribe a more mythical than real significance to the sevenfoldedness. For example, Karl Rahner thinks that we can speak of seven or nine sacraments based on a perspective that is more historical or theological.[‡] Alexandre Ganoczy writes, "The final impression left by the teaching of sevenfoldedness is that of a far-reaching relativity and flexibility."[§] Finally, Herbert Vorgrimler writes, "The question of why, according to Catholic dogma, God wanted exactly seven sacraments, and not one more or one less, is defused if the institutional-sacramental question is imbedded

[*] Ibid., p. 92f.

[†] Ibid., p. 95.

[‡] Quoted in Ganoczy, *Einführung in die katholische Sakramentenlehre*, p. 40f.

[§] Ibid., p. 41

in the framework of a general, sacramental economy of salvation. The number seven itself can be understood symbolically but does not need to be seen as compelling."* The reasons brought forward for why one should not hold absolutely to the sevenfoldedness of the sacraments are plausible. By no means was the number clear from the beginning. On the contrary it took over a thousand years until this understanding appeared. Furthermore, the stories of how each sacrament came into being vary enormously. Baptism and Eucharist were present from the beginning. The others were developed only through a gradual process. A few of them have changed their meaning several times. Finally, the way the sacraments have been performed, their roots in religious practice and their relationship to specific life situations are so different that it could almost appear arbitrary that seven were elevated to the special status as sacraments from the great wealth of church celebrations.

We must also take Luther's reservations seriously. He recognized that Baptism and Eucharist are grounded in the Bible, but at the same time, he questioned whether they had anything in common that would make it obvious that both should be sacraments. In the New Testament, at least, there are no grounds for this. Nowhere is Baptism or Eucharist mentioned and summarized under one umbrella term. Hence, from the point of view of the New Testament, not only is the sevenfoldedness of the sacraments put into question, but also their justification altogether. In any case, for Martin Luther the concept of a sacrament is more an abstract summation of Baptism and Eucharist than the expression of any concrete reality.

* Herbert Vorgrimler, *Sakramententheologie*, p. 57.

Sacramental life in The Christian Community has followed the opposite path. It was clear from the beginning, on the path to its foundation, that the center of religious renewal would be *ritual*, also known as *cultus* in technical theological language. This totality of seven sacraments constitutes the cultus, the ritual; it is given as the *proto-sacrament* and is not derived from historical development. Interestingly enough, in the present-day Catholic Church, Jesus Christ is correspondingly referred to as the proto-sacrament. This is claimed to have been derived from an existing tradition. Augustine called Christ the *mysterium Dei*, the mystery of God. Thomas Aquinas saw Christ as the "fundamental sacrament." Luther says, "Holy scripture knows only one sacrament. That is Christ, the Lord himself."

The term *proto-sacrament* then appears in the twentieth century (by Carl Feckes in 1934), and since then has played a large role in theology—especially after the second Vatican Council,* when reference is made to the *principal sacrament,* meaning the Church itself. This meaning could resonate with the concept of *proto-sacrament.* The theological path of The Christian Community therefore leads from the reality of the proto-sacrament to individual sacraments and *not* vice versa, that is, from individual, concrete ritual actions to an abstract concept of sacrament derived from them. This understanding of the sacraments, that they originate in Christ himself, is fundamental to The Christian Community.

2.3 SACRAMENTALS AND COSMIC CHRISTIANITY

It has always been a tradition for the Catholic and Orthodox Churches to have rituals in addition to the seven

* Ibid., pp. 44ff.

sacraments named in the twelfth century. Since then, these rituals have been called "sacramentals" and are essentially directed toward the *sanctification of the external world.* There is almost nothing natural or manmade that cannot become the object of a sacramental blessing in the Catholic Church; in fact, as civilization has progressed, the entire sector of technology has been included. We can find examples—chosen at random—from a collection of sacramentals.* Blessings now exist for the following:

- For people, e.g., offering and blessing for mothers, blessing for a healthy child, and a blessing for an ill child.
- For nature, e.g., blessings for herbs, springs, fields, alpine pastures, meadows, and bees.
- For food, e.g., blessings for bread, cheese and butter; there is a blessing for Easter eggs.
- For technical products, e.g., for machines, for the generation of electric lights, for a furnace, and for a railroad and its cars.
- For special difficulties, e.g., for a flood, against vermin, for medicines.

Reference is always made to themes from the Old and New Testaments in the liturgical formulas—in a more or less plausible way. For example, the blessing of railroads and its cars refers to an event in chapter eight of Acts of the Apostles, when the apostle Philip climbs into the Ethiopian's wagon; during their journey Philip ultimately converts him to Christianity.

Theological reflection on sacramentals first began in the twelfth century when Peter Lombard† distinguished sacra-

* Dausend, *Die Sakramentalien* (in the series "Religiöse Quellschriften."

† Petrus Lombardus (ca. 1100–1160), teacher at the Cathedral School of Notre Dame, Paris (1140), and bishop (1159).

mentals from sacraments. The sacraments are *signs of salvation* that bring to expression God's actions on behalf of human beings, whereas sacramentals are understood to be deeds of human beings in order to Christianize the world, deeds for which we are jointly responsible. Thus, one can understand the point of view that sacramentals are not directly instituted by Christ but by the church.

When sacramentals are seen to bring Christ's work of salvation not only to human beings but also into the physical world, we see a further dimension of Christianity, which has been insufficiently appreciated in the Western church: its cosmic dimension. There are relevant passages in the New Testament, above all in Paul's letters, that refer to the cosmic Christ. On the other hand, cosmic Christianity has been discredited because it was advocated by early Christian Gnosticism. A Catholic theologian writes in a critical vein:

> Furthermore, the marketing effectiveness of the Gnostics was based on the thesis that, as Christians of a higher order, as "spiritual people," they alone possessed the correct interpretation of cosmic events and thus were alone capable of perfect knowledge of God.*

Today the time has come to reacquire this lost realm of Christianity in a new form. This is a central theme of anthroposophical Christology and belongs to the foundations of Christian Community theology.†

But there are new publications that explore Gnosticism in the Protestant churches, as well.‡ And there are Catholic theologians who speak of a cosmic Christendom in connection with sacramentals:

* Karl Baus, in *Handbuch der Kirchengeschichte*, vol. 1, p. 217.

† Cf. Schroeder, *The Cosmic Christ*.

‡ Werner Thiede, *Wer ist der kosmische Christus?*

> The center of the process of salvation is Christ, in whom the world is created, in whom the world has its existence, who has redeemed the world through his death (Col. 1:15–20), who as judge perfects the world (Matt. 25:11ff) and who will finally bestow a new Heaven and a new Earth (Rev. 21).... The church stands in service of God's salvation history through the cosmic Christ with its sacramentals.... [For it includes] not only human beings but also the world in which human beings live and the cosmos as the body of the cosmic Christ.*

Of course, the question naturally arises here whether The Christian Community also has sacramentals, since cosmic Christianity also plays an important role.† The answer is clear: The Christian Community does not recognize any sacramentals of the traditional kind. This is, of course, not because it does not recognize the task of sanctifying the world. However, a clear boundary is drawn between God's work, which is the bedrock of all true sacraments, and work done by human beings who act out of their own sense of responsibility. The sacraments themselves originate in God's work; even the best spiritual works of humans are not sacramental in the true sense of a sacrament. Such deeds may well benefit the world and many people, but they are not to be confused with spiritual forces streaming into the earth directly from the spiritual world. The call often heard today from many well-intended new-age movements *to make all your actions sacramental* is actually a call to bring more consciousness (mindfulness), more awareness of the spirit behind all things, and hence more responsibility, into one's life.

---

* Auer and Ratzinger, vol. 6, pp. 118, 122.

† As a result The Christian Community has also been accused of being "New-Age Gnosticism."

Think of a polluted river. What would it mean to *bless the river* in such a condition? Are we to pray to God that he clean the river? Or what could it mean *to speak a blessing over an automobile*, praying that angels "exempt it from all danger?" Is it intended that the driver or the other drivers on the road drive more carefully to reduce the risk of an accident for this vehicle? Today we must recognize, perhaps painfully, that humanity bears responsibility for the future of the earth. No one can take that responsibility away—not the church, not even God. Deeds are required that cannot be replaced by prayers or ritual actions. This is also true with respect to sacramentals.

Nevertheless, the healing of the earth is a central theme for the sacraments of The Christian Community. These rituals are considered significant not merely because they bless individual human beings; the process of transformation streaming forth from the altar ultimately takes hold of all of creation. We have a responsibility that goes far beyond any responsibility for the ecological balance of the earth, to which humanity is only gradually awakening. For our very existence, we must thank the kingdoms below us, the mineral, plant, and animal kingdoms, not only in an external sense but much more deeply. The present-day human and animal kingdoms were one kingdom in the past, gradually differentiating only during the course of a long, spiritual/physical evolution. This can be compared to two young boys who want to climb over a wall higher than they are tall. One of them gives the other the chance to stand on his shoulders and thus to climb a wall. As a result, one of them is *above* only because the other, who is now *below*, remained behind. This picture speaks of a profound social law. Those who are *above* are always in debt to those *below* even when they are not conscious of it and imagine they have earned their higher position. In the created world humankind is also above compared to the kingdoms below, which *have remained behind* at various stages of evolution. Hence, we are indebted to them. The *redemption of nature** finds its full expression here. Paul's letter to the Romans (8:19) hints at this secret.

> All around us creation waits with great longing that the sons of God shall begin to shine forth in humankind. Creation has become transitory, not through its own doing, but because of him who, becoming transitory himself, dragged it down with him and therefore everything in it is full of longing for the future. For the breath of freedom will also move through the kingdoms of creation; the tyranny of transitory existence will cease.

The German poet Christian Morgenstern expressed something very similar in a poem titled *Washing of the Feet*:

> I thank you, mute stone
> and bow down to you:
> I owe you my plant existence.
>
> I thank you, soil and blossom,
> and bend down to you:
> you help me rise to the animal.
>
> I thank you, stone, leaves and animal,
> and bow before you:
> You helped me find myself in me.
>
> We thank you, child of man,
> and kneel devoutly before you:
> because you are, we are too.

* Cf. Sloan, *The Redemption of the Animals: Their Evolution, Their Inner Life, and Our Future Together.*

All Divinity gives thanks to One
and all divinity manifest again,
all being is engulfed in thanksgiving.

Thus, humankind has a task with creation that it fulfilled in earlier times through prayer when it was in the bosom of God. Today this prayer is a moral deed benefiting the world. The substance of the sacraments no longer remains in an enclosed milieu of cultic, ritual deeds but rather streams out into the world, transforming it through the actions of human beings. In other words, the world is thereby sanctified, saved and healed. Rudolf Steiner elaborated on this idea:

> What was cultivated symbolically in ancient Christian rituals must be taken hold of by the entire world. The whole world must take hold of what was merely performed on an altar. Humankind must learn to handle nature the same way the gods themselves handled nature. For example, not to build machines in a disinterested way, but to actually perform a service to God with all the activities in everyday life, to bring sacramentalism into everything.*

He goes on to explain how the substance of Baptism flows into the world in a Christian way appropriate to a child.

Sacraments in The Christian Community are to be understood as human deeds in which spiritual substance has been activated. Initially this is only possible with individual human beings. Nevertheless, it remains an important goal that "in all their everyday actions" people increasingly become able to perform a service to God. In this sense, sacraments can inspire people to begin living their lives in a sacramental way.

* CW 172, Nov. 27, 1916.

Indeed, every true spiritual training forms the germinal conditions for sacramental activity in everyday life. This is especially true of the esoteric training path of anthroposophy.

Such entirely worldly deeds, for which humans are responsible, must move into the social space where, in earlier times, ritual acts were appropriate. For it belongs to the essence of Christianity that *God has become powerless with respect to the world. He now works only through human beings.*

In concluding this section, we will consider a series of ritual actions that are performed in The Christian Community, which might have the appearance of being sacramentals because they are directed not toward humans but toward things in the world.

We have the consecration of substances: *water, ash, and oil.* They are needed for the children's burial service (water and ash), Last Anointing and Ordination of priests (oil), funeral (water) and the consecration of chapels (water). However, the substances used for Baptism (water, salt, and ash) need no consecration prior to the Baptism because they are consecrated in the course of that sacrament. The same holds for the other ritual substances (incense, bread, and wine).

Vestments worn by priests are consecrated.
The *rooms, chapels, and church spaces* used exclusively for ritual are consecrated.
The *altar painting* is consecrated.
The *chalice* is consecrated.
The *objects and cultic implements belonging to the altar* are also consecrated.

The formulas for consecration spoken in these rituals are much freer than those spoken in the actual sacramental texts.

Many of these rituals are also performed in a very simple way in the vestry. Indeed, there is a sanctification, a healing of the world that takes place through rituals, which could be seen as the essence of sacramentals. Nevertheless, we are dealing here with something very different. *These rituals consecrate things that serve the sacraments and therefore are explicitly set apart from the world through word and intention.* They are rituals that belong within the inner space of the sacraments, not the secular world.

2.4 Ritual and Sacrament in Anthroposophy

Anthroposophy is science, insofar as it presupposes the human mind applied to understanding the world in all its manifestations. As science of the spirit, it is not religion. Science and religion are very different aspects of the life of the mind, which is why Rudolf Steiner repeatedly emphasizes: "anthroposophy as such cannot appear as religion-forming"* and "anthroposophy does not interfere with anyone's religious faith."† Nevertheless, spiritual science has a different relationship to religion than the science cultivated at universities today. Rudolf Steiner starts from an extended concept of science following Goethe, who was one of the first to speak of a trinity of science, art, and religion. Goethe says: "...all three are one at the beginning and the end of time although separated in the middle."‡ Accordingly an essential task of anthroposophy is to reunite these three areas of human endeavor, but not so that they resemble their original

* CW 343, Sep. 9, 1921.

† CW 72, Oct. 19, 1917.

‡ See chapter titled "Wissenschaft—Kunst—Religion, a prophetic suggestion from Goethe" by the author in Jean-Claude Lin (ed.), *Wirken im Zeichen von Kunst, Wissenschaft und Religion.*

state of union, but rather preserving the fruitful differentiation that arose when they were "separated in the middle" of time. Their necessary separation is to be overcome in such a way that the three are united at the end of time but, as Tertullian wrote, in a different context, "undivided and unmixed."

Anthroposophy begins as a science. It investigates the spiritual world and its beings, as is done, for example, in *An Outline of Esoteric Science* (CW 13), teaching that if we immerse ourselves in the descriptions of the activities of the spiritual beings under investigation, we can develop reverence toward what we are learning. This reverence is a mood of the soul that is more than mere scientific interest. Finally, we can begin to feel the need to establish a conscious relationship to these spiritual beings. Turning to these beings inwardly is the beginning of communication, i.e., religion. Understood in the broadest sense, such communication is prayer.

Communication with our fellow human beings can also become religion if we are addressing the higher self of the other person. Then social awareness and religion grow closely together. In Steiner's work, therefore, in addition to the trinity of science—art—religion, there is also another trinity: science—art—social life (occasionally as a quadruplicity with religion added).* Accordingly, it should be understandable that the sentence "anthroposophy, as such, cannot appear religion-forming" must be supplemented by another of Steiner's sentences (which might initially appear to be a contradiction): "Thus, anthroposophy everywhere

* E.g., CW 333, Dec. 19, 1919; CW 77b, Aug. 21, 1921; CW 343, Sept. 28, 1921; CW 79, Nov. 26, 1921 (these last two locations include religion to make four).

begins with science, enlivens its ideas artistically, and ends with religious deepening."*

We see here that Steiner has not only an expanded idea of scientific knowledge but also an expanded concept of religion. The religious deepening of which he speaks is not to be equated with the religion cultivated in Christian churches. Traditional religion has "faith-based prayer" as one of its foundations, i.e., a direct turning to God, whose existence is presupposed and experienced in faith. A science or knowledge of the spirit is not one of those foundations. In traditional churches a "science of the spirit" is a subject with negative connotations (but by the same token, the world *theology* actually ought to be a problematic word for the churches as well, insofar as it implies "science of God"). Nevertheless, there is a relationship between religious experience and spiritual science: a desire to understand what we have experienced can lead us to an interest in actual knowledge of the suprasensory. In our time religious experience can give rise to the need for understanding and knowledge. Churches are therefore confronted today by this question: To what extent can churches satisfy this need adequately? In this way, religion can become the beginning of a path that leads to a science of the suprasensory. There is also a religious deepening that can result from following a path that has its beginning in spiritual science. The first is the task of a contemporary church, whereas the second is the path of anthroposophy.

Now we do not expect terms such as cultus, Communion or sacrament to play a role in anthroposophy, because they belong to the vocabulary of the church and the religion cultivated by it. It is therefore surprising that Rudolf Steiner

* CW 257, Jan. 30, 1923.

uses these very words quite frequently to characterize facts investigated by spiritual science. What do religious terms have to do with scientific descriptions? If we remain faithful to the anthroposophical method, we must first see them as technical terms, detached from all religious preconceptions. Most of Steiner's statements in which he uses words like sacramental, ritual, or Communion (except when used to describe specific religious facts) have very limited applicability as statements about religion or religious life. However, beyond their mere technical use these words can point to a possible religious deepening on the anthroposophical path of knowledge.

The expression "ground of the world" (*Weltengrund*) is an example. Already in 1886 it appears in *Goethe's Theory of Knowledge* (CW 2). The corresponding passage reads: "Our view has shown that every assumption of a ground of being, which lies outside the idea, is a no-thing, a nothing. The entire ground of being has poured itself into the world, it has been absorbed into it. In thinking it shows itself in its most perfect form, as it is in and for itself. Therefore, if thinking finds a connection, if it makes a judgment, then it is the content of the ground of the world itself that flows in this connection. In thinking, we are not given assertions about some otherworldly ground of the world, but rather the very substance of that ground of the world has flowed into thinking."*

Steiner here uses the terms *ground of being*, (*Seinsgrund*), and *ground of the world* (*Weltgrund, Weltengrund*). The first is a common philosophical term, not religious, even though it has also been frequently understood in personal terms

* CW 2, p. 84 of the 2003 German edition.

in the history of philosophy. *Ground of the world* is not a common expression in philosophy in general but belongs to Steiner's special terminology; he used it philosophically, and he brought it into the context of The Christian Community. In 1907, he spoke clearly of the *divine ground of the world*,* conveying a religious concept.

Finally, in 1921, the expression *ground of the world* was used not only to convey religious meaning but appeared in the rituals provided to The Christian Community at its founding. Prayer is directly addressed to *the ground of the world*. Steiner explained that *the offering is brought to the Father, the ground of the world*.† We can see from this expression, *ground of the world*, the process that begins with spiritual science and can lead to a religious deepening. This term thus acquired a religious deepening the more Steiner developed anthroposophy.

The terms *cultus* (or *ritual*) and *Communion* underwent a similar evolution. In 1887 Steiner wrote: "Becoming aware of the idea in reality is the true Communion of the human being."‡ Later on, he referred to this phrase again and again when speaking of the importance of genuine knowledge, even speaking once of "a sacramental experience of knowledge

* CW 56, Oct. 10, 1907.

† CW 343, Oct. 6, 1921. The fact that The Christian Community, in its Eucharist service, the Act of Consecration of Man, addresses prayer first to *the ground of the world* before the Father God is named has evoked the reproach that it prays to an impersonal God, but this assertion is mistaken. Of course, the Father God is not an impersonal God, and the fact that he is first called *the ground of the world* has a Christological meaning: Christ's help allows us to arrive at a place whereby we are allowed to say *Father*. Paul also says this clearly in the Epistle to the Romans : "Those in whom the spirit of God resides are sons of God. For you did not receive a spirit that makes you slaves and sets you back into fear; you have been given the spirit that makes you into sons of God. He gives us the right to call God our Father!" (8:14f).

‡ CW 1, Dornach 1987, p. 126.

available to anyone." In this context *communion* is a purely philosophical concept. Those who are able to truly behold (i.e., see ideas) experience reality in such a way that they no longer feel separate but one with it in "true Communion."

The archetype of a person who has experienced this Communion is probably Goethe. Steiner frequently mentioned* Goethe's conversation in July of 1794 with Schiller in Jena after a meeting of the natural-science society. Goethe explained his experience of the archetypal plant to Schiller "with some characteristic pen strokes a symbolic plant" created before Schiller's eyes. But Schiller replied, "That is not an experience, that is an idea." To which Goethe could only reply, "It makes me very happy that I can have ideas without knowing it and even see them with eyes." Goethe saw what Schiller called an idea with eyes. "Becoming aware of the idea in reality" was direct experience for him; he experienced his communion with reality. This concept, too, underwent a religious deepening.

In 1922, Steiner further explained how knowledge can become communion. In contrast to 1887 this definitely occurs in a religious context, namely, during the founding of The Christian Community and the establishing of its religious rituals, which included Communion. Here the thinking aspect of knowledge underwent a religious deepening into *spiritual communion* through the addition of feeling and willing to true knowledge. This entire process that leads to union with the reality of the world is what Rudolf Steiner called *cultus*, *cosmic cultus*.

> What would otherwise be only abstract knowledge becomes a feeling and willing relationship to the world.

* For example: CW 6, p. 21.

> The world becomes a temple, the world becomes a house of God, a place of worship. A thinking human being, rousing himself in feeling and willing, becomes a being who sacrifices.... Thus, spiritual knowledge is real Communion, the beginning of a cosmic cultus appropriate to the humankind of the present.*

In addition to the *cosmic cultus*, which is a matter of spiritual knowledge, Rudolf Steiner also spoke of a *reverse cultus*. The cosmic cultus is about the relationship of a thinking human being to the world, about seeing the ideas of the cosmos "with eyes," while the reverse cultus concerns the relationship of thinking human beings to their fellow human beings insofar as they, too, are striving for knowledge. Using Goethe's words, we could say: It is a matter of *seeing with eyes* the ideas of another person. Steiner calls this an *awakening*, a word he uses with a broad spectrum of meanings (his fourth mystery drama, for example, is titled *The Souls' Awakening*). "People awake through encounters with one another, by finding each other again and again. Because each person has gone through something different in the meantime and progressed somewhat in their development, they awake to one another in transformed conditions and contexts."† If, with respect to the reverse cultus, "the actual spirituality common to all" then unites with those who are working together to understand the spirit, this is again a fact that arises entirely from anthroposophic striving for knowledge and can lead to religious deepening.

Usually, the essence of a ritual lies precisely in the fact that it appears as liturgy *for the senses*. But neither the

* CW 219, Dec. 31, 1922.

† CW 257, Feb. 27, 1923.

cosmic cultus nor the reverse cultus has any liturgical form.* They take place purely spiritually. Therefore, to understand them, we need very flexible concepts. Other forms of spiritual or religious life would not be called *ritual*. Nevertheless, by using this term Rudolf Steiner points to the religious deepening that these two processes (knowledge of the world, community building) can undergo.

There is a third cultus that has no liturgical form: the *suprasensory cultus* that occurred in the spiritual world at the turn of the eighteenth to the nineteenth century. It was to prepare human souls to become servants of the spirit of our time. The reign of the time spirit, Michael the Archangel, began at the end of the nineteenth century.† Again we are challenged to imagine a ritual that has no manifestation in the world of the senses. If an earthly ritual depicts suprasensory facts, what facts does a suprasensory ritual depict?

Rudolf Steiner also calls it the *imaginative cultus*, *cultus of imagination*, and *cultus of imaginations*. Imaginations are manifestations of the spiritual world that come closest to the sensory world. They belong to the *lowest* level of the spiritual world, upon which higher beings can reveal themselves. Thus, this suprasensory ritual is a revelation of, or an image in imaginations of a much higher world, in which the human being (in the time between death and new birth) could otherwise not participate consciously.

Finally, let us consider the concept *sacrament*, as it is also very frequently used by Rudolf Steiner. Similar to other words already considered that originally had a religious

* It should be noted here that there are anthroposophical publications in which the cosmic and the reverse cultus are equated. Apparently, this is based on a misunderstanding.

† CW 237 (especially July 8, 1924), CW 238 and CW 240.

meaning, this concept also underwent a crucial expansion in a specific direction. It came to refer to the sacramentalization of all of life. Already in 1904 Rudolf Steiner states the task of anthroposophy: "The human being must again create spiritual life right down into every hand movement and every step; reintroducing this is the task and the endeavor of our spiritual movement. The sacramentalism of earlier times must return.... The essence of sacramentalism is that human beings fill everyday life with consecration."* In this connection, he employed the image of a laboratory again and again. "The laboratory table must become an altar."†

This means that, *to begin with*, our actions in the physical world have the same quality as those brought about by a machine. Religious deepening means that we must become more deeply connected to our actions. When we connect our physical movements and deeds with corresponding thoughts and feelings, they have a different significance for the world than that of a mere machine. What was said above concerning sacramentals in The Christian Community describes what Steiner calls the sacramentalization of all life; the "laboratory table" of our daily work becomes an altar and our attitude toward everyday life is created on that altar.

We have seen that there are religious terms in anthroposophy (such as *ground of the world, communion, cultus, ritual, sacramentalism*) initially used by Steiner without religious intent, but are amenable to religious usage when anthroposophy leads to religious deepening.

It should also be noted that before World War I, Rudolf Steiner also established ritual activities of a completely

* CW 92, July 8, 1904.

† A few examples: CW 98, Dec. 4, 1907; CW 104, June 27, 1908; CW 182, Oct. 9, 1918; CW 216, Sept. 9, 1923.

different kind within the "Esoteric School" led by him. Later he referred to those activities as a "ritual of knowledge,"* in another place "symbolic-ritual activity,"† whose content was "only a demonstration of spiritual-scientific knowledge." That was a ritual, which was actually perceptible to physical senses. The same is true of the services that Steiner gave for the Waldorf school's independent religious instruction.‡ Those services are clearly religious rituals, which may be surprising, because, as we have seen, the anthroposophical path does not proceed from religious experience but from knowledge. But these religious rituals were not originally given for adults but for the children and young people receiving independent religious education.

---

* On July 28, 1922, in a conversation with Bock, Geyer, and Rittelmeyer (recorded by Bock).

† CW 28, chap. 36.

‡ This religious education was introduced by him for children at the request of parents who did not belong to any of the denominations (fundamentally, Catholic or Lutheran) existing in 1922; cf. CW 269.

Chapter 3
Ritual and its Origins

3.1 The Covenant with God

There are different approaches to the question of the origin of the ritual. We want to begin with the example of a human encounter. Whoever wants to enter into a relationship with another person knows that one's own need alone is not enough to bring about a successful encounter; the needs of the other person must also be taken into account. This then leads to possible forms of meeting. In every human encounter form plays a big—often not even conscious—role. These forms vary according to age, culture, generation. Even if one seeks to meet another without formality, informally there will nevertheless be some kind of form. Formlessness is also a kind of form. Forms also play a special role in our relationship to higher beings. In religion this is especially true. We have already mentioned that prayer is a religious form of communication for meeting divine beings. It too always has a form, even if carried out as "free prayer" seeming to need no form. The very fact that we distinguish between prayer and other states of consciousness shows that praying has form. Ritual provides the foundation for the most intense form of prayer. A question can arise here: who creates the forms of a ritual? An obvious answer might be: the praying person him or herself because they express in the forms of their prayer what they want to say, in a way similar to how body language accompanying someone's spoken word can reinforce their message.

Goethe gives a beautiful example of a ritual he created himself in his autobiography *Dichtung und Wahrheit*. As a seven-year-old boy, he once experienced a strong religious need:

> ...to approach the great God of nature directly, the creator and sustainer of heaven and earth,...but the path to this was very unusual. The boy had kept to the very first article of faith. The God who was in direct connection with nature, who recognized and loved it as his work, seemed to him to be the real God, who, as with everything else, could enter into a more exact relationship with human beings, and who would take care of him as well as the movement of the stars, the times of day and year, the plants and animals.... The boy could not give form to this being; he therefore sought him out in his works and wanted to erect an altar to worship him in a good Old Testament fashion. Objects from nature were to represent the world, over these a flame was to burn and signify the mind of man longing for his Creator.*

He set up everything as he saw fit and then held his celebration. "Everything succeeded as desired, and the devotion was perfect." When he wanted to repeat his ritual devotion, something went wrong and the sacrificial flame caused great damage. He was very much affected by this event, "the courage to make new sacrifices had gone out of him, and one would almost like to consider this coincidence as a hint and warning how dangerous it is altogether to want to approach God in such ways."

* Goethe, *Aus meinem Leben: Dichtung und Wahrheit.*

This experience is like an archetype. Goethe, in child-like innocence, arranged a "ritual" according to his own ideas and immediately experienced the inappropriateness of the process.

The archetype for the establishment of ritual-worship is found in the Old Testament. Moses received detailed instructions from Yahweh on how to establish the ritual for the children of Israel (Ex. 25:8ff). In the end, he was not to perform the cultus himself, but to appoint his brother Aaron as the first in the newly established Levitical priesthood (Ex. 28:1ff). The initiative for this cultus comes from Yahweh and is part of the covenant that Yahweh makes with the people of Israel and whose content is *the law*. This covenant was made on Mount Sinai. The two stone tablets with the ten commandments were its symbolic expression:

> Then the Lord said to Moses, "Write down these words. For on the basis of these words I make a covenant with you and with Israel." Moses stayed there with the Lord forty days and forty nights. He ate no bread and drank no water. He wrote the words of the covenant, the ten commandments, on tablets. When Moses came down from Mount Sinai, he had the two tablets of the covenant document in his hand. While Moses was descending from the mountain, he did not know that the skin of his face was emitting light because he had spoken to the Lord.... When Moses stopped speaking to them, he put a veil over his face. (Ex. 34:27ff)

This covenant gave the Old Testament its name, for *testamentum* is the Latin translation of the Hebrew word for *covenant*. But the fact that the Holy Scriptures of the Jews have the "old" covenant as their content is a judgment from the Christian point of view:

> Filled with such hope for the future, we can step forward with great boldness, not like Moses, who had to wear a veil to cover his face so that the Israelites would not see the fading of the brightness that was in decline. In those days human thinking became hardened. To this day, the book of the Old Covenant [Old Testament] has remained covered by the same veil when it is read. The veil was not drawn aside; only Christ takes it away. To this day, those who read the Books of Moses have this covering veil over their hearts. But as soon as one turns to the Lord, the covering is removed. (2 Cor. 3:12ff)

What does *covenant* mean here? Ultimately, it is a contract of the Godhead with humankind, in the highest sense a *legal relationship* in the form of *if–then*. If people fulfill certain conditions, then it can be expected that God will act accordingly for the salvation of people. The fact that God's action is predictable in the context of a covenant gives people a freedom they would not otherwise have. Therein lies the meaning of the covenant: It represents a decisive step in the education of the nation toward the freedom that the divine world grants to humanity. Strictly speaking, the Old Covenant is the summary of three covenants: The first is made with Noah, the second with Abraham, the third with Moses. The covenant with *Noah* brings the predictability of nature independent of human morality (Gen. 8:20ff), the covenant with *Abraham* (Gen. 17:1ff) grants him a great posterity for he was to become the progenitor of the chosen people. The covenant with *Moses* brings the law and with it a path to moral autonomy. The fact that nature becomes predictable, that there are calculable laws of nature, gives humanity external freedom. Do to the apparent unshakable effectiveness of the laws of nature this freedom has also led human beings to the conclusion that there is no God. The freedom that is granted to *Abraham* is the perspective that in the future he will exist through his descendants—the realization that the deeds of human beings have an effect in the future. And finally, the freedom that comes through the Mosaic law is the promise of moral autonomy, which is only in its beginning stages. Those who know the moral law also begin to know possible consequences of their actions. This plants a seed that can grow into inner freedom. In the covenant with Noah the human contribution is sacrifice: Noah builds an altar and sacrifices. And Yahweh "smelled the sweet odor"—and establishes the covenant. With Abraham, we find a willingness to place procreation entirely at the service of Yahweh. The outward sign of this is circumcision. With Moses, the fulfillment of the law forms the human will. This threefold covenant with God is the prerequisite for ritual worship in the Old Testament.

In the New Testament* it is the same. An essential impulse for the Christian ritual of the Lord's Supper lies in Christ's invitation: Do this in remembrance of me (Luke 22:19; 1 Cor. 11:24f). And this then becomes, at the same time, an expression of the New Covenant. Again, the initiative itself comes from the spiritual world and the result is a new freedom—here it is freedom from the Mosaic law, which has been completely transformed into individual moral responsibility through Christ.

Christian worship has its origin in God's New Covenant with humanity. It is a reliable promise of God to be present

* The expression "new" testament (new covenant) is already found in the Old Testament (Jer. 31:31). It is then referred to a few times in the New Testament: in Luke's account of the Last Supper (Luke 22:20) and Paul's (1 Cor. 11:24 f), as well as in Paul's Letter to the Hebrews (Heb. 8–9).

when people properly celebrate the Lord's Supper "in memory of him."

3.2 Collaboration between the Spirits of Form and the Spirits of Personality

A look at the Old and New Testaments has shown us that the source of authentic ritual is found in God's covenant with humankind. This is also true for the rituals of The Christian community. When Rudolf Steiner says that "The Christian Community was founded in reality in the spiritual world by spiritual beings,"* this confirms that the initiative for this new spiritual movement is grounded in the spirit in keeping with the archetype of the covenant. Like all initiatives, this initiative needed an echo. The initiative brought forward by the founders of The Christian Community can be seen as an echo of the initiative coming from the spiritual world. Furthermore, this founding can be understood as a further step in the ongoing evolution of Christianity and as a reconfirmation of God's covenant.

However, anthroposophy also gives rise to another perspective. In the cosmogony described there, the creation of the world and humanity is portrayed as the work of nine angelic hierarchies who carry out God's plan of creation. Steiner named these hierarchies but also continued to use the terms that originated with Dionysius Areopagita,† who was the first to publish the Christian doctrine of hierarchies. In

* CW 346, Sept. 20, 1924.

† Dionysius Areopagite (pseudo-Dionysius; 6th century), pseudonym for a mystical writer who identified himself with Dionysius Areopagite from Acts 17:34. John Scotus translated the writings into Latin around 860. They were taken as original Christian testimonies and enjoyed the highest reputation in the Middle Ages. It was not until 1895 that it could be proven that the writings originated in the 6th century.

the (cosmogonic) evolution there are different epochs (days of creation), greater and smaller, and within these epochs the hierarchical beings unfold their respective powers. The beings that actually create are the Spirits of Form (*Exusiai*) and higher. The angels, archangels, and Spirits of Personality (*Archai*) stand closer to human beings and do not yet participate in the active creation of the external world. Their field of activity is the human soul, influencing human willing, feeling, and above all human thinking—i.e., both the conscious and unconscious inner life. Therefore, during the various stages of human evolution, a special turning point is always reached when a transition occurs from one hierarchy to another. When the Spirits of Form completed their work, it was time for the Spirits of Personality to begin their guidance of humanity.

Rudolf Steiner describes such a transition in the near past. He mentioned the fourth century AD as the focus of this turning point in human evolution, which had begun centuries before and would last until the beginning of the modern era (1450–1850). Until this transition human thinking was guided and influenced by the Spirits of Form. This means that thoughts appeared in the human mind as "given" in a way similar to how objects in the external world simply appear, like a revelation. People did not experience themselves primarily as thinking beings—as we do today. Instead, they *perceived* thoughts—i.e., perceived them as if they originated outside themselves and then appeared as finished and complete. Our present situation came about when the "governance" of thinking was transferred to the Spirits of Personality. Thinking in the modern world is experienced more inwardly, more *personally*. Today we experience our thinking as requiring our inner activity. Indeed, we feel it would not be right if thoughts were simply put into our heads by some outside power. As thinking agents, we are responsible for producing our own thoughts, which also gives us a completely different relationship to reality. This shift from ancient times to the present is reflected in the many philosophical disputes that unfolded from Scholasticism to Kant to our present-day philosophy of science. *However, thinking experienced as something personal also makes it appear subjective.* Then, the "subjective reality" grasped in thinking can very easily appear unreal to us. We can no longer find its connection to the objective world.

The question *how is thinking connected to reality?* is at the center of Rudolf Steiner's philosophical writings (essentially the writings that appeared before 1900). For a thinking human being, there are two factors at play when reality arises in our consciousness: the perception and the thinking that has grasped the perception. If thoughts are no longer given as revelation, but must be brought forth actively, then our experience of reality also depends upon our activity. Steiner says accordingly: "The fact that reality cannot be found through thinking, because *it must first be created as reality through thinking*—that is hardly felt anywhere."* This does not mean, however, that reality thus grasped is unreal, but rather that our creative participation is necessary for its coming into being. The Spirits of Form have handed over the administration of thought to the Spirits of Personality, but they still stand behind perception, which is why our perceptions appear to us as "immediately given."† Therefore,

* Rudolf Steiner speaks of this in several places: CW 186, Dec. 20, 1918; CW 187, Dec. 28, 1918; CW 222, Mar. 16, 17, 18, 1923.

† CW 2, chap. 7.

in the process of knowing that prevails today, the Spirits of Form and the Spirits of Personality work together in perception and in thinking. In ancient times human consciousness was very different; in that era the entire process required in order to know something was subject to and guided by the Spirits of Form.*

From these considerations a bridge can be built to the kind of ritual appropriate for today. To begin with, it is necessary to find a connection to the Spirits of Form. Rudolf Steiner wrote in a letter to Marie von Sivers:

> This should be our ideal: To create forms that express the inner life of human beings. We live in an era of human evolution when human beings cannot see forms and bring them into existence simply by beholding them; this will necessarily cause the spirit to vanish into an abstraction without substance, and reality is forced to mirror this abstract spirit as merely aggregated matter devoid of spirit.... And because one can show spiritualized forms to the masses only through the medium of religion, our work for the future must go in this direction: to shape and form the religious spirit in beautiful, sense-perceptible forms.†

These forms, although they may be "created," come nevertheless from the Spirits of Form and are therefore "immediately given" (i.e., revealed). This applies to every aspect of rituals that is sense-perceptible: the signs, actions,

* From his research Rudolf Steiner describes the transition: "Until the ninth century after the Mystery of Golgotha man stood differently in relation to his thoughts than later. He did not have the feeling that he himself produced the thoughts living in his soul. He saw them as an inspiration from a spiritual world. Even if he had thoughts about what he perceived with his senses, the thoughts were to him revelations of the divine, revelations that spoke to him through the objects in the sense world" (CW 26, Aug. 17, 1924).

† CW 262, letter of Nov. 25, 1905.

and spoken words.* Then, however, rituals must still be carried out, so that they become reality. Today their execution is, similar to thinking, a different process than in earlier times. In former times, the Spirits of Form still stood behind their execution such that their reality was simply a "given." The individual carrying out a ritual had only to execute everything in the proper order—no additional personal contribution was required. This is still largely the case in the Catholic Church today: For a ritual to be valid, the priest must first observe the proper form of sign, action, and word (called *forma et materia* since Scholasticism). But additionally, he must also perform it inwardly correctly—i.e., with the right *intention*.

Here one would expect a personal contribution from the priest, behind which the Spirits of Personality stand, but his intention is precisely not supposed to be personal, but provided "objectively"; it is namely his obligation "to do what the Church does" (*intentio faciendi quod facit ecclesia*). Individual intention does not come into consideration. Apparently, we have here an example of Spirits of Form at work beyond their time. They have, so to speak, not passed on their task and thus have *fallen behind*. Today they are at work where human personality and intention would be necessary but are actually prevented. This happens, however, not only in the ecclesiastical context mentioned, but also in modern scientific research, a realm quite polar to the church. Generally recognized science as practiced today demands

* In the ancient mysteries, the trinity of sign, action and word was also known and in Greek, were called *deiknýmena:* display of what was offered by the priest, especially ritual objects and symbols preserved in the *cista mystica; drómena:* the cultic actions; *legómena:* a recital of religious texts accompanying and explaining the first two; cf. *Lexikon für Theologie und Kirche,* vol. 7, p. 719.

the elimination of everything personal to achieve objectivity. This requirement is one of the first and most important principles of modern science (see chapter 5.2.2.).

Rudolf Steiner's concept of science is different. It is no less objective, but it does include the researcher's personality on the path to truth. This is expressed very clearly in a letter he wrote concerning his book *The Philosophy of Freedom*. He wanted his book to be understood…

> in every line as a *personal* experience.... *I am not teaching*; I am relating what I have *experienced* inwardly. I tell it as I have lived it. Everything in my book is meant personally. Also, the form of my thoughts.... My way of negotiating many difficulties was entirely individual; the way I worked through conceptual thickets was mine alone. Only after you reach the goal do you realize that you have arrived. Perhaps the time for teaching such things as interest me is over. My interest in philosophy now extends almost exclusively to the experience an individual can have.*

The Philosophy of Freedom is subjective and yet its message concerns all human beings. These two aspects of the book belong together—indeed, united by Steiner's entirely personal approach to writing. Today, what is universally valid must be carried and sustained by the personal element if it is to be anchored in reality. That is another way of saying that the Spirits of Form must work together with the Spirits of Personality.

This also applies to contemporary rituals insofar as their forms must be in accordance with the spiritual world. The forms of words and course of action must correspond to strict necessity. Only those human beings whose consciousness can

* CW 39, letter to Rosa Mayreder, Nov. 4, 1894.

extend into the highest realms of the spiritual world can, like Moses on Mount Sinai, receive authentic rituals from the realm of the Spirits of Form. But then, rituals whose proper form has been mediated by such initiates, still need an intention for their execution. That human intention is then fired by the Spirits of Personality in a way similar to how Steiner wrote his book *The Philosophy of Freedom*. This intention must not be arbitrary, but neither can it be provided by any external regulations.

As modern human beings, we can reflect on what we want as our own fundamental intention for this lifetime. If this is in accordance with the objective intention required for the performance of ritual, then we could be called to celebrate rituals and sacraments. We will then be celebrating with our personal intention, doing what we *ourselves* truly want to do. Objectivity and personality will then be united. Similar to Steiner's words, one could then perhaps say: *Everything in rituals is meant personally*—yet, it is precisely because of this personal intention that anyone and everyone can find one's own relationship to spiritually objective sacraments and rituals today. The mission and task of The Christian Community is to cultivate such rituals; it is a task that must always be undertaken anew. Its core reality is found in the interaction between the Spirits of Form with the Spirits of Personality.

PART II:
HOW THE SACRAMENTS HAVE BEEN UNDERSTOOD THROUGH THE CENTURIES

Chapter 4
The Age of the Patriarchs

4.1 Understanding Sacraments

The seven sacraments celebrated in The Christian Community appear to have little in common. They have no common textual form, the duration varies greatly, and their purposes in human lives are very different. Some belong to specific life transitions, such as birth or puberty, while the occasion for others must be deliberately brought about, for example, Sacramental Consultation. Some can be received only once (e.g., Confirmation); others thrive on repetition (e.g., Communion). Most can be received by everyone in the course of their lives, whereas some, only by certain people (e.g., the wedding ceremony). What then justifies speaking of sacraments in an overarching sense? Although the New Testament describes the institution of Baptism and the Lord's Supper, no common generic term for a sacrament can be found there. The leaders of the Reformation also found it difficult to speak of sacraments in general. And finally, even Catholic theologians speak of the "profound difference that prevails between the individual sacraments, and the general doctrine of the sacraments that required over a millennium to emerge as a general, systematic doctrine."*

* Auer and Ratzinger, vol. 6, p. 20.

Rudolf Steiner provided The Christian Community with a foundation for a new understanding of the sacraments.[*] It still needs to be elaborated and further developed; this book is intended to take the first steps toward such a discussion. We begin by examining the history of Christianity to see how a general doctrine of the sacraments gradually evolved.

4.2 Mysteries

In the early days of Christianity, the time of the Apostolic Fathers, people did not yet speak of sacraments. The two celebrations directly instituted by Christ were simply called by name: Baptism and "breaking of bread"[†] or "the banquet of love" (*agape*).[‡] These two ritual celebrations had a common origin, being based on instructions from the Lord, but there was no conceptual framework unifying them. That changed when Christianity entered the Greek cultural sphere, whereupon it had to assert itself in the world of Hellenistic philosophy; Christians had to learn to express the contents of their religion in Greek philosophical terms and to defend Christianity against philosophical criticisms. Quite a number of second-century writers who wrote in defense of the new religion are thus called *apologists*.[§] This greatly influenced Christianity, which, to a certain extent, then merged with Greek thinking. Today, above all in Protestant theology, this process is thought to have been a terrible mistake. It is alluded

[*] Above all in CW 342, June 14, 1921, and CW 343, Oct. 2, 1921.

[†] Acts of the Apostles 2:42; 2:46; 20:7.

[‡] Letter of Judas 12.

[§] Apologia (απολογια) = Reply, defense. One important apologists is Justin the Martyr, born in Flavia Neapolis (today Nablus). After his philosophical education in Ephesus he converted to Christianity and worked inter alia as a Christian philosopher in Rome, where he became a martyr under Prefect Junius Rusticus (163–167).

to as the *Hellenization* of Christianity, which has alienated Christianity from its roots—but one can also see it differently.

Christianity was prepared in Judaism. Already in early Christianity the so-called *typological* approach had considered the Old and the New Testaments as belonging together. This means that a certain figure or event from the Old Testament (type) was related to a corresponding figure or event in the New Testament (antitype), e.g., the prophet Jonah (type) with Christ (antitype). This comparison is even directly stated in the New Testament (Matt. 12:40): "For as Jonah was three days and three nights in the belly of the fish, so also the Son of Man will be three days and three nights in the belly of the earth." The typological approach continued to be used in Europe until the late 13th century, when the so-called *Bibles of the Poor* appeared, in which richly illustrated pictures corresponding to scenes from the Old and New Testament were placed side by side. Apart from the Old Testament, however, one can also speak of a second, Greek–pagan stream preparing for Christianity. To put it simply, the task of Judaism in preparing for Christianity was to create the preconditions necessary for the incarnation of the Messiah, to prepare a bodily nature into which God could incarnate. Hellenism stood in contradistinction to Judaism, *but not to Christianity*. Therefore, Paul took care that Gentiles coming to Christianity were not first required to become Jews through circumcision (Acts 15:1ff). What certain theologians today see as an *alienation* was precisely Hellenism's contribution to Christianity: a philosophical terminology through which Christianity could be understood. Christianity has its roots not only in Judaism and the Old Testament, but also in paganism and its mysteries, especially in ancient

Greek religion; after all, Greek is also the language of the New Testament. This was explained by Rudolf Steiner in his book, *Christianity as Mystical Fact and the Mysteries of Antiquity*, published in 1902,* which was probably the first time this perspective was presented with complete clarity. In his preface to the second edition, he points out "how the source of Christianity created its necessary preconditions in the mysteries of the pre-Christian era. One can see in this 'pre-Christian mysticism' the soil in which Christianity flourishes as a seed of its own kind."

The apologists were the first to introduce a term encompassing both Baptism and the Lord's Supper; it was intended to characterize Christian ritual celebration altogether. Justin Martyr (ca.165) uses the word μυστεριον (mystery) to describe the early Christian rituals. It is not necessary here to describe this word's entire history of meaning—it is sufficient to point out the obvious reference to pre-Christian mysteries. These celebrations, which we call sacraments today, correspond to what were once celebrations within ancient Greek mystery religions. This fact is also clearly illuminated by another of Steiner's descriptions found in the chapter titled "The Gospels" in *Christianity as Mystical Fact*:

> Christianity was to be a means by which everyone could find the way. If they are not mature enough to do so, at least they are not cut off from the possibility that, if only unconsciously, they may become part of the spiritual stream of the mysteries.... From now on, even those who cannot take part in an initiation would be able to enjoy the fruits of the mysteries."

* This understanding of Hellenistic influences on Christianity was given academic credibility in 1910 by the publication of Richard Reitzenstein's book *Hellenistic Mystery-Religions*, which became a widely quoted book and remains in print more than a century later.

What Steiner here calls the fruits of the mysteries, we can understand as the sacraments, which Justin called *mysteries* and are still referred to as such in Eastern Orthodox churches today. The word mystery brings a special inner perspective later lost in the Western Church.* The Catholic theologian Michael Schmaus† describes it as follows:

> The mystery of Christ is proclaimed by the apostles. The church carries it further through time, manifesting it again and again in its cultus. Thus, the word *mysterion* means "cultus." Since Christ is no longer among us visibly, he lives with his salvific work in rituals and cultus.... In general, it can be said that a conviction was prevalent in the ancient church until Augustine that in the execution of the sacraments the Holy Spirit descends into material elements, sanctifies them and communicates to them a sanctifying power. He is called down through acts of consecration through certain prayers and formulas.‡

That "the Holy Spirit descends on the material elements, sanctifies them and communicates to them a sanctifying power" is otherwise called *epiclesis* (recalling) in theology. It is significant that in Eastern Orthodox churches (which still today connect this mood with the *mysteries*) there is a declared view that transformation is brought about by epiclesis in the liturgy (the Mass). In the Liturgy of Chrysostom, for example, the prayer of Epiclesis reads: "We also offer you this spiritual and bloodless sacrificial service and call and ask and implore you: send down your Holy Spirit on us and these gifts here."

---

* At the beginning of the twentieth century a new impulse for a "mystery theology" was given within the Catholic Church by Odo Casel, OSB.

† He is also a representative of the "mystery theology."

‡ Michael Schmaus, *Katholische Dogmatik,* vol. III/2, pp. 3ff.

The Roman Church has no epiclesis in its mass,* works under a different conception of transformation,† and does not call its sacraments mysteries. In the Act of Consecration of The Christian Community, however, the epiclesis of transformation is found in the request that the "power of grace" of the Holy Spirit work "earthward" and thereby transform the bread and wine into the body and blood of Christ. In this point the Act of Consecration of Man is more akin to Orthodox liturgy, although otherwise more closely related to the Roman Mass.

4.3 Sacraments

The concept of mystery is rooted in the Eastern regions of Christianity. For the West, the Occident, another step had to be taken. A further development in terms of content found its expression in the translation of the Greek word μυστεριον into Latin (*mysterium*). In Old Latin Bible translations, this applies to the North African texts, but also to *Itala*, which

* "There is no trace of a customary epiclesis in the documents of the Roman mass" (LThK2 3, 935). In 1999 the Catholic theologian Wilhelm Maas presented a study commissioned by the Theological Research Center of the Freie Hochschule der Christengemeinschaft in Stuttgart (still unpublished), which arrives at the conclusion that the Catholic Mass is, after all, an epiclesis of transformation. In particular, he gives reasons for believing that the Canon Prayer *Supplices te rogamus* is in reality to be understood as an epiclesis. Also, Catholic theology today advocates—obviously for reasons of church policy (Roman Catholic / Orthodox Dialogue Paper, Munich 1982)—the existence of an epiclesis with the view that the Eucharistic prayer *Supplices te rogamus* as a whole is an epiclesis. "Here a future-oriented ecumenical convergence might be aimed at..." (LThK3 3, 716).

† "Whereas according to Catholic doctrine only the words of the Lord bring about the Eucharistic transformation, the Eastern churches that separated from Rome transfer the transforming power either exclusively to epiclesis or to epiclesis in conjunction with the words of institution" (LThK2 3, 935f)

originated in Italy, the Greek *mysterion* is almost always translated as *sacramentum*. This is surprising, because it is actually wrong. The Greek verb μυειν (*myein*) means to close (the lips). The primary meaning of the related noun μυστεριον, *mysterium*, is thus "a secret"—i.e., an inner experience about which one firmly closes one's lips and remains silent. Its spectrum of meaning then goes beyond even that. *Sacramentum* on the other hand, has a strong *will* component, insofar as it involved action: it has to do with the sacred (*sacrum*), but in practical terms meant that in legal proceedings each of two disputing parties must deposit a pledge (*sacramentum*) in the temple—that is, at the holy place. The party who loses the trial forfeits their deposit to the temple. The other meaning is *to vow*, or to vow the oath of allegiance spoken by soldiers. Because *mysterion* and *sacramentum* are so far apart in meaning, in later Latin translations of the Bible, especially in the Vulgate of Jerome (end of the fourth century), the Greek word μυστεριον was mostly translated not with the word *sacramentum*, but with the word *mystery*, understood as a Latin foreign word. Nevertheless, through Tertullian* the translation of *mysterion* as *sacramentum* outside the Bible finally became an important theological and ecclesiastical fact. Where Justin uses the common term *mysterium* for Baptism and Communion, Tertullian uses *sacramentum* as the corresponding word. It is with this word and its meaning that the sacraments, initially Baptism and Communion, came into the Western church. The word *sacrament*

* Tertullian, Quintus Septimius Florens, born around 160 in Carthage as son of a pagan *centurio proconsularis*, received an excellent rhetorical and legal education and probably worked as a lawyer in Rome. After his conversion to Christianity (ca. 195), he dedicated himself in Carthage to the spreading and deepening of the Christian faith until his death (after 220). Whether he was also a priest as well as a catechist, as Jerome reports, remains doubtful.

expresses the obligatory nature of a vow taken by the one who receives them.

The mass as celebrated in The Christian Community—The Act of Consecration of Man—attests to the special nature of this word. One of the founders, Friedrich Rittelmeyer, once had a dream in which he asked Rudolf Steiner about the origin of the Act of Consecration of Man. This was still during Steiner's lifetime, and later the opportunity arose for Rittelmeyer to ask him directly in person. Rittelmeyer reports:

> In that conversation in 1924 we also discussed the origin of the Act of Consecration of Man. In a dream at night I asked Doctor Steiner how the Act of Consecration of Man had actually come about, and he had answered: "I had to go to a place where the German language is taught in mantric language." Dr. Steiner confirmed this response as being accurate, and added, "You mustn't imagine that place in such a way that you could send a postal package there."

We can assume Rittelmeyer hadn't been tempted to do so...

Mantric means language that depends in a special way on the phonetic and rhythmic constellation of words, how they sound together beyond the mere thought content. Words then have a special power and effect. Without this power, ritual worship would not actually be possible, or it would merely amount to empty words spoken in a superficial way. Rudolf Steiner once indicated that elemental beings can even arise through certain mantras. In mantric language, sounds are arranged in regular patterns so that the vibrations of the air are not arbitrary—such as the repeated "o, i, u" heard, for example, in *Dominus vobiscum*. Something spiritually meaningful happens when the priest "makes certain hand movements along with certain sounds; the effect of the repeated sounds is amplified by making certain hand movements, and a sylph is called forth."*

Thus, if, with regard to the Act of Consecration of Man, one speaks of a place where "the German language is taught in mantric," one would expect the mantric quality of the ritual wording in this language to be essential. And indeed, similar to the *Dominus vobiscum* example given by Steiner as early as 1905, one can discover many corresponding word- and sound-constellations in the text of the Act of Consecration of Man (that act in this mantric way). It is noteworthy that the wording of the Act of Consecration of Man consists almost exclusively of words from the actual German language, that is, with no foreign loan words. Even fully assimilated foreign words, for which there seems to be no equivalent in the German language, such as "*Mystery* of Golgotha," appear in a form displaying their Germanic roots, in this case "Deed of Life and Death on Golgotha" (German: *Lebens-Todestat auf Golgotha*). The very few foreign words that are nevertheless in the linguistic body of The Act of Consecration of Man then stand out as singular representatives of other languages and obviously with a special mantric power. These include: *Evangelium* (gospel), *physisch* (physical), *Materie* (matter), *Amen* (amen), *Substanz* (substance), *Äther* (ether),† *prophetisch* (prophetic), and finally, in a prominent place and emphasized by the syntax, *Sakrament* (Sacrament). Four of these foreign words represent

* CW 93a, Oct. 30, 1905.

† The word *ether* appears only in the St. John Tide epistle of the Act of Consecration of Man. On the other hand, in the main body of the mass, the words *Formative Forces* serve to convey the concept that might elsewhere be referred to as "etheric forces."

the Greek language; *Amen* represents the Hebrew language; *Matter, Substance,* and especially *Sacrament* represent the Latin language. These are the three languages in which Pilate wrote the reason for Jesus' crucifixion on the cross.* We can therefore assume that the word *sacrament* appears in the German ritual of The Christian Community because it brings the mantric power of the Latin language in an appropriate way. This contrasts completely with Zwingli's opinion, who said on one occasion: "I very much wish that the Germans had never included the word *sacrament* in their vocabulary."

4.4 AUGUSTINE: SIGNS AND SEALS

Greek theologians spoke of Baptism and the Lord's Supper in mystery-cult language and placed ritual experience in the foreground. The Latin theologian Tertullian emphasized the will side, the ethical action, in the sacraments. With Augustine† an understanding of the sacraments begins. He introduced a concept that proved to be fundamental for sacramental theology: sign (*signum*). A sign points beyond itself to what is designated, namely the thing (*res*). Thus, a sacrament

* "Pilate also had a sign made and fastened to the top of the cross; the inscription read: Jesus of Nazareth, King of the Jews. Many Jews read this sign because the place where Jesus was crucified was near the city. The inscription was written in Hebrew, Latin, and Greek (John 19:19ff).

† Aurelius Augustinus, born in 354 in Thagaste (Numidia), died Aug. 28, 430, in Hippo Regius (Numidia), ecclesiastical teacher, son of a pagan official and a Christian woman (Monica). He decided to become a rhetorician. The reading of Cicero's *Hortensius* led Augustine to philosophy. For many years he was a follower of Manichaeism, then briefly of skepticism, later of Neo-Platonism (in particular, Plotinus, ca. 205–270). In Milan, finally, the personality of Bishop Ambrose and his synthesis of Neoplatonism and Christianity won him over to Christianity for good. He dedicated himself to an ascetic life. In 387, he was baptized and, in 395, named bishop in Hippo Regius near Carthage.

as a sign points beyond itself to a holy "thing"* (i.e., grace or Christ). The important thing is, of course, not the sign itself, but what it points to, the designated thing (in scholasticism one then spoke of an *external* and *internal* sacrament). The signs themselves are still differentiated into word and element by Augustine—for example, when considering Baptism. The element in the case of Baptism is water, while the word is the baptismal formula. "When the word comes to the element, the sacrament is created" (*accedit verbum ad elementum et fit sacramentum*).

Augustine's distinction between *signum* and *res*, between sacramental sign and divine grace to which the sign points, contains the dualism of earthly, sensible sign and spiritually transcendent grace. This statement is an expression of thinking shaped by Neoplatonism.† Signs and grace belong to different worlds; the sacraments as external signs are only symbols of what they point to. It is all the more astonishing then that Augustine also asserts the truth of the polar opposite—namely, that the sacraments actually do what they indicate. "The church Father, despite his platonic, idealistic way of thinking, thus professes a sacramental realism."‡

Consider for a moment the content of the following

* "*Signa, quae, cum ad res divinas pertinent, sacramenta appellantur.*" English: Signs that point to the divine, *res divinas:* the divine things, the holy thing, are called sacraments. Quoted from Auer and Ratzinger, vol. 6, p. 38.

† Neoplatonism is the last great system of Greek philosophy (ca. AD 200 to 500). In addition to Platonic terms, Aristotelian, Stoic and terms from the mysticism of late antiquity were also included in Neoplatonism. Ammonias Saccas (AD 242) is considered the founder of Neoplatonism, but the most important Neoplatonist was his student Plotinus. Rudolf Lorenz writes in *Die Religion in Geschichte und Gegenwart,* vol. 1, pp. 740ff: "Augustine learns through Plotinus to seek the truth beyond the physical world and to recognize the invisible perfection of God through created things."

‡ Ganoczy: *Einführung in die katholische Sakramentenlehre*, p. 18.

statements. The second sentence alone could seem like the name of a magical act, insofar as the sacrament itself brings something about—namely, grace. It does so through the vehicle of the priest performing the sacrament. Even today many people still experience some echoes of this magical understanding of sacraments. On the other hand, however, the first sentence speaks of the sacrament being a sign that refers to something that *does not have to be performed because it already exists.* So, the two sentences carry each other and protect each other from a one-sided understanding. With these two basic statements, he combines Neoplatonic and Aristotelian thinking:

> The sacraments are visible signs of an invisible grace.
> The sacraments are signs that bring about the designated grace.

Augustine hereby laid a permanent foundation for a sacramental theology, on which the Catholic Church continued to build until the Council of Trent (1545–1563).

It may now come as a surprise that The Christian Community's new understanding of the sacraments follows Augustine's line of thought. In the sacrament of Ordination, it is stated that when a priest acts sacramentally then what he or she "does in sign" should be understood as "done in spirit." This is in accord with Augustine inasmuch as sacraments are signs that refer to the spirit, and inasmuch as they create a spiritual fact.

But it must also be noted that there is an implied tension between the two basic statements. A great thinker like Augustine could unite them within himself but later theologians often could not. As a result they understood sacraments in a one-sided way, and ultimately came to very different views of the sacraments even while attributing the views to Augustine. In the Middle Ages there were those who mainly saw the first sentence as more fundamental and saw in the Lord's Supper only an external symbol for the reality of the presence of Christ. And then there were those who placed the second sentence at the center of their understanding and concluded that the real presence of Christ in the Lord's Supper was brought about almost magically. This led to the great theological nominalism/realism controversy.

There are two further characteristics of sacraments, not entirely newly named and described by Augustine; through him, however, they became an accepted aspect of sacramental theology. One question was whether the effectiveness of a sacrament depends on the worthiness of the bestower—a very obvious question, which today still occupies many participants in the rituals. In the fourth century, this question originated from the so-called Donatists, the followers of the counter-bishop (since 313) Donatus of Carthage (ca. 355). For them, the effectiveness of the sacraments depended on the dignity of their bestower, which is why in 312 they did not recognize Caecilian's episcopal consecration. The consecration was invalid because the co-celebrating bishop was accused of having handed over Holy Scriptures to the Roman authorities during the time of persecution, which was considered a mortal sin. The conflicts of this North African church with the Roman Church continued throughout the fourth century. When Augustine became Bishop in Hippo, he turned with all his intensity against the Donatists with the response that even a heretical priest could administer valid sacraments. He justified this by arguing that the one actually celebrating the sacraments is not the priest, but God—implying that the priest is the vehicle for that divine force. The individual characteristics and beliefs of the priest therefore do not play a (great) role (in the effectiveness of the sacrament).

We want to pause again and ask ourselves what consequences are connected with this question. If the church had decided that the dignity of a priest was of decisive importance for the effectiveness of a sacrament, then as a consequence the faithful would have to live in complete uncertainty as to whether a sacrament was really effective. A personal element would have entered the church, revolving around the personality of the priest. Sacraments would have become subjectively bound to the priest and his moral condition, his dignity. It was obvious that Augustine had to fight against the Donatist view, but with the statement that the effectiveness of a sacrament is not bound to a priest's dignity, one could draw the one-sided and therefore wrong conclusion that the ideological or moral constitution of a priest does not matter at all. This view was actually widespread in the dark centuries of the church before its reform councils.

In the controversy with heretics, theologians became aware of a third characteristic of the sacrament. It was the question whether heretics, when they ask to be admitted to the church, must once again be baptized, but this time *correctly*. As with the Donatists, this question was answered in the negative. Following a passage in Second Corinthians,* the biblical word *seal* had gradually acquired just one

* "But God, who strengthens us and you in faithfulness to Christ, and who has anointed us all, it is also he who has put his seal on us and given the Spirit as a pledge in our hearts" (II Cor. 1:2f).

meaning by the fourth century. Augustine's understanding of the baptismal seal is based on the Roman practice of "burning the sign of the emperor or commander into the skin of the soldiers."* This "mark of men" (*character domenicus*) as a permanent seal became then the proof of Baptism that had been validly administered, regardless of the priest. Because of this seal the Baptism cannot be repeated; it is a permanent, objective effect of the sacrament.

Here again there is tension: The sacrament is an objective fact for the priest (regardless of his dignity) and for the one baptized (the seal), but if a sacrament works objectively in this way, is the goal not already achieved in light of the effects of grace? Does it then still require an additional personal effort? What is the personal contribution of the priest, if any? What is the personal contribution of the one who receives a sacrament?

These questions, anchored by Augustine into sacramental theology, also play an important role in The Christian Community, but with a more evolved understanding. We will discuss this in the following sections.

We will now consider Augustine's personality. What qualities of soul were at work in him that made it possible to form concepts still valid today, polar concepts that can easily lead to contradictory conclusions? These soul qualities embody the tension of the words *this as well as that*.† In

* Auer and Ratzinger, vol. 6, p. 72.

† What is meant here is an active, tension-filled *this as well as that*. In the Eastern religions of Asia there is an ancient form of *this as well as that*, which has a rather passive character (in every situation there is always something that is *justified*). Such a serene approach that *begins* with an attitude of having already risen above the situation does not lead to the kind of dynamic advancement described by Goethe. His process involves a polar tension that *culminates* in a rise to a higher perspective, a higher principle governing the phenomena.

anthroposophy, the ability to contain and live with this tension is called the *consciousness soul.* It is the most mature form of the soul and it is to be developed gradually in our time.* Augustine obviously had some of this ability already—Rudolf Steiner said that Augustine "lived long before the first emergence of our age, but he prepared it; he is the spirit in whose writings we find the first dawn of our age, long before the sun actually rises, the age that is entirely tailored to the consciousness soul. In every line of Augustine's writings, this can be perceived. A sensitive reading will find that every line of Augustine differs from all that was possible in ancient Greek."†

Augustine thus gives us three characteristics of sacraments in which he finds signs and seals. These characteristics are fundamental for an understanding of the sacraments.

1. The two basic statements already discussed concerning an external sign (*signum*) and supernatural grace (*res*). They also apply to the sacraments of The Christian Community.

2. The validity of the sacrament does not depend on the worthiness of the priest. This statement is also significant for The Christian Community; however, there are nuances reflected in an evolved understanding of this issue.

3. The sacrament of Baptism causes a permanent seal (*character domenicus*). In The Christian Community one can also speak of the seal of the sacraments; again, there is an evolved understanding of this issue.

We must bear in mind that Augustine was in a position to establish a conceptual outline of sacramental theology

---

* "Our time" is described in anthroposophy as the fifth post-Atlantean cultural epoch. It began in the fifteenth century and lasts approximately 2,000 years.

† CW 145, Mar. 26, 1913.

even though he had only the sacraments of Baptism and the Lord's Supper in mind.

4.5 Medicine

There is a further essential aspect of sacraments in The Christian Community, which seems to be a distinctive feature of Christian Community theology. This is the sacrament's therapeutic effect. One can find a whole spectrum of references to it in the ritual wording of the sacraments, particularly the mass (ACM), but the one that stands out the most is the term "the sickness of sin."* The term *original sin*, which is usually used in theology, emphasizes the ethical aspect of the Fall, which can be seen as problematic insofar as before eating of the forbidden tree of knowledge, there was no capacity to distinguish good from evil. Personal ethical behavior was not yet in play. For this reason, we choose to speak of the pathological aspect of the Fall instead. For example, Lessing writes in *The Education of the Human Race* (§ 74): "As for the doctrine of original sin...how, if finally, everything were

* First used by Rudolf Steiner in 1922 in the translation of the Mass for Hugo Schuster: "May your body, O Lord, which nourishes me, and your blood, which has strengthened me, penetrate my soul forever and in me erase the sickness of sin as the pure and healing sacraments" (CW 343, Oct. 7, 1921). Apparently, the same term already occurs with Augustine in his *Confessions* (2nd book, chap. 7), in the translation by Georg Rapp, 1838: "And whoever is called by you and follows your call, whoever avoids what he reads here about me, and what I myself confess about myself, do not laugh at me, that the same doctor healed me of my illness, who saved him from it or caused him to fall ill less. Let him love you likewise, even more, when he sees me healed of so great a sickness of sin by him who saved him from it himself." On closer inspection, however, it becomes clear that the term used by Augustine (*languores peccatorum*) is not the *sickness* that becomes the constitutional cause of sin (this is the meaning of *sickness of sin* in Steiner), but the mental *weariness* as a result of sin. Hermann Hefele (1958), for example, translates *languores peccatorum* as *lingering illness* (*Sündensiechtum*) accordingly.

to convince us that the human beings, standing on the first and lowest level of their humanity, are not so entirely master of their actions as to be able to obey moral laws?" Since we must nevertheless bear the consequences of the fall of humankind, the responsibility for the fall has been imposed on us. Although we do not at first have that responsibility, we must gradually grow into it, as it were, later as a result of our maturation. Seen in this light, salvation has not only a moral but also a therapeutic aspect. The phrase *sickness of sin* points to this, and leads us to the thought that redemption is healing.

References to healing also abound in the sacraments of The Christian Community. In the creed of The Christian Community the Holy Spirit is called the *Healing Spirit*. In the Pentecost prayers and in the prayer to Michael the archangel, there is also reference to the *healing Spirit*, and beyond that also to *the Spirit who brings healing*, and the one *who heals as a world physician*. Finally, the *healing medicine* is found in the Communion, which is identified with the Sacrament itself and is to bring about *the healing of the sickness of sin*.

In this focus on healing we find a new approach to the theology of sin. Rudolf Steiner then expanded this approach into practical life when he held the *Pastoral Medical Course for Doctors and Priests** of The Christian Community. The theme of illness and sin is dealt with here in a very unexpected way, and a foundation is provided for a deepened collaboration between members of both professions.

This aspect of the sacrament as a healing medicine was already mentioned in early Christianity by Ignatius, Bishop of Antioch. All that is known of his biography—besides that

* CW 318, Sept. 8–18, 1924.

he suffered martyrdom in Rome between 110 and 117—has been gleaned from seven letters he wrote to different churches, in which he addressed important topics. In his letter to the church in Ephesus he characterized the Lord's Supper as a *remedy for immortality* (*pharmakon athanasias*). This corresponds to the healing remedy spoken of in the ritual of The Christian Community and is a very important description of the sacraments' therapeutic effect. However, it has been largely neglected and has barely played a role in the sacramental theology of the church. Alexander von Hales,* a medieval theologian, also expressed this thought, although it never gained any significance. In his *Glossa* (written 1223–27) he wrote of a sevenfold infection (*infectio)* of the human soul caused by different kinds of sins, and then contrasts them with the sacraments, which serve to heal those sins:

1. Baptism: *medicina curatoria* (preventive medicine);
2. Confirmation: *medicina conservativa* (preservative medicine);
3. Ordination: *medicina meliorativa* (refining medicine);
4. Marriage: *medicina praeservativa* (protective medicine);
5. Last Rites: *medicina mitigativa* (soothing medicine);
6. Communion: *medicina conservativa, meliorativa et confortativa* (preservative, refining and strengthening medicine).†

---

* Alexander von Hales, about 1170–1245, born in England, studied theology in Paris. Around 1231, he became a Franciscan and founder of the older Franciscan school. Despite the many works wrongly attributed to him there are some verified: *Glossa in 4 libros Sententiarum.*

† Auer and Ratzinger, vol. 6, p. 87.

Chapter 5
Scholasticism

The groundwork for sacramental theology was laid during the time of the church Fathers. To a certain extent, The Christian Community builds on that foundation. In scholasticism,* this foundation was elaborated with great precision by theologians employing a specific philosophical-theological method. They examined extremely subtle aspects of intricate questions. Some issues have become much clearer through their method, but some have also been narrowed and led to legalistic paths, which make it difficult to experience the original meaning of sacramental celebrations. Here the relationship to Christian Community theology becomes more complicated. In some areas we find a direct connection to scholasticism—e.g., in the recognition of seven Sacraments. In other areas, scholastic concepts need to be expanded and

---

* *Scholasticism* is the term used to describe the philosophical–theological speculation that took place between the Carolingian period and the Renaissance, first at cathedral and monastery schools, then at universities (especially Paris and Oxford). In terms of content, it is characterized by the combination of Christian doctrine of revelation with philosophical thought. Its goal was the rational foundation and systematization of the contents of faith. The main problems of early scholasticism (ninth to twelfth centuries) were the relationship between theology and philosophy and the problem of universals (realism, nominalism). In high scholasticism (thirteenth to early fourteenth century), when new universities were founded, the Franciscans and Dominicans entered scientific life, and the scientific writings of Aristotle became known. Late scholasticism (late fourteenth and fifteenth centuries) brought a kind of schooling intent on preserving the philosophy of high scholasticism.

brought into dialogue with modern consciousness. There are also areas in which The Christian Community finds itself in opposition to the sacramental theology of scholasticism.

5.1 Why Seven Sacraments?

A long interim follows Augustine, in which the legacy of the Patristic era continues but is not further developed. "The early Middle Ages were a time without theology."* The next theological impulse arose with scholasticism. With regard to sacramental theology Augustine's legacy consisted of a clear description of the structure of a sacrament: sign (*signum*) and designated grace (*res*), as well as the relationship between them. Furthermore, he established the idea of a sacramental (baptismal) seal and the fact that sacraments are effective independent of the beliefs and moral worth of the officiant. Scholastic theology from the twelfth century onward examined these ideas. Augustine had achieved the amazing feat of laying the foundation for a general doctrine of the sacraments, despite referring solely to Baptism and the Lord's Supper. What Augustine had to say about the two sacraments was found in high scholasticism to be applicable to all seven sacraments, justifying the further development of Augustine's thoughts.

The question of the number of sacraments first needed to be clarified, but no number was fixed until the twelfth century. Until then, the number varied "between five and twelve, some theologians even counted thirty."† The number seven was probably first written down in 1147 in a treatise by

* Vorgrimler, p. 66.

† Ganoczy, p. 39.

Gilbert of Poitiers (or his student).* The fact that the number seven became established very quickly, however, is due to the decisive influence of Peter Lombard, who wrote about it in his *Libri quatuor Sententiarum* around 1155 to 1158. In 1208, it is mentioned for the first time in a church document (see section 2.2). It is astonishing how easily the number seven became established, without lengthy theological disputes. Less than a hundred years later, Thomas Aquinas (1225–1274) begins his theological work with this assumption, and in 1274, representatives of the Orthodox Church at the Council of Unions in Lyon also adopted this view. It is then found in 1439 as official doctrine of the church in the *Dogma to Be Taught to the Armenians*.

Why was the number seven taken, so to speak, as naturally as a ripe fruit falls into one's hands? There was hardly any valid external justification for it. Even today some authoritative Catholic theologians do not accept the number (see section 2.2), but there are also theologians who have no problem with it, such as Johann Auer,† who describes the number seven as self-evident. The systematization, which was achieved by the "method of salvation history as well as the dialectical method" led to "establishing the actual number of seven sacraments given by tradition." We have seen how little facts and traditions contributed to the precise number of *seven* sacraments. Herbert Vorgrimler‡ also makes things easy for himself by not stating any reason: Seven as the number of sacraments prevailed, "not least because the sacraments of the New Covenant were finally to be separated

* Gilbert Porreta, ca. 1080 in Poitiers, taught in Chartres and Paris and became bishop of Poitiers in 1142.

† Auer and Ratzinger, vol. 6, pp. 87ff.

‡ Vorgrimler, p. 67f.

from the broad 'sacramental range' of the natural sacraments, the Old Testament sacraments, the sacrament-like ordinations and blessings. New Testament sacraments were accorded outstanding dignity and assured effectiveness." No explanation is given; it is up to the reader to interpret why theologians concluded that the number seven is the appropriate one for the number of sacraments.

So, a mystery remains. Skeptics say that people of that time were simply following a mystical preference for the number seven. But one could also see it in reverse, namely that "sevenness" is a spiritual truth that lives beyond people's everyday consciousness and it took people more than a thousand years to wake up to it. After what seems to have been an intuitive discovery, a justification had to be found. In the Eastern church, for instance, the seven sacraments are connected to the "seven gifts of the Holy Spirit."* Catholic theologians (H. Schell) have also established a connection with the seven letters in the Apocalypse (chapters 2 and 3).† Friedrich Rittelmeyer made the discovery that the seven signs described in John's gospel can be connected to the seven sacraments; Rudolf Steiner then confirmed this. These analogies or indications that one specific *sevenness* is connected with other groups of seven are important, but hardly constitute proof.

Thoman Aquinas was the first to attempt a justification; he connected the sevenness of the Sacraments with seven biographical stages in human lives. Rudolf Frieling also gives

* "But out of the stump of Jesse's tree a sprig grows, a young shoot from its roots bears fruit. The Spirit of the Lord settles on him: the Spirit of wisdom and insight, the Spirit of counsel and strength, the Spirit of knowledge and piety. He fills him with the spirit of godliness" (Isaiah 11:2f).

† Auer and Ratzinger, vol. 6, p. 88.

a description of this in an essay on the sacraments that is worth reading.* Herbert Vorgrimler gives a brief summary of Thomas's remarks: "The most important achievements in the development of man, birth, growing up, nutrition, are healed and perfected through Baptism, Confirmation and the Eucharist; what threatens man and makes him ill is also turned to healing through penance and anointing of the sick; human social existence is led to prosper before God through consecration and marriage."† The persuasive power of Thomas's reasoning can be left aside. It was a first attempt. At the end of the Middle Ages it was not yet understood why the organism of the sacraments is sevenfold; it was accepted but was not yet understood. The Catholic Church agreed with Thomas, and at the Council of Trent it laid down the sevenness of the sacraments as an indisputable dogma.

Rudolf Steiner, who links an understanding of the sacraments to the idea of evolution, has provided a completely new way to understand the "law" of sevenness to a greater depth. This is entirely appropriate for anthroposophy, which includes the idea of evolution in every field of spiritual or human endeavor. Actually, the consistent inclusion of evolutionary change and development is what distinguishes anthroposophy fundamentally from other spiritual teachings. We will discuss this in a later section.

5.2 The Threefold Nature of the Sacraments

Scholastic theology understands the sacraments to have a threefold structure. Pope Innocent III first officially described

* Frieling, *Die sieben Sakramente in der Geschichte der Christenheit.*

† Vorgrimler, p. 70f.

them in 1202.* Accordingly, three things are to be distinguished "in the most exact" (subtle) way:

1. The ritual act (*sacramentum tantum*)
2. The sacramental reality (*res et sacramentum*)
3. The grace of the sacrament (*res tantum*)

5.2.1 The Ritual Act (Sacramentum tantum)

Scholasticism asked the question: what conditions are necessary for a sacrament to be performed *correctly?* The newly discovered writings of Aristotle (384–322 BC) played an important role in high scholasticism. He was *the philosopher* and had the authority of a church teacher. The two Aristotelian principles form and matter (*forma et materia*) became important for sacramental theology.

Rudolf Steiner used these two principles to explain the philosophical foundations of anthroposophy. The reality we perceive is created when our thinking brings together our perceptions (or percepts) with the ideas or thoughts that explain them. Expressed in the conceptual language of Aristotle, according to Steiner, perception would correspond to matter and thinking to form. Steiner explains:

> [Aristotle] is clear that with regard to all things that form our world of experience, it is important for cognition that we grasp form, because form gives things their essence, not matter. There are personalities in our time still who have a correct understanding of Aristotle. Vincenz Knauer, who was a university lecturer in Vienna in the 1890s, explained the difference between matter and form to his listeners by means of an illustration that

* In a letter to the Archbishop of Lyon. Cf. Piault, *Was ist ein Sakrament?* p. 57; and Debus, *Anthroposophie und die Erneuerung der christlichen Kirche*, pp. 29ff.

> may be mocked, but is nevertheless accurate. He said that one should think how a wolf that may have eaten nothing but lambs for a time in its life, how it is actually made up of the matter of the lambs—and yet this wolf never becomes a lamb! If you follow it correctly, that gives the difference between matter and form. Is the wolf a wolf through matter? No! He has his essence as wolf through form—we find the "wolf form" not only in this wolf, but in all wolves. So, we find the form by forming a term that expresses a universal, in contrast to what the senses grasp, which is a special, single thing.*

Just as Rudolf Steiner applies these two principles to the act of knowledge and relates them to perception and thought, they were also applied to the sacraments in scholasticism. The first to do this in the strictly Aristotelian matter-form *(hyle-morphe)* sense was Hugo of St. Cher.† Following the Augustinian division of the sacramental sign into word and element, he connects the element to matter, and the word to form. The perhaps surprising connection between word and form becomes understandable when we consider that the meaning of the element (e.g., water in a Baptism) is only revealed through the word, the *formula*. However, the significance of priestly action was still an open question, as were such sacraments as Confession and Marriage, which have no material element at all, but only human action.

Therefore, a further distinction was necessary, which was made by John Duns Scotus.‡ He allocated the term *matter*

* CW 35, *Philosophy and Anthroposophy,* Aug. 17, 1908.

† Hugo of St. Cher, ca.1190–1263, important theologian, became a Dominican in Paris in 1226 and cardinal in 1244.

‡ Johannes Duns Scotus (ca.1270–1308), Doctor subtilis, is considered the most astute thinker of scholasticism. Born in Scotland, he became a Franciscan and studied at Oxford. After teaching in Paris, he returned to England in 1305/06. He died in Cologne.

not only to the material element, which he calls *materia remota* (distant matter), but also to human action, which he called *materia proxima* (near matter). This offered the possibility to answer the question of how form and matter are related in all sacraments and helped to explain what is essential for a sacrament to come into being in the first place. The result was applied in the *Dogma to Be Taught to the Armenians,*[*] written at the Union Council in Florence in 1439. Three examples are given:[†]

- For Baptism, the following applies: *Matter*: "True and natural water, whether warm or cold." *Form*: "I baptize you in the name of the Father and of the Son and of the Holy Spirit."
- For the Lord's Supper: *Matter*: "Wheat bread and grape wine, to which a small amount of water must be added before Ordination." *Form*: "Words of the Savior with which he administered this sacrament, because the priest administers this sacrament by speaking in the person of Christ the words of institution[‡]."
- For Confession: *Matter*: "The penitential activities: remorse of the heart; the sinner's oral confession; the amends for sins (prayer, fasting, almsgiving)." *Form*: "I absolve you, etc."

Thus, the minimum requirements are defined. If form and matter are in accordance with these indications, the sacrament has been performed appropriately. Everything else can be determined by circumstances.

[*] By recognizing this decision the Armenians achieved union with Rome in 1442, which was urgently needed militarily against the Ottomans but was of no help and (therefore) only lasted for a short time.

[†] Neuner-Roos, *Der Glaube der Kirche in den Urkunden der Lehrverkündigung*, pp. 365–450.

[‡] A particularly delicate point, because according to the Eastern church's view the transformation is not brought about by the words of institution but by epiclesis, i.e., this should be the *form*.

For The Christian Community it would be unthinkable to consider some aspect taken from the whole of the ritual as essential and to think that the performance of the sacrament depends especially upon that one aspect. Nevertheless, the pair of concepts form/matter can be used profitably for an understanding of the sacrament if one begins at the same point as Rudolf Steiner:* Just as, in the process of knowing, what is given to us by the senses (pure perception) and the thing to be created (the concept) exist as matter and form of knowledge, likewise in ritual there is the given and the thing to be created. The substances, the actions (gestures) and the words that are spoken by the celebrant of the sacrament can be thought of collectively as what is given, for they are provided to the celebrant, who has no say in changing them. These three—substances, actions and words—constitute the *matter* of the sacrament. (According to Catholic theology, substance and action would also be matter, but the wording would be the form.) But for the sacrament to become a reality, it must be performed (i.e., celebrated). This is the creative part for the human being, the celebrant; it is the form of the ritual that corresponds to the actual thinking that brings about knowledge. Everything Steiner said about the process of cognition can be said in the same way about ritual† and can lead to a deeper understanding, especially of the human role in the fulfillment of ritual. (This applies today to the congregation as well as to priests.‡)

---

* Cf. Debus, *Anthroposophie und die Erneuerung der christlichen Kirche*, chapter on knowledge and worship."

† Cf. chapter 2.4 in *Ritual and Sacrament in Anthroposophy*.

‡ At this point, confusion could easily arise as to the terms used. In the chapter "Collaboration between the Spirits of Form and the Spirits of Personality," we have stated that the Spirits of Form provide the given, "but then the ritual given as form is still in need of an intention for execution, fired by the Spirits of Personality." But what comes from

Rudolf Steiner gives profound indications of what human beings must contribute in order for a sacrament to be a reality. He refers first of all to pre-Christian mysteries because initiates in ancient times had to anticipate the future—that was the purpose of their initiation, so they could give impulses for spiritual development. In his 1902 book, *Christianity as Mystical Fact*, he mentions the fact that the sensations and feelings of students of the mysteries must undergo a transformation in order for a higher world to become reality. And then everything depends on the mood:

> To begin with, for an initiate, everything depends upon the mood in which he approaches what he feels to be the highest answers to the riddles of existence.... A deity comes to meet you! He is either nothing or everything. He is nothing if you meet him in the same mood in which you encounter everyday things. He is everything if you are prepared for him, attuned to him.*

The importance of transforming and creating new feelings and sensations runs through the whole of anthroposophy. It is only through this that human consciousness can prepare itself for higher worlds. All knowledge obtained from the suprasensory world and conveyed through anthroposophy has meaning for the higher development of the human being only if it is transformed into feelings and sensations not based on the sensory world. In "meditation we have, so to speak, been given the technique for our esoteric life. This consists of letting thoughts, so to speak, act upon one's mind and through those thoughts awaken sensations and feelings

---

the Spirits of Form is matter in the Aristotelian sense, and what comes from the Spirits of Personality is, in Aristotelian terms, form!

* CW 8, pp. 20, 27.

that do not originate in the physical world."* And so we understand what is meant when Steiner says that those who celebrate sacraments must be trained and learn to sense and feel spiritual reality in order to celebrate rituals, in order for the act of worship to become real. "You must bring these feelings and sensations to your religious deeds; only then will what happens become what it should be."†

The same applies to individuals in the community: the ritual depends upon their inner activity, upon their ability to sense and feel religious reality. Such feelings no longer come naturally to modern human beings, so a modern church must also address people's need for knowledge. They need this knowledge to create a foundation upon which a new life of sensation and feeling can arise. The religious experience of ritual is not a given today, but must be created in the soul in the same way that thoughts are produced in the process of cognition: Form (concepts) is brought to the given (percepts) when reality arises in human consciousness. As Steiner applied Aristotle's epistemology, when form (spiritual concepts and feelings) joins percept (external ritual act) a ritual becomes "what it should be."

This gives us a whole new approach to understanding ritual. In the early centuries of Christianity—i.e., during the epoch immediately preceding modern times (the fourth cultural epoch in anthroposophic terms)—the word had a significance different from that of today. Similarly, during this epoch, the *administrative oversight* of these thoughts gradually passed from the Spirits of Form to the Spirits of Personality, with the result that they can no longer simply be *given* from outside but must themselves be *brought forth*

* CW 266/2, Jan. 17, 1911.

† CW 344, Sept. 7, 1922.

within the human soul. The same applies to the spoken word, especially words spoken in ritual. In the past, those words still had power in themselves, with an almost magical effect, and could thus serve as the actual form or shaping force by themselves. Augustine said: "When the word comes to the element, the sacrament is created" (*Accedit verbum ad elementum et fit sacramentum*).

Today the Spirits of Personality must participate in the word, and language thus becomes more personal. It no longer has a formative effect by itself and therefore must be seen as providing the *matter* of a sacrament today. There is no need for us to examine the sacraments individually, as the Catholic Church did in Florence in 1439 with the question where form and matter are to be seen in the individual sacraments. The same is true for all the sacraments in The Christian Community. If we follow the way Rudolf Steiner uses the Aristotelian terms form and matter in all the sacraments of The Christian Community, the external substance (as provided for each sacrament) as well as the action and the wording provide the matter. What must be added by human beings today, however, is form—namely, sensing and feeling that arise from spiritual knowledge. The sacraments in The Christian Community can thus be characterized as ritual using the terms form and matter. Innocent III called this *sacramentum tantum*.

5.2.2 Sacramental Reality (res et sacramentum)

The spiritual essence (Augustine used the word *res*) of a sacrament is yet another aspect of a sacrament. The external ritual points to it and brings it about. In scholasticism it was called grace. What does that mean?

A girl—let's call her Clara—is baptized. The act of Baptism (*sacramentum tantum*) is performed. What is the effect? Is it temporary or is it permanent and objective? How is it noticed? Can a teacher later distinguish baptized from unbaptized children? Can we recognize from Clara's behavior that she has been baptized? And if we cannot: has Baptism been effective at all? These questions can be used to illustrate how scholastic concepts were formed. If we assume that sacraments do have an objective effect, then we can say that some *effect* has resulted. Clara has been baptized, she is no longer the same as before Baptism. But a completely different question is whether Clara, in the course of her life, *shows* herself to have been baptized. That may not happen and then Baptism has perhaps not proven fruitful. Being baptized as such is not yet everything; it is not the final goal. Baptism also wants to radiate into life. So, Baptism has a twofold effect. The first is the enduring fact that she *is* baptized, which causes certain hidden changes in the human constitution. This is the sacramental reality that Innocent III called *res et sacramentum*: Clara *is* baptized. The second effect, which does not always occur or occurs only partially, requires follow-up attention after the Baptism in order for a sacramental deed to go on working. This is the real goal, the real grace of the sacrament: Clara *shows* herself to have been baptized. Innocent III calls this *res tantum*.

We turn first to the initial effect of a sacrament: *res et sacramentum*. If a sacramental deed is "proper" in everything, we expect it to be effective, even if the child has cried throughout Baptism. Neither do we want to check whether the priest was one hundred percent attentive in everything he did, or whether he was perhaps irritated for a moment or otherwise distracted. We also assume that the value of a Baptism does not depend on the particular priest performing it. In short, we expect a sacrament to be objective. Whether there are limits to this objectivity may occasionally preoccupy us, but we feel that an answer to this question will probably be exceedingly difficult. Even the desire to draw *objective* limits in such situations can prove problematic, especially when it involves the effort to grasp the inner soul condition of a priest.

The objective effects of a sacrament became an undisputed article of faith in the Catholic Church through Augustine following the dispute with the Donatists. Even a priest's attitude does not invalidate the effectiveness of a sacrament (even a Baptism performed by a heretical priest is considered valid). In terms of the scholastic threefold division of the sacrament, this is due to the middle link, the *res et sacramentum*—the spiritual reality. If this first effect is an objective fact, it will leave a lasting imprint in the one blessed. As we have already seen, Augustine saw this lasting effect at Baptism as a *seal* impressed on the soul of the person, comparable to the *domenicus* character of Roman soldiers. Augustine had only two sacraments in mind and, in relation to the seal, only Baptism. Scholasticism found it necessary to make a similar decision regarding all seven sacraments, so it was decided that Confirmation and Ordination also imprinted a seal—this was now called the *indelebilis* character (the indestructible, indelible characteristic). These three sacraments can therefore not be repeated during one's lifetime. The spiritual reality, the first and objective effect of a sacrament is therefore an indelible result of these sacraments.

Catholic theology has found nothing corresponding to this attribute for Confession, the Last Anointing, or Marriage. "When asked why only Baptism, Confirmation, and Ordination convey this indelible characteristic, to begin with, one can only say that tradition attributes the indelible effect to these three sacraments alone."* Confession, the Last Anointing and Marriage can therefore be repeated. But here, too, the first objective effect (*res et sacramentum*) is found *in the person* who has received them. In the Eucharist, the Mass, however, the spiritual reality is seen in a different way: it appears *at the altar*. "In the Eucharist *res et sacramentum* is the real presence of the Body and Blood of Christ.... The Body and Blood of Christ are thus the first reality of the sacrament."† This expresses the special position of the Mass in relation to the other six sacraments. What is actually and objectively brought about by the sacrament occurs in the other six sacraments *on and in the human being*, but in the Mass, it occurs *outside* the human being at the altar. We will be looking at this aspect of the sacraments when we consider The Act of Consecration of Man.

We have seen that a problem arises along with the desire to know whether a spiritual reality always comes into existence when a sacrament has been *properly* performed. Establishing a precise definition can be very tricky. But scholasticism drew some clear limits: first of all, the correct execution of a sacrament presupposes form and matter are proper, that substances, actions, and words are correct. In addition,

* Auer and Ratzinger, vol. 6, p 74.

† In the past, the Last Anointing was said to be repeatable after recovery from illness in case death threatened later. Today it is "anointing of the sick" and can be repeated. A second marriage can be performed sacramentally when the first marriage has been ended by the death of one spouse.

however, the priest's correct intention must be added. If he has "the intention to do what the church does" (*intentio faciendi quod facit ecclesia*), his intention is correct. His feelings and sensations, his insights and knowledge are not decisive: the integration of his will into the will of the church is the essence. Beyond this determination of his intention, scholasticism has also clarified the degree of consciousness that is necessary. Three types of intention are distinguished:

1. The actual intention: A priest celebrating a sacrament must always be fully aware of his intention. He is completely focused with his consciousness.
2. The virtual intention: A priest celebrating a sacrament made a decision at one time as to the direction of his intention and has not revoked it since. In celebrating any given sacrament, however, the decision may not always be conscious.
3. The habitual intention: The actor has an inner predisposition that he may not even be aware of, which has not yet become a conscious intention and decision.

For a priest (to do what the church does), the virtual intention is the minimum requirement. The habitual intention is sufficient for a parishioner to receive a sacrament; only a will opposing the blessing could prevent the objective efficacy of the sacrament.

High Scholasticism then developed additional concepts to express the objective effects of a sacrament. If form and matter are correct and the priest has the right intention—at least virtually—the objective efficacy of the sacrament is in any case preserved, indeed, absolutely, regardless of the consciousness and attitudes of the persons involved. Then it does not matter how a person being baptized behaves during their Baptism, because they have the habitual intention to be baptized. And it does not matter if a priest is somewhere else with his or her thoughts during the celebration of a Baptism. Such absentmindedness does not have an adverse effect so long as the priest makes no mistakes and has not inwardly revoked the decision previously made "to do what the church does." That was called—probably for the first time by Peter of Poitiers*—an effect *ex opere operato* (by virtue of the execution). This concept has aroused a great deal of dispute during the past 450 years. Catholic theologians today think they can explain it by putting it into historical perspective. Thomas Aquinas did not use this formula, but at the Council of Trent it was established as official church dogma.

This understanding led to extreme views among some clerics, as expressed in a pastoral letter from the Archbishop of Salzburg dated February 2, 1905.† "Glorify the priests, for they have the power to consecrate...to make present the Body of the Lord with His precious Blood, with all His holy humanity and His Divinity in the form of bread and wine; bread and wine transform into the true Body and the precious Blood of our Lord, what a high, sublime, marvelous power!...The Catholic priest cannot merely make Him present on the altar, close Him up in the tabernacle, take Him out again and offer Him to the faithful for their blessing; he can even offer Him, the Incarnate Son of God, for the living and the dead as a bloodless sacrifice. Christ, the only begotten Son of God the Father, through whom heaven and earth

* Peter of Poitiers (1130–1205), student of Peter Lombard, whose method he taught at the University of Paris as it was being established (since 1167 as a professor of theology, since 1193 as chancellor of Notre-Dame).

† Johannes Baptist Katschthaler (1832–1914): "The honour due to the Catholic priest," in Mirbt, *Quellen zur Geschichte des Papsttums und Römischen Katholizismus*, pp. 497–499; quoted in Steiner, CW 196, Dornach 1992, p. 317.

were created, who bears the whole universe, can be willed here by a Catholic priest."

With regard to the formula *ex opere operato*, it must be noted that this principle, which is now a principle of modern mechanistic science, was established and employed by the church at the end of the twelfth century (see section 3.2). Today's prevailing scientific ideal of objectivity with regard to the effectiveness of medications is found in so-called *double-blind*[*] experiments. Ironically, this is an *ex opere operato* procedure applied to materialistic research. The aim is to rule out any conscious or unconscious causation contributed by doctor or patient when evaluating a drug's effectiveness. Only the active substance should be effective, regardless of the (conscious) state of the participants.

The question concerning the objective effects of the sacraments is also central for The Christian Community, and even played a decisive role at its beginning. Friedrich Rittelmeyer reported that during his time as a preacher in Berlin he experienced an overcrowded church during his services, which deeply moved him. However, this overcrowded church attendance was not transferable to his colleagues. So he asked whether it was right for church attendance to depend so much on the personality of the preacher and whether a more objective form of service might not be more appropriate. "A preacher who has a sense of responsibility must not feel satisfied today that he himself has 'a full church'...but he must ask himself: Are there no more possibilities today of a Christian community in which people come together for

* "Method for determining the real effects of medicinal products in relation to placebo effects. In double-blind tests, the physician and the test person are not informed concerning the type of substance administered [placebo preparation or active substance]" (Brockhaus).

reasons greater than the personality of an individual?"* For him personally, as a Protestant pastor, this was an important moment to realize the necessity of an objective ritual.

How can this spiritual objectivity be understood? This is what Catholic theology calls the *indelible attribute* of a sacrament and whose mode of operation it refers to as *ex opere operato*, the formula we discovered that kills everything connected with the actual process. It is not sufficient for many people today simply to say that this attribute is imprinted on the soul. This brings us to the anthroposophical worldview and the concept of the human being presented by Rudolf Steiner (see section 14.3).

We have already mentioned the intention of a priest in The Christian Community (see section 3.2). It is no longer possible today for intentions to come from outside a priest (doing what the church does). That would amount to an intention still under the rule of the Spirits of Form. Intention today must be personal, arising from the innermost center of a human being. This can be seen in words written by Rudolf Steiner in a letter to Rosa Mayreder, in which he described his approach to writing his book, *The Philosophy of Freedom*. This book has an objective significance, meaningful for every human being—and yet Rudolf Steiner claims " My way of negotiating many difficulties was entirely individual; the way I worked through conceptual thickets was mine alone."† Those who share Paul's courage ("For the Spirit searches all things, even the depths of the Godhead." [I Cor. 2:10]) and have the firm intention to understand the mystery of the incarnation of Christ, to grasp how God could live into the reality of earthly life, will as a consequence eventually find

* Schühle, *Entscheidung für das Christentum der Zukunft*, p. 143.

† Cf chap. 3.2 (CW 39, letter of Nov. 11, 1894).

and embrace the earthly order that arises from that incarnation. He will understand the *incarnational structure** of the sacraments, which extends into the social realm. The commitment naturally arising from a truly *personal* intention does not require additional intentions introduced from outside. In this way priests will also be able to accept responsibility for what they teach. This commitment arising from personal insight and intention has become the foundational bedrock for the work of a priest in The Christian Community in the twentieth century.

5.2.3 The Grace of a Sacrament (**res tantum**)

We now come to the third area of a sacrament, sacramental grace, which occurs when one can say: Clara *shows* that she has been baptized. What does that mean? And how is this grace to be distinguished from grace from Communion, when one says: Clara *shows* that she is someone who has received Communion? During the counter-Reformation the Council of Trent arrived at the formulation: The sacraments confer *justification*—the central Reformation theme—and are therefore *signs of grace*, "through which all true justice begins, grows or is restored after loss."† They convey "sanctifying grace." What this means in concrete terms remains somewhat unclear, at least compared with the otherwise unsurpassed precision of scholastic theology. Moreover, the differentiation of individual sacraments into several different effects of grace makes it difficult to give an overall view.

Sacramental grace (*res tantum*) is the actual goal of the sacrament, but the church does not have the power

* Adam, *Sinn und Gestalt der Sakramente*, p 12.
† Schühle, *Entscheidung für das Christentum der Zukunft*, p. 143.

to command this kind of grace; the church cannot *make Clara show* that she has been baptized. It has power only over the sacramental act that brings about Clara's Baptism. Thus, Catholic sacramental theology (and expectations among the faithful) focuses on the sacramental reality, *res et sacramentum*, which has a lasting effect and works objectively (*ex opere operato*). Today, authoritative theologians place "what is called *res et sacramentum* at the center of each sacrament."* But sacramental grace (*res tantum*) originates in God's free will to bestow it. One must also admit that God is free to grant his grace also outside the sacrament; any other understanding would limit God. Catholic theology thus conceded already in the twelfth century (Peter Lombard) that Christ did not bind his grace solely to the sacraments. Thomas Aquinas also argued several times that the "divine power of salvation is not tied to the sacraments."† Above all, *spiritual communion* seems important to Aquinas, i.e., participation in the Mystical Body of Christ, not in the sacraments.‡ Along these lines, the theologian Johann Auer comments: "The decisive thing remains that the sacraments are not only received bodily, *sacramentaliter*, but in the spirit of Christ, *spiritualiter*, and in the right way."§ Here we find within the Catholic view a surprising bridge to what we have already touched upon¶ and what Rudolf Steiner called *spiritual communion*. Nevertheless, in practice the Catholic Church is far from acknowledging that God's saving action is possible outside the sacraments. It would be "disastrous to misjudge the

* Auer and Ratzinger, vol. 6, p. 50.
† Ganoczy, p. 42.
‡ Auer and Ratzinger, vol. 6, p. 94.
§ Ibid., p. 57.
¶ Chap. 2.4 Ritual and Sacrament in Anthroposophy.

high importance of the sacramental way of salvation in the church of the incarnate Son of God."*

A need for salvation was one of the topics that also arose at the Council of Trent with respect to sacraments: "Whoever says that the sacraments of the New Covenant are not necessary for salvation but superfluous, and that people without them or without the desire for them can by faith alone attain from God the grace of justification—admittedly, not all sacraments are necessary for every individual—is expelled."† Not all sacraments are necessary for every individual: e.g., Marriage or Ordination to the Priesthood. Indeed, the common theological argumentation today is that the sacraments are not an absolute necessity, but an *appropriate* path to salvation. The real goal of a sacrament is the sacramental grace (*res tantum*); it is the least tangible in conventional sacramental theology and it is beyond the power of the church.

We will return to the question of sacramental grace in a later section (14.3) with regard to the anthroposophic view of humanity.

* Auer and Ratzinger, vol. 6, p. 56.

† Neuner-Roos, Nr. 509.

PART III:
THE SACRAMENTS OF THE CHRISTIAN COMMUNITY

Chapter 6
Historical Development

The boldness of scholastic theologians in applying the Aristotelian concepts of *form* and *matter* to the sacraments corresponds to the boldness with which Rudolf Steiner applied the idea of evolutionary development to the sacraments. The idea of evolution—not as a word, but as a concept—is not old.* In fact, it emerged only gradually during the eighteenth century. Lessing (1729–1781) was among the first to use this term as it is currently understood. His small booklet *The Education of the Human Race* appeared shortly before his death, in 1780. Working with the idea of evolutionary development, he was led to the idea of reincarnation. In two places the word *evolution* already appears explicitly with its modern meaning.† Goethe uses this word with incalculable frequency, especially in his *Wilhelm Meister* and in his writings on natural science. And finally, the term moves into the natural sciences, where it becomes—in complete contrast to Goethe—the basis of a materialistic

* Frank Teichmann, *Die Entstehung des Entwicklungsgedankens in der Goethezeit.*

† § 5: "And just as education is not indifferent to the order in which it develops the powers of man; just as it cannot teach man everything at once: just as God, in his revelation, also had to keep a certain order, a certain measure." § 46: "I call a hint what already contains some seed, from which the still held back truth can be developed..." Lessing also uses the word very often in earlier works, but initially in a different meaning, such as a dramaturgical polarity of entanglement and development.

world view. Since Darwin and especially Haeckel, the idea of evolution has ultimately transformed the human being into a higher mammal.

For Rudolf Steiner, the idea of evolutionary development was decisive for understanding modern consciousness and conducting spiritual research. But he also describes quite clearly "what the newer evolutionary theory is actually suffering from." For if one stops at the "general trivial idea of development," one comes to see the human being as only "the most perfect of animals."* This is because the idea of development had been one-sidedly understood as physical evolution, as it were, as an unfolding of something already existing. Being an essentially materialistic idea, this thought is completely opposed to a spiritual worldview. Steiner saw that it needed an addition, and already struggled to develop it in his youth as a "correction to the concept of time."†

The true essence of time is a duality: time flows not only from the past to the future, but there is also a spiritual counter-current that comes from the future, flowing through the present and into the past and carrying our will impulses. Steiner informed Édouard Schuré that this is called the "double current of time." An analogous duality is also found in a similarly *complete* idea of evolutionary development. About his conversations with Rudolf Steiner, Schuré wrote: "We are all aware of the outer stream of evolution, which draws all beings of heaven and earth, stars, plants, animals, people, with it, and which allows them to move forward into an infinite future without us becoming aware of the original force through which they are pushed and which restlessly continues to push them forward. However, there is also a

* CW 67, April 15, 1918.

† Letter of June 20, 1882, to Friedrich Theodor Vischer, CW 38.

reverse current in the universe, which moves in the opposite direction and constantly intervenes in the first current. This is the stream of *involution*, through which the principles, the forces, the beings, and the souls that come from the invisible world and the region of the eternal, incessantly penetrate visible reality. No evolution of matter would be comprehensible without this constant *involution* of the spirit.... Thus, the spirit, which contains the future in seed form, becomes involved in matter; and matter, in receiving the spirit, evolves toward the future."*

The *complete* idea of evolution thus contains a duality of evolution and involution. It may be surprising that already at the beginning of the eighteenth century, long before the idea of evolution as such appears in general culture, we can find intimations of it in the writings of Gottfried Wilhelm Leibniz (1646–1716). The concepts of evolution and involution appear already in seed form in his *Monadology*, written in 1714. In every external unfolding outward there is always a countercurrent of drawing backward and within, similar to the process of seed formation in plants; it can be pictured as a reverse flow.

The workings of the spirit are comprehensible only when seen out of an involutionary current. Rudolf Steiner makes it clear in his book *The Philosophy of Freedom* that because of this, thinking in fact works against the human bodily organization: "The essence of the activity of thinking has a double duty: first, it suppresses the human organization's own activity, and second, it puts itself in its place."† To the extent that the external forces of (bodily) evolution are *repressed*, involutionary forces are at work and mental activity takes

* CW 262, Dornach 2002, p. 28f.

† CW 4, chap. 9.

place in human consciousness. This implies that mental/spiritual activity is always at the expense of nature, but what it "takes from" nature it can "give back" to nature in a mental/spiritual form as meaning. Nature acquires meaning only in and through culture, i.e., culture understood in the broadest sense. Nature is carried by the evolutionary stream—one could also say, the birth stream. If we stop at that, we see the world only physically/materialistically. All mental–spiritual activity is born out of involution, the time stream which comes from the future and proceeds from death.

This concept lays the foundation for a new understanding of the sacraments inaugurated by Rudolf Steiner. He described this new understanding for the first time on June 14, 1921, to a small group of eighteen participants who had asked him to address the question of religious renewal. With his help The Christian Community, Movement for Religious Renewal was founded fifteen months later. On June 14, 1921, he said:

> In modern times the Catholic Church knows nothing of the preexistence [of a human being]. [A human being] is only a thought of God, and this [human life] "growing forth from a thought of God" is presented in seven stages. Each of these seven stages must be met by other forces. Birth is an evolution, puberty is an evolution, and each form of evolution is met by a form of involution: birth by Baptism, puberty by Confirmation. Each sacrament is the inverse of a natural stage of evolution. One can see a biography as consisting of seven stages of evolution, which are in turn contrasted with "seven stages of involution, and these are the seven sacraments, four of which are earthly, namely Baptism, Confirmation, Eucharist,

> Penance.* These four are as universally human as our physical body, etheric body, astral body and "I." When you rise higher, you reach the Spirit Self, the Life Spirit, and the Spirit Body.... These are the seven sacraments, the last of which are the Last Anointing, Ordination, and Marriage. These are simply the inverse processes for the natural processes that take place and the corresponding sacraments are designed to bless accordingly.†

Steiner considered it self-evident that there are seven sacraments. The fact that Protestantism accepts only two sacraments is, according to him, connected with the fact that, even during the time of the Reformation, one "had no feeling for the inner numerical constitution of the world."‡ It took the medieval church until the twelfth century to find its way to the seventh of the sacraments. Thomas Aquinas was the first to explore how this sevenfold nature might be connected to the logic of human biography—i.e., "to understand it from its anthropological function." In doing so, he arrived at a particular order of the sacraments: Baptism – Confirmation – Eucharist – Penance – Last Anointing – Ordination – Marriage. His efforts represented a nascent attempt to understand, because during his time (in the thirteenth century) it was not yet possible to begin with the idea of evolutionary development. Steiner's approach also sees the sacraments as fulfilling an "anthropological function." However, unlike Aquinas settling on the number seven by chance, as it were, Steiner saw the number seven as lawful, being the result of the role played by numbers in the essential constitution of the world. Steiner understood that every evolutionary

* *Penance* and *atonement* are sometimes used as synonyms for Confession, or the sacrament of Consultation.

† CW 342, June, 14, 1921.

‡ Ibid.

development proceeds according to the law of seven. Up to the middle of a cycle of development ascending forces, the evolutionary forces, predominate; then the descending forces, the involutionary forces, come into play. The sacraments are in this sense involutionary forces added to the corresponding evolutionary stages. According to the above, they belong to the stream coming from the future as the counter-current of time. They are polar to the birth current of evolution as a death current—that is, as a current that creates space for the work of the spirit. To put it in a nutshell, what gives natural development, or evolution, its deepest meaning arises from the evolutionary stream. The renewed sacraments of The Christian Community are then, as involutionary events, sources of meaning in biographical development that work from the depths. This mystery is spoken out directly in the Easter prayers of the Act of Consecration of Man, the Eucharist service of The Christian Community: "Christ has risen to you as the meaning of the earth."

Rudolf Steiner's understanding of the sacraments in their anthropological function goes even further by placing them in the context of the bodily nature of a human being, hereby also applying the saw of seven. There are four *earthly* "members," or "sheaths," which a human being brings to birth, or allows to emerge, at seven-year intervals beginning with the birth of the physical body. The etheric body then comes into its own around age seven, the astral body with puberty, and the "I" around age twenty-one.* These *births* are not moments, but processes that take place over a seven-year period. The three *spiritual* bodily members of the human being will only reach their full form in the future. Those

* See Steiner, *The Education of the Child* (CW 34), p. 309.

three reach beyond the earthly framework of personal biography and therefore relate to death and to the community tasks that, from the outset, are supra-personal, corresponding thus to the sacraments of Last Anointing, priestly Ordination, and Marriage.

Three and a half months later the second course of lectures was given to the founders of The Christian Community. In those lectures the sacraments were differentiated in greater detail into four *earthly* and three *spiritual.** Only the births of the four earthly bodily members of a human being are actually stages of evolutionary development. Death is not an evolutionary step in life but is itself an involutionary event. Also, Ordination into priesthood is not based on anything earthly, but on spiritual factors that reach, so to speak, from the spiritual world into the earthly world. Similarly, this involves a completely new understanding of marriage, in which marriage is in its very essence a spiritual reality that has its reflection in the earthly. Last Anointing, Ordination, and Marriage are thus inverse processes (hence, evolutionary) to each of these spiritual facts of involution. Each corresponding sacrament represents the transition of a spiritual fact into a fact of external, evolutionary life. This is perhaps most obvious in the case of Ordination into the priesthood, but also clearly visible in the Last Anointing, wherein a celebration takes place in life, referring to life after death. In marriage, this aspect is most surprising. One might rather expect the reverse, namely that the Marriage sacrament

* CW 343, Oct. 2, 1921. It should be mentioned that the thought of *Evolution/Involution* and their *relationship to the sacraments* had already been expressed in 1893 by the English theosophist C. G. Harrison in *The Transcendental Universe: Six Lectures on Occult Science, Theosophy, and the Catholic Faith.*

would celebrate life unfolding, as a stage of evolution. This would be completely in keeping with the traditional conception of marriage. The fact that it is understood the other way round in The Christian Community points to a new understanding of marriage that is yet to be developed.

The seven sacraments are therefore understood as stages of human biographical development coming to meet evolutionary and involutionary events. Consequently, their sequence is:

Baptism
Confirmation
Act of Consecration
Confession, or Sacramental Consultation
Last Anointing
Ordination
Sacrament of Marriage

This sequence agrees with that of Thomas Aquinas (who was following Peter Lombard), albeit for a different reason.

Chapter 7
Baptism

Three things are to be emphasized in the Baptism celebrated in The Christian Community: first, it is for *infants and children;* second, the child receives its *name* through the Baptism; and third, certain *substances* are used. Baptizing children and bestowing a name are sacramental deeds apparently similar to Baptisms performed in Protestant and Catholic churches, but there are no similarities to Baptism in early Christianity. Let us first examine these three aspects (for children, name, and substances) of Baptism in The Christian Community.

7.1 Infant Baptism

Early Christianity did not have infant Baptism. Until about 400, adult Baptism was predominant; it was understood as the sealing of the new faith, combined with a conscious decision after much previous instruction in the Christian faith (catechumen instruction). According to Justin (ca.165) we are born without our having willed it but are reborn (in Baptism) by our own will. There are reports from around 125 that even adolescent children were baptized if they had been taught and had genuinely become Christians, that is, children who are of school age in the modern sense. Infant Baptism is attested to by Tertullian (who fought against it) for the first time around 200.

Around 220, Hippolytus I considered what relatives needed to do for adults, children and infants who are not yet able to answer the baptismal questions. Soon after the middle of the third century, infant Baptism was not only considered possible, but demanded. Cyprian* argued that infants should be baptized as early as the second or third day of their life because they are subject to original sin and their salvation should not be endangered. Augustine's doctrine of original sin reinforced this proposal, and in 418 the Synod of Carthage adopted the doctrine that unbaptized children are condemned according to John 3:5.† Child Baptism was then obligatory.

As a result of this development, the Baptism's emphasis has shifted within the Western church. Originally, Baptism was the transition *from death to life*, which was inconceivable without a personal conversion.

> Before Baptism, one must vow to lead a new life and change one's profession if it is immoral or mixed up with idolatry. Baptism is a contract made with God; Tertullian takes it as an "oath of allegiance," he even demands that one earn the grace of Baptism and compensate for the former life of sin through fervent repentance.‡

Baptism is understood as the forgiveness of sins. In early Christian times, therefore, exorcism preceded it, and

* Thascius Caecilius Cyprianus, canonized father of the church, was born around 200/210 and died as a martyr in Carthage in 258. Cyprianus was an effective church writer. He is also the origin of the doctrine of the church's need for salvation: *extra ecclesiam nulla salus.*

† "Jesus answered, Amen, Amen, I say to you, unless one is born of water and the Spirit, he cannot enter the kingdom of God" (John 3:5).

‡ *Religion in Geschichte und Gegenwart,* vol. 6, p. 638.

immediately afterward the *bestowal of the Spirit* took place through the laying on of hands and anointing—the latter corresponds to today's Confirmation. One cannot make these demands of a child or an infant. Baptism thus acquires a new content: it is liberation from original sin, in which every human being has a share through birth; through the water of Baptism it is "washed away." The doctrine of original sin, which in the West was particularly shaped by Augustine (the Eastern Church does have it), was tightly connected to the meaning of Baptism, which is how it became the decisive justification for infant Baptism.

The step from adult Baptism to infant Baptism was thus dogmatically completed, but not liturgically. Although the laying on of hands together with an oil anointing was separated from Baptism and gradually became an independent sacrament for older children (Confirmation), the baptismal act itself (published as binding in the "*Rituale Romanum*" in 1614 by Pope Paul V) is only a shortened version of adult Baptism, separated from water consecration and Confirmation. The preceding exorcism remained. It was not until the Second Vatican Council that a new baptismal liturgy for children was created—the first real infant Baptism in two thousand years in the (Catholic) church. Even the Reformation did not change anything essential in the Baptism of adults as applied to children. As early as its founding in 1922, however, The Christian Community took the liturgical step toward genuine infant Baptism.

In The Christian Community the sacrament of Baptism is carried out as a rule only up to the age of 14—i.e., no longer on adults. Certain questions arise here: How should one imagine the effect of a sacrament to which the recipient cannot give conscious consent? And since it is also difficult to imagine that a person (through Baptism) *without conscious consent* could be removed from his or her original sin, the further question arises as to the meaning of Baptism. What sacramental act can be meaningfully performed on a child without interfering with his or her religious freedom?

7.1.1 Christian Community

At this point we need to make an insertion and look at the role played by community in an individual's life. It is present at the very beginning of every individual's development. Those who have not yet attained inner maturity and autonomy need a community to support them while also providing them with norms for behavior, guiding them concerning good and evil. This applies to children especially. They need a supporting community, which is normally (even today) represented by the family. It not only forms a temporary foundation for life on earth, but also creates the first contours of an internalized morality, a conscience.

At this stage, conscience is certainly not yet individualized, but merely a mirror of the community (family, school, people, etc.). What one must do or not do varies according to community. If we take larger ethnic or even linguistic communities, the spectrum of what is considered good or bad becomes immeasurably large and reflects the whole range of what we today call cultural diversity around the earth. Accordingly, conscience, i.e., what someone individually considers right or wrong, is initially nothing more than the internalized result of an individual's socialization. The interests of a community provide orientation at this stage. They must take precedence over the interests of an individual, who must fit in and, if necessary, must also expect sanctions if rules are broken. Every morality that comes from outside, everything that has the form of moral law, belongs to this stage. For normal, everyday life, such arrangements with a legal character are necessary and justified (for example, the fair distribution of emergency services among the members of the family, or in governmental regulation of highway laws.) They are based on the fact that everyone should be equal before the law. This is what Rudolf Steiner calls the rights sphere of life.*

In the sphere of morality, however, people are not equal but quite individual. Therefore, there is not only the conscience that reflects socialization, but also individual conscience, which, however, *cannot* be educated from the outside but must be developed independently from within. This is what Paul has in mind when he seems to speak against the law: "Thus the law has been our educator toward Christ, that we might be justified by faith. But after faith has come, we no longer need an educator" (Gal. 3:24f). The original Greek word for *educator* is *pedagogue*. Morality imposed from outside has a pedagogical value for development (toward Christ) of an individual morality (faith). There we are free, and with regard to the social organism—in anthroposophical terminology—we are no longer in the sphere of legal rights, but in the sphere of spiritual life. Therefore, where an independent, spiritually autonomous individual is concerned, the legal sphere of rights has no role to play; it is the spiritual life that is all important. It is one of Rudolf Steiner's fundamental clarifications that criminal law is not actually part of the sphere of legal rights but of the spiritual life, and that judges are needed

* Steiner, *Towards Social Renewal* (CW 23).

who have the freedom to decide an individual's fate without being constrained by legally predetermined outcomes.

So, there is a path leading from community to individuality. An educator leads this child or adolescent along this path of *lawful*, legitimate development. Rudolf Steiner discovered this fundamental law of sociology as early as 1898:

> ...which I would like to express approximately in the following way: Humankind strives in the beginning of cultural societies for the emergence of social organizations; the interests of an individual are first sacrificed to the interests of these organizations; further development leads to the liberation of the individual from the interests of the organizations and to a free unfolding and expression of the needs and powers of the individual.*

These "social organizations" are those I mentioned above: family, folk, language community, etc. It is wholly legitimate that these communities gradually lose their power to influence and determine behavior. If this process unfolds positively, it leads "to the liberation of the individual," but such liberation will not necessarily be the result of patterns that govern human biography. In his *Philosophy of Freedom*, Steiner makes this clear: Human beings "can make only *themselves* into *free* beings," and "human beings must give themselves the final polish."† The question then arises as to whether there is any perspective beyond human beings as "liberated beings," or whether communities have then perhaps served their only purpose.

The answer is that in the future a new kind of community could come about in which human freedom is fully affirmed

* CW 31, p. 255f.

† CW 4, *Intuitive Thinking as a Spiritual Path,* chap. 9, p. 159.

and even, to a certain extent at least, presupposed. As early as 1894 in the *Philosophy of Freedom* there is a first indication of this:

> But how is it possible for humans to live together socially if everyone is striving merely to express his or her own individuality? This objection is characteristic of misguided moralism, which imagines that a society of human beings is possible only if they are all united by a commonly determined ethical order. Such moralism fails to understand the unity of the world of ideas. It cannot conceive that the world of ideas that is active in me is none other than the one that is at work in my neighbor.... The difference between me and my neighbor consists not in our living in two completely distinct spiritual worlds, but in my neighbor's receiving intuitions other than my own out of the world of ideas common to us both. My neighbors want to live out their intuitions, I mine. If we all really draw from the Idea, and follow no external (physical or spiritual) impulses, then we cannot but meet in the same striving, the same intentions.*

In other words, the diversity of people, when they follow external influences, are led to a clash of opposites. *If they act from different intuitions from the common world of ideas (i.e., if they are "free"), they will complement one another in their differences.*

Later, Steiner goes much further in characterizing such new communities:

> [One day in the future] we will live in communities that people will create by forming groups they themselves create according to self-chosen perspectives while fully respecting each other's freedom and individuality.... By

* Ibid., pp. 154–155.

> voluntarily letting their feelings shine together, something beyond a merely emancipated person is created. The emancipated human being has an individual soul; it is never lost again once it has been gained. But when people come together voluntarily, they group around a focal point and this gives opportunities to spiritual beings to act as a kind of group soul but in a very different way from the group souls of old. All the earlier group souls were spirits that made human beings unfree. These new beings, however, are entirely compatible with freedom of the individual human being. We could even say that, from a certain perspective, they derive their existence from the unity of human beings. *

This is similar to the situation in which the Apostles awaited the day of Pentecost: "All these were always together in prayer with the women and Mary, the mother of Jesus, and his brothers" (Acts 1:14). In the original Greek text, "with one accord" expresses roughly what Steiner calls "letting feelings shine together." They were also grouped around a central point, as expressed in many Pentecostal representations; often the mother of Jesus is depicted in this way as the representative of a "new kind of group soul." In the Pentecost event itself, a new community of apostles is created: in his own way, each is representative of the whole and yet no one is the same as the other. Everyone receives different intuitions from the common world of ideas.

A truly Christian community or congregation would not be led hierarchically from above, but from the center. Only then will the name "Christian" be truly applicable. By orienting themselves toward the center, those who are being led gradually become leaders themselves,

* CW 102, Jan. 6, 1908.

representatives of the whole. The individuals do not need to free themselves from this community but find that their own individual possibilities are increased because they are strengthened by the center.

7.1.2 *The Baptismal Congregation*

In The Christian Community a congregation has an important and prominent role to play. In the words of the ritual, the people attending are referred to as the "congregation gathered for this Baptism." Those in attendance of, say, a wedding or Confirmation have an important task as well, but are not directly called upon as they are in the sacrament of Baptism. This is due to the fact that it is an infant Baptism, where the will of the gathered congregation stands in for the will of the child. The congregation is responsible for the Baptism on behalf of the child. Such a vicarious role is not necessary to the same extent in any of the other sacraments. With each succeeding sacrament the congregation gradually assumes a different role until, at the far end of the scale, so to speak, at the wedding ceremony, it functions purely as witness. Who takes on responsibility in a Baptism? Rudolf Steiner describes it as a *vow* that the baptizing congregation takes to receive the child and, insofar as this can be done in harmony with Christian ideals, to watch over his or her development as a Christian.*

Have we not then arrived again at the point where community as a "social association" is set above an individual and the interests of the individual are sacrificed to the interests of this community? We can clarify this with an example: A teacher may demand of a student (let's just

* CW 343, Oct. 10, 1921.

call her Ella) that she do things that she would never do on her own initiative. Ella the student may well complain a great deal. Many years later that teacher might receive a letter from Ella thanking him or her for all that was demanded of her, because it turned out to have been of great importance in the rest of her life. Indirectly, such a letter confirms in retrospect that the teacher had indeed acted in the student's best interest. In short: it was not the complaining student who was acting on behalf of her own true individuality, but the strict teacher. Ella may well have experienced the severity of the teacher's demands as limiting her freedom, but later realized that the teacher had actually led her to greater freedom, namely, to be herself, to fill her potential. It was the teacher's job to guide the student on a path that her higher self actually wanted to follow. One could aptly call such a pedagogy *Christian*. In this sense, The Christian Community has the task of welcoming the newborn soul and of watching over its development as a Christian so that the child can find its way to itself, to its own true freedom. Baptism is the starting point for this development. It is not simply a deed to be accomplished so as to state that the child is now completely baptized; it should be seen more as the beginning of a process deserving a continuing *education toward freedom*.

These are concrete reasons for infant Baptism. It is a misunderstanding to think that Baptism can only be meaningful when adolescents are old enough to decide for themselves. Acceptance into a Christian congregation, as it is understood here, is not meant to preempt someone's later decision to be baptized; neither does it imply that an individual has officially become a "registered" member of The Christian

Community. It is intended as a strength-giving blessing to mark and initiate the beginning of a path to inner autonomy and freedom.

7.2 Bestowing the Name

Until the fourteenth and fifteenth centuries, officially naming an infant was separate from Baptism. Only then did the *baptismal name* become common practice. This means that all the sacramental theology developed up to that time, including within scholasticism, had not yet investigated the act of bestowing a name during Baptism. Here is another area in which The Christian Community has explored a new and essential aspect of Baptism. From the point of view of the structure of the Baptism, naming is even at the center. Naming as such, for which there have always been forms aside from Baptism, has always played a role in Christianity insofar as the content of the name was concerned. It was natural for early Christians to carry on their pagan names after they had been baptized as adults; for them it was only important that they be allowed to call themselves Christians. Thus, in the third century the martyr Carpus, when asked his name, answered his judge: "My first and most important name is Christian. But if you ask my name in the world, my name is Carpus."*

Over time, Christian names gradually became established, names from the Old or New Testament, names of martyrs and apostles, and finally new names were created that had a connection to Christ (e.g., Cyril), Christian salvation (Renatus) or Christian virtues (Fides). A completely new treasure

* *Religion in Geschichte und Gegenwart*, vol. 6, p 1494.

of names was thus created between the fourth and seventh centuries. In Europe, north of the Alps, Christian names were introduced by Christian missionaries in the eighth and ninth centuries. In the tenth century, however, the Benedictine mission left the old Germanic name treasure untouched, with the result that the Germanic names were again almost solely dominant in Germany in the tenth and eleventh centuries. Then, until the fourteenth century, Christian naming gradually dominated again, and became associated with Baptism. In the Roman Catechism, published in 1566, the church took an official position on naming for the first time and demanded that the baptismal name be taken from a list of saints. In any case, this had become common practice in the sixteenth century. From the seventeenth century onward, it became customary to have several first names. Then church instruction required that at least the second name of the child should be a saint's name.

At the birth of a child, members of the Anthroposophical Society repeatedly asked Rudolf Steiner to suggest a name, especially in the last years of his work. Eighty-nine names suggested by him have become known (since 1911).* With two exceptions, there are always two names. Rudolf Steiner once said to Emil Bock in 1924: "The first of the two names characterizes more the ethnic character, i.e., what can be understood from the inheritance. In your case it is therefore the Germanic element; the second name is then the Christian one, because it indicates the future, the goal into which the child grows."† The names he gives almost always fit this

* Eighty-six of these names were published by Erwin Schühle ("Names given by Rudolf Steiner") in *Mitteilungen aus der anthroposophischen Arbeit in Deutschland*, Apr. 1955.

† Emil Bock, "How Dr. Steiner gave names for children," in *Mitteilungen aus der anthroposophischen Arbeit in Deutschland*, Easter 1954.

pattern with few exceptions when two Christian names come together, such as Martha Johanna, Maria Elisabeth or Johannes Michael. Furthermore, there are many repetitions, almost exclusively with the Christian names. Their numerical diversity is correspondingly small compared to the names that express their ethnic nature. One can therefore have the impression that the names that express the goal of Christian striving are more general, and therefore few names can encompass the whole. The ethnic names are more specific, and here Steiner was also occasionally active in language creation, depending on the particular personality of the child; so naturally some of these names sound very unusual to us. One has the impression that the starting point is a kind of linguistic raw material in sounds and syllables, from which a name was formed in accordance with the personality. The Christian names, on the other hand, already have their content and their history.

Although Steiner's guidance concerning two names reminds us of the Catholic Church's demand that at least the second name of the child should be that of a saint, he chose few names from the abundance available in the calendar of saints. In The Christian Community naming the child is at the center of the Baptism. It is stated that "the Christian congregation that is baptizing the child also accepts it into the community."*

In a sense every community "baptizes," i.e., it gives something like a name to its members, even in secular life. The naming is not always explicit but is expressed in the fact that every member—sooner or later—is seen to play a certain role in their community, perhaps more negatively (black

* CW 343, Oct. 5, 1921, morning.

sheep) or positively (trusted person). There are many possible roles that reflect the abilities or inabilities of an individual concerned. One has then "made a name for oneself." Role and name belong together—they are two sides of the same thing within a community.

However, when a Christian congregation baptizes, something quite different happens. The congregation does not assign roles to the child. Nor can one make a name for oneself in the congregation through certain activities. The only role to play is to become one's own true self, which is often a mystery enough to the individual. In such a community we are always expected to be who we really want to become, even if we can only slowly grow to meet this expectation. The community does incite and motivate us to make a name for ourselves, but only the right one. The two different developmental movements, from the individual toward the community and from the community toward the individual, become one. In this way, we also recognize that a properly functioning Christian community is compatible with complete freedom of the individual. It should be noted, however, that a Christian community is of course not protected in principle from assuming the features of a secular association with a corresponding purpose, expectations, and role assignments. However, this is not in keeping with the essence of a *Christian* community.

The two names given could also be seen as reflecting the Baptism process itself. Through birth we are born into certain contexts, into family, people, language, culture. We find ourselves in a social unit. In this way we are, as it were, stamped with an initial character, but not given freedom. This is expressed in the name, which expresses the ethnic character.

Then, in Baptism we are born again into a community compatible with freedom of the individual, even if this ideal only finds its complete realization in the future.* This second birth is represented by the Baptism with the name. The second,† the Christian name, expresses this ideal of freedom. In order that this whole process from the old (social unit) to the new (Christian) community may proceed in a salutary way, not only the Christian but both names are given in the Baptism.

7.3 Baptism with Substances

From the very beginning of Christianity, water has been regarded as the proper substance for Baptism. This is already implied by the word Baptism, which in the original Greek text derives from a verb meaning to immerse, submerge, wash off, and clean. The noun *baptism* even has its own form in the original text. Aside from the New Testament, however, it is not found in the Greek language, which means that it cannot be explained through its usage in other contexts. Our only explanation of its meaning in concrete terms derives from its use in the New Testament, namely what John the Baptist performed in the Jordan. It is also used in the New Testament in a figurative sense, for example when Jesus says with reference to Golgotha: "But I have a Baptism to be baptized with, and how very distressed I am until it is accomplished" (Luke 12:50). One must infer that he was referring to John's Baptism.

* Of course, this does not exclude the possibility that the social unit present at the beginning of a biography can also be a community in which internal (not only external) freedom can evolve. That would truly be a Christian family in the sense of the word being developed here.

† The words *first* and *second* name do not necessarily mean the external sequence spoken but are only meant to distinguish between kinds of names, one reflecting what is, and one representing what can be.

It is similarly perplexing in the Baptism of The Christian Community (as well as in other churches)—there is no real explanation of what one is to do with the substances. If one asks the priest, he/she can only answer: *I baptize; at least that is what it is called in the wording of the ritual: "I baptize you with water..."* etc. The classical baptismal formula of the church accordingly states: "I baptize you in the name of..." But that statement does not include an explanation of what the formula means. John's Baptism provides the archetype for this act, in which people were actually immersed in water, and while it is simply assumed that everyone knows what it means to baptize, in fact, no one actually does. There is no other sacrament in which its very name (*baptism*) also designates the actions of the priest. It is therefore necessary to give here an account of what it means to baptize.

In the ritual of The Christian Community the word *baptize* is directly connected with specific substances. Here Baptism occurs with a narrower meaning. Obviously, this no longer refers to immersion or cleansing, although the theology of other denominations speaks of washing away sins. Instruction given for a Protestant baptismal specifies: "The Baptist pours three times with his hand on the head of the person to be baptized..." However, this represents only a symbolic immersion (the temperature of the water may also be warm). After a conversation with Rudolf Steiner, Emil Bock made the brief note: "The baptism that has taken place so far (three handfuls of water, with the words: I baptize you) is not a ritual at all, but at most, merely a symbol. The Christian Community's understanding of baptism is therefore not simply a continuation or further development of John's Baptism."

In order to understand what distinguishes Christian Baptism from John's Baptism we need some concepts provided by anthroposophy. Rudolf Steiner sees John's Baptism as clearly connected with pre-Christian mysteries. One must bear in mind here that the principles found in the ancient mystery religions were at work not only among the pagans, but can also be found among all peoples, also in Judaism,* which is why we can see in the Baptism in the Jordan an echo of one of the trials experienced in the mysteries—a trial connected with the elements. In his book *How to Know Higher Worlds,* Steiner describes the equivalent of these trials for modern human beings, including the water trial,† and in response to a question after a lecture, he explained that the Baptism of John is an echo of the water trial of the ancient mysteries.‡ At the end of the *Magic Flute*, Mozart drew from the initiation in the Masonic context in representing Tamino and Pamina's trials by fire and water.

However, the time of the old mysteries is past. We can understand the words spoken by the priest to mean "I baptize you with water for a change of heart and mind; but he who comes after me is stronger than I, and I am not worthy to wear his shoes; he will baptize you with the Holy Spirit and with fire" (Matt. 3:11). The baptism "with the Holy Spirit

* "That we find, as it were, grafted onto the same Judaism mystery views which have proved to be a common good of the Greek and Egyptian spiritual life: we need not be surprised about that ..." (CW 8, p. 115).

† "This trial is called the water test, because during the test in these higher spiritual realms the human being lacks any support from his external surroundings, just as when moving in water, whose bottom cannot be reached, the support is missing" (CW 10, p. 82).

‡ "If we want to understand Baptism correctly, we must go back to its original meaning. Baptism originally meant one of the first stages through which a human being gradually ascended to higher knowledge. It was present as a so-called water trial in the ancient mysteries" (CW 53, Oct. 20, 1904).

and with fire" points to the event of Pentecost and is understood as a baptism in the Spirit. These words were added to the early Christian adult Baptism after immersion in water with a subsequent laying on of hands. They were combined with the chrism (a mixture of oil and balm) anointing (this is still done today in the Orthodox Church, even for babies). In the West, from the third century onward, this form of baptism in the Spirit was separated from Baptism and became the sacrament of Confirmation. But does John's Baptism with water become a Christian Baptism simply by adding the baptismal formula found at the end of Matthew's Gospel?*

The Baptism in the Jordan is an echo of the ancient mysteries in yet another respect, connected with the loosening of the bodies† of the individual to be initiated. In the mysteries of antiquity, separating the life body from the physical body led to clairvoyant states. Something similar happened in John's Baptism in the Jordan. Through prolonged immersion in water, the resulting separation from the physical body led to what is today called a *near-death experience*. However, because the human physical body is

---

* "Go therefore and make disciples of all nations, baptizing them in the name of the Father, the Son and the Holy Spirit, and teach them to observe all that I have commanded you" (Matt. 28:19).

† Rudolf Steiner's description of a human being's *bodily nature* includes, in addition to a physical body, a body (here sometimes referred to as a "sheath") that enables and sustains life, a body that enables and sustains conscious thoughts and feelings and finally a body that carries and allows a person to experience him or herself as an "I." The usual terms for these aspects of a human beings are physical body, life (or etheric) body, astral body, and "I." The German word for all four is *Wesensglieder,* literally "members or limbs of a person's being." The term points to four aspects or "bodies" of a human being that continuously interpenetrate and influence each other during life on earth. Here these sheaths will be called physical body, life (etheric) body, astral body and "I." Occasionally, when the term *Wesensglieder* refers to all four bodies collectively, it will be translated as the human *bodily nature.*

nowadays so tightly bound to the other sheaths, such a separation should not be attempted voluntarily—it would be extremely dangerous, with a high likelihood of the deadly consequence that the bodies could not be reunited. But in ancient times, after appropriate training, such a loosening caused experiences of the spiritual world and led the initiate along inner paths.

In John's time his Baptism was an echo of these ancient mystery initiations, an echo carried out in public, symbolically displaying a (water) trial associated with a path of initiation. Rudolf Steiner describes this process for the first time in detail in his lectures on John's Gospel held in Kassel.* However, this Baptism and the attitude toward life that it created had consequences for many people. According to Steiner, "...in no way does history describe it at all accurately"—for those baptized then withdrew to the desert and began monastic lives. In the Jordan River Baptism, the intention was that, by loosening the etheric body, baptized individuals would feel themselves, in their consciousness, transported back to the time before what is called "the Fall." The individuals felt that they had taken a wrong path because of the Fall, and if they were to continue on this wrong path, it would not end well for them. Therefore, they felt a need to tear themselves away from what the world has become since the Fall and return to desert solitude to lead a monastic life.

Steiner asserts that the times call for a different approach. "This is what John the Baptist meant when he said, 'There will come one who will baptize with the Holy Spirit.' John could save people from the consequences of the Fall only by tearing them out of the world. Christ Jesus wanted to

* CW 112, June 29, 1909.

save them in a different way; he wanted to leave them in the world and nevertheless save them."* This means that *a Christian Baptism begins with an affirmation of the world and does not seek to separate the baptized individual from that fallen world.*

The Christian Community sacrament is based on a new understanding of Baptism. Steiner explains:

> If you take John's Baptism, it was based on the fact that someone was immersed in water, an adult was immersed.... He experiences that he belongs to a spiritual world. This is actually also expressed in the baptismal ritual. We cannot do that with a child. We must have a ritual with the child that expresses how the child is received into our community, and the suprasensory religious substance that lives in the community must flow over into the child. We must express this in the rite of Baptism.†

But what is the *community's suprasensory religious substance?*

Here a theme is raised that applies equally to all the sacraments in The Christian Community: the substance that is always at issue is the *soul* substance. This is seen similarly in traditional theology; at any rate, the objective effect of a sacrament was described in scholasticism as follows (in relation to the sacraments that form *character*): They imprint a *character indelebilis* on the soul. But the basic forces of the soul are thinking, feeling, and willing. The important questions for each sacrament are then the following:

What role do these three play in each sacrament?
What transformations do they undergo?
What goals are set for them?

---

* CW 175, April 10, 1917.
† CW 342, June 14, 1921

This trinity of human soul forces is connected with other trinities in human nature, e.g., with the threefold division into body, soul, and spirit. Ultimately, this threefold aspect of human nature reflects the divine Trinity, for man is made in the image of God. This was also widely understood in the first centuries of Christianity.

> The Platonic and the Gnostic traditions, as well as some phrases from Biblical tradition, seemed to point out that it was wrong to understand the human being only as body and soul, and that one rather...had to distinguish from the soul in general the "spirit" as a brought-along, even if buried, remnant (body, soul, spirit—anthropological trichotomy...). Wherever anthropology was trichotomous, even in the background (as in Origen's case), a predetermined proximity of man to God was reckoned with. An anthropological *dichotomy* ultimately became the church dogma (Council of Constantinople, 869–870).*

The Christian Community, however, assumes *anthropological trichotomy* (that the human being consists of body, soul, and spirit) as foundational for its theology. It also therefore assumes that the human being enjoys a certain *proximity to God*, but does not understand this closeness as simply given; it is rather a constitutional orientation presenting us with a task. This closeness to the Trinitarian God is inscribed in every human being because the anthropological trichotomy is not limited to Christians. In an essential way there is a Christ-orientation present in every human being, even if it is completely unconscious. The objective event of Baptism begins the process of becoming aware of this Christ-orientation, of becoming a Christian.

* *Religion in Geschichte und Gegenwart,* vol 1, p. 414f.

Therefore, for an infant Baptism, it is of great importance that The Christian Community watch over the Christian development of the individual being baptized. Every human being, because of the very way their bodily nature is constituted, has an objective, meaningful relationship to Christ. But only when people become aware of this relationship do they become real Christians. In this regard Rudolf Steiner says:

> Here, however, you see how different this is from those people who, so to speak, wish to know nothing about the mystery of Golgotha. Christ did his earthly work on Golgotha for their bodies, for the possibility of their life on earth. He also did it for the unbelieving Gentiles. However, for the soul and spirit it is necessary that...human beings consciously acknowledge and confess the content of the mystery of Golgotha.... So, you see now how there is a difference between those who confess the mystery of Golgotha with their inner powers of faith, knowledge and feeling, and those who do not confess to it.*

In The Christian Community there is no water baptism, but the substance that lives in the community and flows over into the child—representative of what Steiner referred to as the "community's suprasensory religious substance"—is threefold: water, salt, and ash. It is an image of the Trinity, an image of the trichotomous human (body, soul, and spirit) and an image of the soul in its powers of thinking, feeling and willing. All three references appear in the sacrament of Baptism, and all three substances go back to Paracelsus (1493/94–1541), which he referred to as *mercur,*

* CW 224, May 7, 1923.

*sal, sulphur.** A phenomenological, goethean view of these substances shows them in their relationship to earth and to each other. Salt is related to the earth; it is the only one of these substances that we consume in mineral form. It has a preserving power, which, on a spiritual level, corresponds to remembering, without which we cannot lead an independent life on earth. Finally, its crystallization as a cube also points to a "law of *fourness*" that belongs to the earthly (four cardinal points, seasons, bodies of the human being, etc.). In the Apocalypse (the Book of Revelation), the new earth, the new Jerusalem, also has the shape of a cube: "The length and the breadth and the height of the city are equal" (Rev. 21:16).

In contrast to this, ash, which results from a burning process, falls by its own weight into completely chaotic matter. Ash represents the end of all form; at the same time, however, precisely because it represents chaos, it is completely open to new forms, just as the mythical phoenix rises from the ashes. In early Christianity, the resurrection was associated with this myth.† In a spiritual sense, burning fire corresponds to pain. The process that takes place is separation. When a metal become liquid through fire, the impurities that float to the top as slag can be skimmed off, leaving the metal to be extracted in its pure form. Such a purification process can also take place in the human soul when the inessential is separated from the essential. Although this process is always

* In anthroposophy, these three principles play a role in various contexts. There is a series of publications on this subject, for example from Hermann Beckh, Willem F. Daems, Volker Harlan, Armin Scheffler (see bibliography). Here we would like to point to three essays by Volker Harlan in the monthly periodical *Die Christengemeinschaft*, issues 1, 3, 4 / 2003.

† First letter of Clement; cf *Religion in Geschichte und Gegenwart*, vol. 2, p. 674.

associated with pain, it is often the beginning of something completely new. Finally, water stands in the middle as a balance. It has no external shape of its own but adapts completely to its surroundings. Water also has a mediating effect, so to speak, between different chemical substances when they are dissolved in it.

A picture for these three basic forces, which is more than just an analogy, appears in the disciples' vision of the Transfiguration on the mountain: Christ between Moses and Elijah. This motif plays a major role in the history of painting—especially in iconography of the East, but also an important motif in the West, finding supreme representation in Raphael's work. A key to understanding this scene is given by Steiner when he said that the well-known parallelism of Buddha's life according to legend and that of Jesus' life according to the Gospels goes only as far as the Transfiguration. "Buddha ended in a sublime manner. On a hike he felt ill. He came to the river Hiranja, near Kushinagra, where laid on a carpet spread out by his favorite disciple Ananda. His body began to glow from within. He ended up transfigured, as a body of light, while saying, 'Nothing is long-lasting.'" Comparing the death of Buddha to the transfiguration of Jesus implies that everything that follows in the Gospels goes beyond Buddhism.*

The core of the Buddha's teaching was based on the insight that all life on earth is suffering. His four noble truths concern suffering, the origin of suffering, the cessation of suffering and the path to the cessation of suffering. Suffering is abolished when a human being on his or her path overcomes the thirst for existence and thus no longer needs to be

* CW 8, p. 104 f. Editor's note, p. 192: Steiner refers to Rudolf Seydel, *Buddha and Christ*, Breslau 1884, pp. 8ff.

reborn. Two gestures speak here: Rejection of suffering and rejection of the earth as the place of incarnation, because incarnation means suffering.

On the Mount of Transfiguration, Christ is as far as Buddha at the end of his life: he has become free from the earth and its attraction—and has become weightless, as Raphael masterfully portrays it. But he does not leave the earth. In conversation with Moses and Elijah, who appear as spiritual figures beside him, this decision is confirmed. The words "And as they came down from the mountain..." (Matt. 17:9) express this gesture of affirming earthly existence. But because Buddha is correct—that being on the earth really does mean suffering—Christ Jesus must also perform the affirmation of suffering. He turns his inner eye to Jerusalem and sees how he will do so: his passion in Jerusalem. John the Baptist, his forerunner, had already suffered the Passion when Herod had him beheaded: "But I say to you: Elijah has already come, but they did not recognize him, but did with him what they wanted. So also the Son of Man will have to suffer through them" (Matt. 17:12).

In the spiritual conversation on the mountain, Moses affirmed the earth. He looked back into the past and described how the people of Israel arrived on earth as the Promised Land and what laws were needed to live there properly. Elijah looks as a prophet into the future, but he knows that the future must always be suffered: the essential must be distinguished from the inessential in complete objectivity. This can be experienced as burning pain. This also brings to mind how he ascends to heaven in a chariot of fire.

In this gesture of earthly affirmation we recognize the inner quality of salt. In the Sermon on the Mount Jesus said to his disciples: "You are the salt of the earth" (Matt. 5:13). The next step, the affirmation of suffering, is connected with the inner quality of ashes. Both actions of affirmation belong to the inner essence of Christianity. Both can also certainly lead to one-sidedness: the affirmation of the earth to materialism, and the affirmation of suffering to a rapturous escape from the earth. This was repeatedly evident in Christianity up to the Baroque period in view of *the vain world*. But if both work together and keep in balance, a positive Christian attitude toward the earth and the tasks that must be fulfilled here can arise, as well as a positive inner attitude toward the gravity of life, from which the senses wish to be released but which give life its depth. In the middle between salt and ash we find the water of life, just as we find Christ between Moses and Elijah: "But those who drink the water that I shall give them shall never thirst, for the water that I shall give them shall become in them a spring of water springing up into eternal life" (John 4:14).

The arrangement of the substances in a triangle on the baptismal table corresponds to this inner relationship between the three substances: in the middle (at the apex of the triangle) is the water, at the other two points on the right and left are salt and ashes, respectively. Thus arranged, the substances reflect the body (salt), soul (water) and spirit (ashes) of human beings *as well as* the Trinity: Father (salt), Son (water) and Holy Spirit (ashes).

But in another part of the Baptism ritual these three substances are arranged in a different manner: When a child is baptized with the substances, a triangle is drawn on the forehead with the water, and this act of Baptism is related to the Father God. A square is drawn on the chin with the salt which here reflects the Son God, and a cross is drawn on the chest with the ash, which then reflects the Holy Spirit. The substances have a spatial arrangement on the baptismal table, while here they appear in chronological order. This can appear as a logical contradiction. Should the salt be associated with the Father or the Son? And the water: is it related to Christ or the Father? The founders of The Christian Community asked Rudolf Steiner this question. He said:

> There is a bit of a difficulty here, because one cannot properly express in time what is present. When I talk about the physical body, etheric body, astral body, sentient soul, mind soul, consciousness soul, spirit self, life spirit, spirit man, I string them together consecutively—as if they exist one after the other. But that is not true. I would have to have two currents flow into each other [drawn on the blackboard] if I wanted to draw it properly. I'd have to do it like this: physical body, etheric body, astral body, sentient soul, mind soul, consciousness soul; and now I wouldn't have to draw the spirit self in the same plane with it, but in another direction, here I'd have to bend it over and draw it three times in a different direction.... That is the same in the [Baptism] ritual.... You cannot connect [these elements] directly; *they are oblique to each other*.

So, the second sequence of substances, which is at an oblique angle to the first, is: water (Father), salt (Son), ashes (Spirit). This sequence calls to mind the Rosicrucian verse:

> *Ex deo nascimur* (We are born of God).
> *In Christo morimur* (In Christ we die).
> *Per Spiritum Sanctum reviviscimus* (Through the Holy Spirit we receive eternal life).

Everything—as the Greek philosopher Thales already

said—is born from water. This can be understood physically, biologically: without water there is no life; it can also be understood spiritually: everything that crystallizes within consciousness as a thought initially existed in fluid form, that is, in indefinite thought movements. Here, through water we can experience the divine primordial ground of existence from which all Being is born: *Ex deo nascimur.*

Salt expresses something different. When it crystallizes out of solution into solid form, the fluid movement of the crystal comes to an end. Whenever we give form to something it loses its original life—a process comes to its end and dies. Rudolf Steiner gave an even more profound perspective on the nature of salt using the example of seasonal change from summer to winter. First of all, in winter we gain a consciousness that is more awake than in summer, but we also experience the dying processes in nature as the price we pay for greater alertness. *Consciousness is always at the expense of life.* This is true in the evolution of living organisms: generally speaking, the lower a living being is on the evolutionary scale, the duller its consciousness and the greater its vitality. The same applies within human physiology: brain cells that enable consciousness are the least vital. Thus, the loss of life in winter makes greater consciousness possible. Seen this way, winter is not only a reality for us but also becomes a symbol.

> In order to live with the earth in winter in the physical world, we must immerse ourselves in the dying. But after the mystery of Golgotha, we submerge ourselves by taking the Christ impulse with us into this dying: *In Christo morimur.*[*]

[*] CW 162, May 23, 1915.

Paul expresses it in this way: "If we have died with Christ, we believe that we will also live with him" (Rom. 6:8). Christmas can thus become an expression of the fact that *we go with Christ into the death of earth in winter* and believe "that we will also live with him."

However, this wintry earth, on which we experience death and consciousness, also has a relationship to salt. For suprasensory vision, what characterizes the wintry earth is "the deposits of what is salt-like." That vision also shows that the earth in winter is permeable to the spirit in a special way, because "where there is salt, there the spirit has unobstructed space, so to speak. The spirit can enter where there is salt."* Thus, with the help of anthroposophy, we have a deeper perspective on earth in winter, which is at the same time a deeper understanding of salt, because the earth takes on a salt-like character in winter. The summer life of earth dies into the crystalline forms of earth in winter. But this *salt crystal* is spirit-permeable for the gift of God's grace. What salt "tells" us is that movement and life die into form. It also tells us that form is spirit-permeable; and finally, that Christ himself followed this path from life in the cosmos into the form of an earthly incarnation all the way into death. Since that time, we can connect and unite our dying with Christ—*in Christo morimur*—and thus open ourselves to life in the spirit.

This brings us to the third substance, ash; through the Holy Spirit we receive eternal life, *per Spiritum Sanctum reviviscimus*. The truth of life is that the forms, with which we live on earth can no longer be dissolved; there is no going back to a time before birth or before the decisions

* CW 229, Oct. 6 and 7, 1923.

determining our destiny. With these forms imposed upon us, we are to bring everything to an end; that is, we must learn to die with Christ. Then the forms can be shattered. But from the ashes of what has been shattered, new goals can take wing, like the phoenix bird, born out of fire.

We have now considered two different sequences for the three baptismal substances. Both sequences are a picture for the Trinity. The first sequence, which finds its expression in the spatial arrangement of the triangle on the baptismal table, expresses an aspect of the Trinity as found in the physical world: salt is assigned to the Father, water to the Son, ash to the Holy Spirit. The second sequence, which unfolds in time, follows a line from the forehead, to the chin, and then to the chest of the person baptized. This sequence brings to light the aspect of the Trinity found in the human being which is connected to the Rosicrucian saying: *ex deo nascimur–in Christo morimur–per Spiritum Sanctum reviviscimus*. Water is assigned to the Father, salt to the Son, and ash to the Holy Spirit. The two sequences are not to be directly lined up with each other; they are, so to speak, oblique to each other.

Finally, we will consider what the substances themselves contribute to a Baptism. Augustine's formula: "When the word comes to the element the sacrament is created" (*accedit verbum ad elementum et fit sacramentum*) still contains much wisdom. Fundamentally speaking, elements—that is, substances in and of themselves—cannot really contribute to the sacrament, at best symbolically. Our previous thoughts concerning the relationship of the three baptismal substances to the Trinity, for example, could then be misunderstood, as if the significance of the substance were merely symbolic. On the contrary, just as Rudolf Steiner introduced the idea of biographical development into the doctrine of the sacraments, another great achievement of anthroposophy is the introduction of the idea of evolutionary development to an understanding of substances.

We should not imagine that matter as we experience it today has always been the same. Substances develop and evolve—and we are not speaking here of a chemical process, but a spiritual-physical one. Like human beings, substances have also undergone a process of transformation as they became earthly matter, for they originally consisted of pure *spiritual materiality*,* which was still a *process, a movement or gesture*, in the spiritual world.

> That was the important thing in ancient times, to look at what had to happen in the world process in order for a certain substance to acquire a certain form. That was the first thing. Substances were evaluated only after that step. Today we start from the substance, whereas back then people started from the process—and every substance is just a process, a process stopped at some stage.†

Only a substance at its initial stage, when it is still all process, all spiritual movement, can contribute to a sacrament. This was Paracelsus' understanding of these three substances. Instead of salt, water, ash, it is therefore better to say (expressed in the Latin words of Paracelsus): *sal* process, *mercur* process, *sulfur* process. Earthly baptismal substances are therefore consecrated in order for their material form to be reconnected with their original spiritual processes or gestures. "Consecration means making what is solid fluid."‡ In

* CW 343, Oct. 10, 1921.

† CW 318. Sept. 18, 1924.

‡ CW 345, July 11, 1923.

a sense, the materiality of these earthly substances serves as an anchor for them to be present in the world of the senses. Consecrating* them restores the process character to earthly substances, allowing them to exist in their original *spiritual materiality*. This consecration, which takes place during the Baptism ritual, makes the water, salt, and ash, real and not merely symbolic factors in the sacrament.

7.4 The Form of the Baptism

The basic structure of the baptismal ritual is sevenfold. In the first act the priest expresses his or her intention *to lead the soul* of the person baptized into the "community of the Christ Jesus"—a masculine gesture. With this intention the spiritual world is addressed. It is referred to with the unusual appellation *spirits of worlds*, which may at first sound very pagan. To understand what is meant by *spirits of worlds* it helps to see how Steiner used these words in other contexts.

The Christian Community does not regard Steiner as the source of its rituals. It sees the realm of ritual as preexisting in the spiritual world but, like any ordinary thought, needs a linguistic body in order to appear on earth. Just as 2,000 years ago the Greek language of that time (*Koiné* Greek) was suitable for receiving the revelation of Christianity in linguistic form *vertically*, so to speak, from above, in the form of the New Testament (after which translations have come into being *horizontally*), similarly with modern spiritual science. *Anthroposophy* first appeared *vertically* in the German language and required for its expression much of what Böhme,

* To avoid possible misunderstandings, it should be noted that the consecration of substances is a fundamentally different process than the consecration of bread and wine that takes place in the course of the Eucharist, The Act of Consecration of Man.

Fichte, Hegel, Novalis, Goethe, and other great spirits have brought into the language.

Because their gifts were not quite enough for expressing certain nuances, Rudolf Steiner introduced even more expressions into the German language, words that go beyond merely technical terminology (such as *astral body*).[*] He created additional expressions within the German language to make it even more suitable for the contents of spiritual science and also for ritual wordings that reflect the spirit. From this point of view (but only from this point of view), the rituals of The Christian Community also bear the mark of Rudolf Steiner. Certain words such as *ether* or *formative forces* can also be found in ritual wordings. They originated in his unceasing effort to find new formulations in the German language for spiritual realities that he was perceiving. This does not contradict the fact that Steiner himself did not author those wordings.

Steiner generally used the expression *spirits of worlds* to denote the totality of creative forces in the world, insofar as they positively advance evolutionary development. We can think of these forces as consisting of the hierarchies, but they could also be the Logos. Here are two examples, with italics added:

> We come to know ourselves in a living sense as standing within a stream of evolutionary development. We come to know, so to speak, how *spirits of worlds* have intended something with our existence, and how what they intend is becoming more and more apparent in life.[†]

A few years later, Steiner also said, "We recognize

---

[*] Cf. Martina Maria Sam, *The Challenge of Spiritual Language: Rudolf Steiner's Linguistic Style*.

[†] CW 60, March 9, 1911.

ourselves as instruments of *spirits of worlds*, who want to enter into a relationship with us. And this gives our life great wealth and an assurance that cannot be lost."* We see here the keynote, or the tone given to Baptism when the priest first turns to the spirits of worlds.

In the second act of the Baptism the congregation is told that it should *receive* the soul of the child being baptized and *bear* it into the communion of the Christ Jesus. This is a feminine gesture in which one can recognize a kind of conception and pregnancy. At the same time, the congregation is also instructed concerning the child's origin in body, soul and spirit, whereby the Trinity is reflected in this trichotomy: The body comes from the realm of God the Father, the soul from the creative word of the Son. The spirit is an earthly task in light of the Holy Spirit's goals for the future.

In the third act the godparents are appointed. The wording makes it clear that the godparents have come forward of their own initiative—even if they were initially asked by the parents. The godparents are guardians, though not in any legal sense. There are essentially three meanings of this word as used by Rudolf Steiner. First, it refers to the *guardian of the threshold*, then to the guardian angels of individual human beings, and finally, to the human conscience. Steiner describes the origin of conscience: at a certain moment in history everything was designed "to awaken the ego, and as the guardian of the ego, as the voice of God within, to let conscience arise."† These three areas impressively describe the spiritual tasks of godparents.

The fourth act is the center of the Baptism: the naming. This was discussed in section 7.2.

---

* CW 64, Jan. 15, 1915.

† CW 59, May 5, 1910.

The fifth act is the Baptism with substances. There is meaning to the signs that are drawn on the forehead (triangle), the chin (square) and the chest (cross). Steiner spoke of this in various ways.

> The triangle and the square are only precursors of the cross. The cross is what underlies the whole formation of human being.... Is it not true that what lives in the sign of the cross, the physical and the etheric human being, is completely unconscious? What lives in the astral body is semi-conscious; it is best expressed in the square, while what lives in the "I" is expressed in the triangle. So, we see the "I"—the triangle, the astral body—the square, and the entire human being, living as an "I" and astral body within the physical and etheric body—the cross."*

A third meaning for the cross is found in the notes that Emil Bock wrote after a conversation with Steiner: "Triangle, the divine; square, the inner life on earth; cross, connection of both." We have three different descriptions of the cross: connected to the lower elements, connected to the triangle and rectangle, connecting the upper elements with the lower ones. Everything in human beings is connected with the cross. And since triangle and square are only preliminary stages of the Cross, the emphasis is on Baptism with ash, that is, "with the Holy Spirit and with fire." This also indicates to what extent Baptism is a sanctification of an involutionary process. Already with the first breath a human being takes, very quietly a dying process begins.† "The human being must in a certain way sanctify the process of involution, which is the opposite process to evolution. Evolution is what is natural, it is a gift of nature.... But when we feel the involution process

* CW 343, Oct. 9, 1921.

† Cf. chap. 6 "Historical Development."

begin, which seizes us as a process of dying, then it must... be sanctified, that is, what proceeds from the Christ impulse must be inserted into it.... What birth is *as an evolutionary process*, Baptism shall become *as an involutionary process*."* The ash part of the Baptism in The Christian Community is the sanctification of a process of involution.

In the sixth act, Baptism is brought into connection with the Trinity. The ancient formula, *in the name of the Father, the Son and the Holy Spirit,* is now expressed in more differentiated terms: in the Father's *substance of worlds*, in Christ's *streaming of the Word* and in *the Spirit's brightness of light*. In this way Baptism unfolds its blessing power into life.

The seventh act is a review of what happened in the Baptism and a look ahead to the future. The soul of the child has now been led *into the community of the Christ Jesus* with the participation of the congregation. This is a fact; the child is baptized (in terms of what was presented in section 5.2.2, "The Threefold Nature of the Sacraments," this would be *res et sacramentum*). But this does not mean that Baptism is concluded, for now the responsibility of the congregation toward the baptized child comes into play. By its very nature, this responsibility represents a vow that the community will "of itself watch over the child's development as a Christian," so that the child will be shown more and more to be one who has been baptized (*res tantum*).

One can see in these seven acts a step-by-step passage of the soul through the planetary spheres (understood geocentrically), concentrated in reverse order in the ritual, how the soul ascends again through the planetary spheres after

* CW 343, Oct. 2, 1921.

death.* The first act is colored by the Saturn mood, the second act (*instructions* for the congregation) by Jupiter, the fourth (the naming) by the Sun, with the seventh act as retrospection in the reflection of the Moon.

Then the child arrives on earth, and the Lord's Prayer is added after the actual Baptism has been completed. This prayer has a special effect at this point, because it accompanies the beginning of a life on earth, a biography. Each of the seven petitions has a biographical dimension that can be heard, as it were, in view of the next seventy years: divine will, may it always be done; the daily bread that the baptized person will need spiritually and physically; the guilt that will inevitably befall the person; the evil that they will encounter from outside and within themselves. And how will the same Lord's Prayer resound again at the grave when a human lifetime, filled with deeds and sufferings, has come to an end? The eighth act is the step from the lowest level of heaven (the moon) to the earth.

Baptism also has a wider meaning in The Christian Community. If an adult who has not received Baptism and Confirmation wishes to become a member of The Christian Community, neither Confirmation nor, as a rule, Baptism is necessary. Both sacraments are linked to specific ages when an *involution-evolution* transition occurs in life. In the two thousand-year history of Christianity, it has always been felt that Baptism is an essential step for those seeking membership in the church; it makes them into Christians. It has even been regarded as *the sacrament* per se—which corresponds to the Protestant view that there are no other sacraments apart from the Lord's Supper and Baptism. However,

* Ibid.

someone wishing to join The Christian Community can remain unbaptized. This is not merely accepted but considered correct.

The Christian Community understands the sacraments as seven developmental forms of *one single organism*. This organism is the *proto-sacrament*,* the archetype for all sacraments. No matter how different they are from one another, each of the individual sacraments reflects this proto-sacrament. Those who, for reasons of personal destiny, could not receive Baptism and Confirmation at the designated age will nevertheless be able to participate in the wholeness of the sacramental stream through other sacraments (e.g., Sacramental Consultation and Communion). This original sacrament is also called Baptism in a broader sense in The Christian Community. This is expressed in the ritual of priestly Ordination when the word *baptism* is understood to include the celebration of all the sacraments. Thus, those who immerse themselves in the sacramental stream, especially through the Act of Consecration,† receives baptism in the broader sense. Understood thus, there is also adult Baptism in The Christian Community in the form of a reception into the sacramental stream of The Christian church. Baptism of children is only one way to enter into this larger stream of baptism and is linked to a particular age.

The reality of the sacraments, as is evident in the Baptism ritual, is intimately connected with the reality of the congregation. One must ask what Baptism would mean—what

* Cf. section 2.2, "Sacraments in the Catholic, Orthodox, and Protestant Churches."

† The Act of Consecration of Man represents in a special way the totality of the sacraments as the proto-sacrament; cf. in this volume section 14.2, "The Act of Consecration of Man in Relation to the Other Sacraments."

reality would it have?—if it were not connected to a congregation. The sacraments require a social echo and recognition. Even an Ordination to the priesthood within The Christian Community has no earthly reality except within The Christian Community. For example, it would have no reality in a Catholic congregation. It is not an abstract, magical fact.

One could also ask whether a newborn child should be baptized if it is known that the child's young mother will soon move to a country where law demands an entirely different religion be followed by all, and where there is no possibility for a Christian education. Would that resemble some kind of spiritual inoculation that would then continue working by itself without human participation? The idea that the sacraments have a magical effect simply by themselves (*ex opere operato*), so to speak, is still quite common, but no longer appropriate in our time. Nevertheless, sacraments do have an *objective* effect. This creates a tension that today can be balanced by the personal contribution of human beings.* The objectivity of the sacraments requires human participation in order to become real. The contribution made by people participating in a congregation is also an essential aspect of this reality.†

* Rudolf Steiner already described this tension in another field in 1886 for today's cognitive process: "As unusual as the idea may be to us that we ourselves actively manifest something objective, that we not only perceive a phenomenon but also produce it at the same time, this idea is not inadmissible" (CW 2, p. 52).

† What is really meant is the concrete baptismal congregation of The Christian Community. Baptism, like Ordination to the priesthood, has a reality above all with regard to this congregation (i.e., The Christian Community). This is a *spiritual* fact, not yet a description of the management of valid membership in the congregation etc. From the baptismal liturgy it is not evident to what extent Baptism could be real without a baptismal congregation (i.e., The Christian Congregation). In this respect it is consistent—albeit for quite different reasons than what theological argumentation shows—that other churches may not recognize the Baptism of The Christian

Community for themselves. The Christian Community has no reason to expect this, any more than it expects this for its priestly Ordination. A problem arises only where the Christianity of The Christian Community is judged. For example, Baptism in The Christian Community is not recognized as Christian by the Council of the Lutheran Church in Germany (most recently in a decision of 1969), partly because it does not contain the baptismal formula of Matthew 28:19. This is true. But even the words of institution in the Roman Mass do not correspond to any of the four biblical wordings (Matt. 26:26ff.; Mark 14:22ff.; Luke 22:17ff.; 1 Cor. 11:23ff.) but have their own *non-biblical* form. In this sense the baptismal formula of The Christian Community is also non-biblical, but why should it therefore be non-Christian? Fortunately, in individual cases there are also places for a dialogue between representatives of the Protestant church and The Christian Community where Christianity is not formally judged. A very commendable recent example of this is the publication of the results of the work of such a discussion group by the Protestant Oberkirchenrat Stuttgart (*Zur Frage der Christlichkeit der Christengemeinschaft* [The question of the Christianity of The Christian Community]).

Chapter 8
Confirmation

8.1 The Sunday Service for Children

A period of about seven years begins when a child enters school. These years can be blessed by the Sunday Service for Children. Seven years contain 365 Sundays, during which time a child could in principle experience this celebration; that would amount to an entire year of Sundays. The congregation received the child to be baptized and thereafter carries them *into the communion of the Christ Jesus*. They are on a path to themselves in their congregation. In the first seven years, there is no need for children to attend church, except perhaps to participate in a Baptism or wedding ceremony. During the second seven years the inner life of the child changes. "Therefore, it is also necessary for religious development to begin during this time."*

An important step is now taken through experiencing this religious service in a form appropriate to the child's age. For the first time the children experience themselves as members of the congregation. They enter the room one by one and are received at the door—the threshold—by a priest or server who then takes their hand while saying, "You know

* CW 96, March 4, 1907.

you are going to the service that will lift up your soul to the spirit of the world." Then this brief moment alone with the server or priest ends and each child joins the community of children standing before the altar, while the adults remain in the background. It is appropriate that the priest addresses the little community of children as *we*. The priest stands at the altar facing the children, spiritually and physically in a different place, and yet that difference is suspended by the spoken word *we* which includes both priest and the community of children.

The word *we* emphasizes that there is no doubt that the adults must lead the children. An example from everyday life would be: *Now let's tidy the room!* This statement usually means that only the child is cleaning up, but the adult is there with their (guiding) consciousness and therefore says *we*. The same thing is happening during the first part of the Sunday Service for Children, which concludes with a prayer spoken by the children. The *we* is introduced once again by the priest with the words "We will now pray." The old Latin Mass also contained an *Oremus*, "Let us pray," which is connected to the childlike state of consciousness prevailing during the millennium before the modern age. The *we* expresses the great distance between priests and the worshippers, who were not considered to have come of age religiously.

At the end of the children's common prayer, the *we* stage is left behind, and each child is addressed individually. The priest takes the child by the hand and speaks to the children one on one with a simple statement, "The Spirit of God will be with you when you seek him." The children's response is similarly simple, yet speaks to their future lives: "I will seek him." The course of action has now led to this central point: from us, through you, to me. This is similar to the journey to the birth of each child's sense of responsibility. The community, which received and now bears the child, actually seeks to lead him or her to come of age religiously, i.e., to that very sense of responsibility. The final step on that path is Confirmation. After the answer, "I will seek him," the curtain of *we* is pulled away; the children now experience the priest in his or her words as a person standing across from them and thus experience themselves as individuals—hinting at their future maturity. The priest then shifts from the *we* to the *"I"* form and addresses the children as *you*. Now they can hear the Gospel, only to be released after a song. The Confirmation contains an important look back over the years when the children were led in this way, back to how they had been guided into their own autonomy, from the *we* to the *"I."*

8.2 The Age of Confirmation

In early Christianity, adult Baptism was combined with a subsequent act reserved for the bishop, which consisted of a laying on of hands and an anointing of the forehead. The accompanying prayer was an invocation of the Holy Spirit to descend upon the person to be baptized. This act was later given the name *confirmatio* (English: *confirmation*). It was immediately followed by the confirmand's first participation in Holy Communion. These three actions were experienced as belonging together, as a rite of initiation into the church of Christ. In the Eastern Church, this trinity of actions is still performed today as infant Baptism (Communion for infants is only in the form of wine). In the Western church, with the appearance of infant Baptism, Confirmation and First

Communion were separated from Baptism. At the same time, Baptism was understood more and more as a sacrament of purification, while anointing was understood not only as an imparting of the spirit, but as a perfecting and completing of Baptism (*perficere*) necessary at a later age: "Baptism gives life from God, Confirmation alone gives maturity to this life from God."* After the fourth Lateran Council of 1215 had set the seventh year of life (the so-called age of discernment) as the age of First Communion, the age of Confirmation began to move toward this age as well. In the nineteenth century, there was a tendency to consider the age when children left school as suitable. Confirmation was then rather understood as a sacrament of transition from childhood to youth. Thus, the early Christian sequence of Baptism–Confirmation–First Communion was gradually abandoned; Confirmation came last.

The Protestants did not follow the Roman Catholic view of Confirmation. All churches resulting from the Reformation created a successor form of Confirmation but understood it differently. It was unacceptable to the reformers that Baptism as such should be thought of as incomplete, somehow still needing to be completed. For Luther, Catholic Confirmation was almost a devaluation of Baptism, which already conveyed the gifts of salvation without restriction. Afterward, the baptized person can only be sent to the congregation gathered for the sermon and the Eucharist, where his or her faith is awakened and strengthened. Any further sacrament was out of the question; neither does the New Testament attest to it. Thus, a radical break was made and any attachment of Confirmation to Baptism was completely

* Auer and Ratzinger, vol. 7, p. 93.

abandoned. For Luther, however, the catechism became important in a completely new way. His interest in teaching followed by *confirmatio* was therefore primarily catechetical. It was concerned with catching up on baptismal instruction (which, in any case, was not done with infants) and acquiring the knowledge necessary to participate in the eucharist with understanding. It was essential that those who attend the Lord's Supper know what they are doing. Luther had no interest in Confirmation as a ritual, but he was not against a blessing service with intercessory prayer. Thus in the Protestant church a service developed which bears the Latin name of the rejected sacrament of Confirmation (*confirmatio*) but whose essential elements lie in the Reformation catechism and in an educated admission (*admissio*) to the Lord's Supper with a blessing associated. Now in modern times, ongoing catechism examinations are being discontinued and religious instruction is increasingly concluded with Confirmation. In the eighteenth century, the spread and prestige of Confirmation in bourgeois society grew once again due to the influence of the Enlightenment, which saw in it a kind of bourgeois rite of maturity associated with the graduation from school. For the age of Confirmation, the fourteenth to fifteenth year of life thus became the norm in the Protestant church. Today, however, this is again being questioned intensely; in particular the connection between Confirmation and admission to the Eucharist is also under scrutiny.

The Confirmation age in The Christian Community is fourteen to fifteen years. Initially this is not connected with theological considerations (completion of Baptism, admission to the Eucharist), but with considerations related to human development.

> The second evolutionary process that occurs in our life is the one that shows itself in all its strength as human beings become sexually mature, when their physical body and their etheric body have reached a certain development and the astral body begins to take on a special role in their development, that is, when what separates in every sleeping state is connected in a new way. The sleeping state is such that the physical body and the etheric body remain in bed and the astral body and the "I" leave.

So, throughout life there is an intimate connection between the physical body and the etheric body, whereas there is a "looser connection" between the etheric and astral bodies, so they can separate from each other every night.

> But this connection is modified in a certain way when it actually comes to maturity [in the fourteenth, fifteenth, sixteenth years of life]; it only comes to a proper interaction with what we have separated in sleep from the physical–bodily, which remains in bed during sleep. The correct interaction only enters in the fourteenth, fifteenth, sixteenth years of life.*

The process of evolution here therefore refers to puberty, to sexual maturity. The sacrament, however, refers to the associated involutional process, to what is regressing, so to speak, *what is lost*. In ordinary experience this would be called the loss of childhood, being cast out of childhood's paradise. From the point of view of anthroposophy, this is the liberation of the astral body which is simultaneously the beginning of human self-centeredness. Children now experience a new, a modified, relationship between the physical and etheric bodies. The two poles of the polarity of sleeping

* CW 343, Oct. 2, 1921.

and waking move farther apart. The world of sleep and the world of waking are much closer in children. This has great significance for their relationship to morality, which, for the child, rightly still comes as a moral law completely from outside, mediated by their educators. The path to morality for children before puberty leads through the senses, through a healthy perception of the world and through the formation of good habits, that is, through the formation of the physical and etheric bodies. At that age children's astral bodies, their inwardness, is still completely secure with their physical and etheric bodies. This changes at puberty. What the astral body (with the "I") goes through separately from the physical and etheric body during sleep at night become more and more the source of morality originating completely from within, and from which an individual conscience gradually grows.

Without the possibility of self-centeredness, there could be no individual conscience. Without the possibility of bringing moral impulses from the sea of spiritual night experiences to the shore of day-consciousness, self-centeredness would cut us off from the reality of the world. This insight can give us important themes for a sustainable education of youth (e.g., arousing interest in the world). The evolutionary process leading to the self-centeredness arising with puberty is blessed by the involutionary deed of the sacrament of Confirmation. This sacrament can strengthen the nascent individual morality and help the youth to guide and lead themselves.

8.3 The Threshold Leading to Youth

The central motive of Confirmation in The Christian Community is blessing the passage from childhood to youth. The ritual has three main focuses: the first is still on this side of the threshold, thus it refers to childhood; the third is beyond this threshold and refers to youth. The second, the middle focus, is the threshold itself, which also has its own ritual form. A connection with Baptism definitely exists; it is expressed outwardly by the fact that only baptized children can be confirmed. But The Christian Community would say—in agreement with the Reformation and disagreeing with Catholic theology: the point of Confirmation is not to perfect and complete Baptism. Baptism conveys a complete blessing in itself; but this is only true when applied to infants and children, for when the child becomes an adolescent, the next step is due. Through Baptism, a child is connected to Christ primarily in its *life forces*. Through Confirmation, a foundation is laid for this connection to become more and more *conscious*. To this extent, The Christian Community—together with Catholic theology—would say: Confirmation is the sacrament of the Holy Spirit and a necessary *continuation* of Baptism.

What does it mean, then, when in Confirmation children are told that they are rising from childhood to youth? First of all, it is a wording characteristic of initiation. The initiation of adolescents into adulthood used to be the transition from one age, in which traditional values had to be adopted and accepted, to another age, in which those traditional values had to be advocated to a younger generation. But the values themselves were never questioned. Questioning used to be reserved for the leaders, the initiates. All new cultural development came about as a result of a *revolution from above*; cultural development was—as Lessing says—*an education of the human race*. When a new level was due in this school of the human race, the learning material was developed accordingly, and a new cultural impact came from the suprahuman world above. The wheel, the plough, the cultivation of grain, the art of building pyramids, etc., were not inventions in the modern sense, but rather "gifts" from wisdom beyond everyday human awareness. Those gifts were made public and thus became cultural progress. Cultural progress always meant revolution in relation to traditional values, revolution from above. This meant not only that it came from the ruling leaders, but ultimately in the past from the spiritual guidance of humanity.*

Rudolf Steiner describes how such an initiate sees the world: initiated leaders had insight and knew what was spiritually necessary. Even after initiation an initiate remains completely a citizen of the sensory world but sees another reality beyond. To see the normal, ordinary world *immersed in a higher reality* is a prerequisite for recognizing what new impulses a culture may need.

> That is right for the eye. Nor is it deprived of its due by the spiritual eye. It is only that the spiritual eye permits us to see the things of sense in a higher light. Nothing perceived by the physical eye is thereby denied; and yet a new glory radiates from what is seen, showing that the former perception was only of a lower reality. What is seen remains exactly the same as before, but now it is merged into something higher—into the spirit."†

It is an intermediate state between the child (accepting traditional values) and the adult (upholding and representing

* That there is a guiding force behind cultural evolutionary development is of course an unusual understanding of history that is also no longer fully valid for the present. On the concept of "spiritual guidance" see Steiner, *The Spiritual Guidance of the Individual and Humanity* (CW 15).

† CW 8, *Christianity as Mystical Fact*, p. 4.

traditional values): the prevailing tradition from the past is seen and questioned *in a higher light*. Other and new values must then arise out of this higher light. It is a state between *no longer* and *not yet*. This state shall be called *youth* here. In the past the only truly youthful people were the leading initiates—they alone were allowed to introduce new revolutionary values into the culture.

Christianity has made public the wisdom contained in the ancient mysteries. It has, so to speak, published those mysteries.* *Being youthful* as a possibility—or even preference—has thus also passed over to universal Christianity. Being youthful is part of the Easter message: "And they [the three women] went into the tomb and saw a young man† sitting on his right hand, wearing a long white robe; and great wonder overcame them" (Mark 16:5). It is this young man who then tells them the Easter story.

One can see from this that Christianity represents and is an altogether youthful force. It questions traditional values. The law from the past is fundamentally questioned. The values are not simply replaced with new ones, however, for new ones are meant to be sought as goals arising from within individuals. This truth lies in the sentence that is usually misunderstood: "This is my commandment, that you love one another, even as I love you" (John 15:12). The Greek word used here for *commandment* (*entole*) has a broader meaning than just command. It is derived from the word *telos*, which means goal. Christ does not give orders, external commandments (see section 7.1 Infant Baptism), but rather suggests goals that then need to be sought and found individually.

---

* "For nothing is veiled that will not be revealed, and nothing is hidden (occultum) that will not be made known" (Matt. 10:26).

† *Neaniskos*, Greek for young man, or youth.

The love of people for one another is the Christian goal that sums up everything. It took a long time for youth to become a reality in Christianity, first among the privileged classes, the nobility, and then later among the upper middle classes. In the lower classes, for a long time childhood continued to pass into adulthood at the age of fourteen. The adolescents in the upper classes began to study. Those who studied laid the foundations for their own, new values. When they started, they were allowed to free themselves from the old values without being obliged to represent any new values. In this way, the picture of a *young student who is learning* became the archetype of gradually emerging youth. In Germany at the beginning of the twentieth century this finally led to the *Wandervogel** youth movement, which was open to all young people. What is important here is that originally youth was always associated with education.

Furthermore, new values can take hold in a society only when individuals acquire the ability to introduce them correctly into the world *as it is*. This requires developing one's own abilities and a deep understanding of existing society and how it got that way—in short: it requires study and training. Today it is taken for granted in Western societies that everyone can have a period of time for youthful exploration; it is no longer necessarily connected to study and training.

It is also worth noting that, as this period of youthful exploration was being democratized, the first publication

* *Wandervogel* is the name adopted by a popular German youth movement from 1896 to 1933. They protested against industrialization by hiking in the country and communing with nature in the woods. They were influenced by medieval wandering scholars and were known to sing folk songs while walking as well as in their gatherings.

(1906) appeared on the group delinquency of youth,* portraying youth as no longer a privilege of the upper classes, but also a phenomenon that could potentially fail. One form of failure is juvenile delinquency, the reasons for which are usually insufficient study and training. But the transition known as initiation in the past has now in any case definitely passed over to youth. Today young people look at the modern world with its traditional values (in a society that has become valueless, a "traditional value" would be precisely this valuelessness)—and they judge it. Because they are young and still close to the spiritual world, their ideals are still powerful and felt as true. *When they see the world in the light of these ideals, their relationship to the world is similar to that of the initiates of old:* "One now sees the same thing; but one sees it immersed in a higher world, in the spirit."† From this, the question arises as to how any intuited new values can become a reality in the world.

Goethe's *Faust* is described as a young man who tears himself away from the old ways in order to confer new values upon the world. This breaking away is depicted in the first part of *Faust* and is done with the help of the cosmic naysayer (Mephistopheles), who appears as the liberator. The break actually leads to complete external liberation but at the same time to enormous catastrophes. The last scene of the first part occurs at a place totally lacking in freedom, in the dungeon where Gretchen, Faust's beloved, is left alone awaiting execution the next day. She had killed her mother with poison and drowned the child she shared with her lover.

* Günther Kaiser, "Youth as a social mass phenomenon," in Schäfer (ed.), *Gewaltkriminalität Minderjähriger,* vol. 1, pp. 70ff.

† CW 8, p. 21f.

Her brother had been killed by Faust. Faust's outer freedom was purchased at great cost: overwhelming guilt and subjection to his ostensible liberator. In order to move forward, to really find himself and move on to a true version of the new, Faust must now free himself from Mephistopheles after he has made his contribution. Faust must follow paths that Mephistopheles, the one who appeared to be superior in everything, cannot follow. Goethe imagines this as the path to the *mothers*, the path into nothingness:

> MEPHISTOPHELES:
> And if you had swum the ocean
> The boundless there,
> Then you would have seen wave after wave,
> Even if you are terrified of going under.
> You would see something.
> You would see something in the green....
> Thirst quenched seas are stroking dolphins;
> You would see clouds rolling in, sun and moon
> and stars—
> You will see nothing in eternal empty distances,
> And not hearing the steps you're taking,
> Finding nothing solid to rest upon.
> FAUST:
> We will go for it! We want to fathom it,
> In your nothingness I hope to find everything.

Mephistopheles can point out the way, but he cannot accompany him on the path into nothingness, for it is the path into death, which finds its continuation only through the power of resurrection. This is the path of Christ. To free oneself not only outwardly but truly from all supporting pillars, in the symbolism of the New Testament, means to "abandon father and mother" (Luke 14:26), to prepare oneself *to find everything in nothing,* which means to walk with Christ through death and resurrection. Of this Paul writes: "If we have died with Christ, we will also live with him" (2 Tim. 2:11). Only through this experience do we gain a right relationship to the new values created by our ideals. Only then can our new values take hold in the world. This is how individual conscience is created and shaped. Confirmation awakens the formation of individual conscience, the courage *to find everything in nothingness* with the help of Christ. Thus we take responsibility for our lives, our biographies. This requires continued interest in the world (study) and continued work on oneself (disciplined training).

What comes after youth? The anthropology of the sacraments says: death. Biological puberty—however one may define it—can come to an end. The inner condition of being young, the state where one must detach from the old with courage to seek the new in nothingness, must never end if a biography is to remain alive. Today one can no longer be a human being in the full sense of the word without study and training, without genuine interest in the world and continually working on oneself. Being human is then, in truth, being young. This is not a question of outer age. Expressed in exaggerated form, *those who stop being young die, even if they continue to age*. This implies that there are only two real stages of life today: childhood and youth. Confirmation is the transition, lying in the *qualitative* middle of life, between birth and death.

8.4 The Form of the Confirmation Ritual

Essentially, Confirmation is a sacrament of transition, and the ritual is correspondingly structured. The first step is based on childhood, which is now being completed; its form is similar to that of the Sunday Service for Children, whereby the confirmands are also received at the door and these words are spoken directly to them: "Remember the importance of this moment in your life." This motif appears two more times, and the third time occurs at the conclusion of the Confirmation. The priest speaks directly to the children, no longer with the *we*-form, but with the "I–You" form.

Every threshold experience begins with a review of the path leading up to this moment. Only when we know how we have arrived at this point can we turn our gaze forward to enter new territory. Therefore, we now look back with the children on the path they have followed. They have been led by people whose destiny was to guide them. But in addition to this awareness, that their earthly guidance was an expression of spiritual guidance, a mature person must also be aware of the points of view at work in their previous guidance. These points of view are spoken out loud. This is a speech act that amounts to an impressive publication of what, up to now, was only a concern for those who led the children: Their parents and teachers were concerned that the soul forces of the children, their thinking, feeling, and wanting, should be filled with the "Spirit of God" and that Christ should be present, influencing their fate as "their highest leader."

This retrospective view has a corresponding form at a later age, which Rudolf Steiner describes: "If you often practice a kind of retrospective view of what you have experienced or done in life, you will make a peculiar discovery about yourself." Ultimately, this discovery can lead through many stages to the certainty that we can rise above ourselves to something that at present is already growing beyond us, and that will continue to grow from life to life. What do we have in us, in this sense? Truly a higher, a divine self; a higher self we can feel permeating us in a living way. Thus, we can say: *This higher self in me is my guide.*[*] The retrospective look back upon their childhood is intended to awaken the children to discover—inwardly, "supra-consciously," so to speak—this guide in them, who is actually the Christ. He should increasingly replace the external guidance that guided them up to this point.

The second step is then the central prayer to Christ, the request that Christ no longer influence the children's thinking, feeling, and willing merely through the intentions of their educators, but that his light should shine in them directly, indeed until the moment of death.

The third step is the High Priestly Prayer (John 17), which Christ—as on Holy Thursday evening for the disciples—is now speaking *in the present moment* for the children. This prayer may later be spoken again in an individual's biography at the Last Anointing.

The fourth step is the blessing, connected with the laying on of hands. It contains again a review of their previous guidance and a preview of their guidance by Christ himself as a reality now beginning.

The fifth step is a sermon by the confirming priest. In the Sunday Service there is usually no sermon, so in the Confirmation the young people hear their first sermon, often followed by the children singing a song as a kind of response. The sixth step is their dismissal, with which the Confirmation could be considered complete. However, there is a question:

---

* CW 15, pp. 9, 21.

what is the first thing these young people, now come of age religiously, will do?

The first actions taken after being assigned a new responsibility in life are always important and often have a formative effect: the first Mass of a newly ordained priest, the first independent operation of a licensed surgeon, the first lesson of a young teacher. In this case the first thing these newly confirmed young people do is to co-celebrate the Act of Consecration, the Mass, together with the priest and congregation. It ends with the confirmands receiving their First Communion. We have already discussed the relationship of Confirmation to Baptism. The relationship to First Communion is not merely admission to the Lord's Supper. First Communion is actually an integral part of Confirmation. The first Act of Consecration of Man celebrated in community with others is an act of transformation oriented toward the future. The priest speaks again in the *we* form, but now in the sense of equality. He or she is also facing the altar with the congregation facing the same direction. After this act, all later deeds of the young people will be secondary in the true sense of the word. A fundamental attitude toward action has been instilled. This attitude belongs to the second half of life, which now begins.

Between the first part of Confirmation and the celebration of the Eucharist, a transition occurs, which becomes visible as a ritual action: the priest takes off the vestments he wore during the first part of Confirmation and then puts on different vestments that will be worn during the Act of Consecration of Man. The subtle inner transformation of the child into a young person thus appears in an impressive picture: in the time after removing the Confirmation vestments and before donning vestments for the Mass the confirmands see the priest clothed only in a cassock. This is the black robe in which he or she otherwise never appears before the congregation. It is an image of death which we all carry within us, even bodily as a skeleton. Here, the words of Pilate could be spoken (John 19:5): "This is truly the human being!—*Ecce homo*." Thus, the motif of death appears for a third time. The first time occurs when the moment of death is mentioned. Then the High Priestly Prayer resounds, which is also the Gospel for the Last Anointing and, as such, also a reference to death. And finally, and most impressively, *they directly see an image of the passage through an experience of death, which is essential to every real transformation.* In this way, confirmands are shown a crucial truth for their lives; in the course of their further lives this truth can increasingly grow into the courageous impulse embodied in these words: "In your nothingness I hope to find everything." Everything—i.e., the universe itself, is what is truly new.

Chapter 9.
The Act of Consecration of Man

The Act of Consecration of Man is the central ritual of The Christian Community, which as a regularly performed celebration, is at the center of community religious life. The name is still unusual even after more than a century. In Rudolf Steiner's lectures preparing for the launch of the new movement, he mostly used the traditional name, *the Mass*, when speaking of our Eucharist service. He occasionally also used it later, naturally employing the traditional term in order to make himself understood. Since most of the founders came from Protestantism, the question of a different name arose as early as 1921. Steiner, however, considered it a matter for the founders themselves to find new names. "It is not actually an anthroposophical task to intervene in the reality of community and church formation."*

When the young men and women who were to establish The Christian Community gathered in Dornach in the autumn of 1922, there was only one suggestion from Rittelmeyer for the new name of the Mass: *Sacrificial Celebration.* But Steiner said, "Surely this would not express the inner meaning of the Mass. It would imply a celebration of sacrifice, but that's not what it is."† Finally, on the third day of

* CW 343, Oct. 10, 1921

† CW 344, Sept. 9, 1922.

the gathering, he himself brought the new name: *The Act of Consecration of Man* (*Die Menschenweihehandlung*). One day later he gave an initial explanation for this:

> It would not be possible for me, for example, to find an expression for the Mass other than *act of consecration of man*.... Therein lies a concept that absolutely belongs to the Mass, that it is a community undertaking and that it is done in a gathering...the community coming together belongs to a Mass, and this is expressed in the words *act of consecration of man*. But it is an act of consecration; the word *consecration* [*Weihe*] has survived as a German word for the ancient word *initiation*. *Consecration* is connected with *immersion*, with immersing oneself in something; and it has become customary to think and feel that one is being immersed in the spirit of original revelation when one speaks of consecration. Of course, the term *initiation* is much more appropriate to the matter. Both consecration and initiation mean that a human being is led back to his divine origin in God. That is what the word *consecration* might make clear.*

So we see that the process of finding a name for the new service shows how the old and the new come together in The Christian Community; this is especially clear in the Act of Consecration of Man.

> This ritual takes into account the historical development of humanity. In its details and in much that affects its totality, it is a continuation of history. But it also carries everywhere the impact of the new: what can be revealed only today from the spiritual world to suprasensory consciousness."†

* Ibid.

† CW 257, Sept. 14, 1924.

In this way, the Act of Consecration of Man is "a metamorphosis of the old, in which still-valid elements from the past are preserved but have taken on a form that flows today out of the spiritual world."*

There is much literature in The Christian Community introducing the rituals and sacraments, especially the Act of Consecration of Man. Therefore, the following sections will be limited to fundamental theological questions.†

9.1 The Fourfold Structure of the Act of Consecration

The Act of Consecration has a clear structure: the four main parts—*gospel, offertory, transubstantiation* or *transformation, communion*—as well as an Epistle,‡ which changes with the course of the year, and, if necessary, an *insert prayer*. Since the Act of Consecration carries a continuation of the historical within itself, one would expect that this four-part structure also has a history in earlier rituals. But this is not the case. Although the four parts (*gospel–offertory–canon,* or *transubstantiation–communion*) are also known in the historical mass, these four do not represent its essential structure, but are parts of a more manifold whole, consisting of the liturgy of the word and the eucharistic celebration. Tracing the historical

* CW 346, Sept. 14, 1924.

† Some examples: Fischer, *Die Menschen-Weihehandlung—was ist das*; Lenz, *Die Menschen-Weihehandlung*; Rau (ed.), *Vom Kultuserleben*; Schroeder, *Vom Erleben der Menschen-Weihehandlung.*

‡ The epistle is now a "letter" in name only (from the New Testament). In the appropriate place in the Roman Mass, it is read out loud. A new name has not yet been found for it in The Christian Community, for Rittelmeyer's suggestion "Prayer for the Time of Year" has not come into widespread use.

development of the Christian service, one does not find a predetermined fourfold unity anywhere.

The individual prayers of the mass have developed gradually, always prompted by the needs of concrete situations. They follow no recognizable blueprint. It is all the more astonishing that Rudolf Steiner always presented the fourfold structure as constitutive for Christian worship, long before the founding of The Christian Community. We are reminded of the seven sacraments, for whose occurrence in the historical process there is also no law recognizable by theology. In this sense, one can say that it took more than a thousand years for the sevenfold nature of the sacraments to become known and it has taken two thousand years for the fourfold division of the mass to become recognizable.

The reason for the hidden fourfold division is Christianity's connection to the mysteries of antiquity (cf. sect. 4.2, "Mysteries"). In 1905, Steiner gave a lecture in Cologne on *the meaning of the Mass in terms of mysticism*, in which he also spoke of its four parts. The Christian Mass had its origin in the mysteries, in Persia and Egypt (in later years he described this in more detail).* This idea was completely foreign to the theology of that time. Later, in the temporal periphery of the foundation of The Christian Community, also in the Catholic area, *mystery theology* came into being (the Benedictine Odo Casel writes first in 1918 and then in 1922 about the Mass as *celebration of mysteries*), which was critically evaluated at first, but since the Second Vatican Council has been regarded positively.

The second key idea in this lecture then refers to the four

* "The offering of the Mass, with all that comes with it, is a continuous development of the Mithras mysteries combined in a certain way with the Eleusinian mysteries" (CW 175, Apr. 24, 1917).

parts of the Mass. The connection between these two concepts (the origin of the Mass in the mysteries and its four parts) was, however, not yet made clear in this lecture. In later lectures Steiner will explain that the Mass did not originate with the Lord's Supper on Holy Thursday. He states that "the offering of the Mass is often considered to be a continuation of the Maundy Thursday Lord's Supper described in the Bible, but this interpretation is nonsense unless one first projects it into the biblical scene. The offering of the Mass with its wonderful ritual, its imitation of the four stages of the mysteries, was created precisely because the Risen Christ was the teacher of those individuals who were able to understand the depths of these esoteric teachings."*

A note by Emil Bock from 1922, following a conversation with Rudolf Steiner, also describes the Mass as being older than Christianity: "The offering of the Mass was accepted by Christ only after the resurrection. It already existed before that." In 1913, Steiner spoke about the four stages of initiation into the mysteries, calling them:

Coming into contact with the experience of death
Passage through the elemental world
Seeing the sun at midnight
Meeting the upper and lower gods†

They correspond to the four parts of the Mass:

Gospel reading
Sacrifice
Transubstantiation
Communion

A historical source for these four stages in the mystery religions can be found in the Roman writer Apuleius, who

* CW 211, April 13, 1922.
† CW 144, Feb. 3, 1913.

wrote the novel *The Golden Ass* in the second century AD. In the last chapter of the novel, an Isis initiation is described, and these four basic experiences are described. Within the esoteric school led by Rudolf Steiner in 1912, the corresponding sentences of Apuleius were then used almost literally in a slightly rhythmic form:

> I went to the border of death
> I entered Proserpine's threshold.
>
> And after I traveled through all the elements,
> I turned around and came back.
>
> At midnight I saw the sun
> With bright white light radiant.
>
> I went to the lower and higher gods
> From face to face and worshiped them
> From the closest proximity.*

The Christian form of the Mass is therefore originally a replica of this path in the mystery religions. We can *hear the gospel as the word of God* only if we understand it not as a secular message (which could be analyzed by means of biblical criticism, for example), but as a message from beyond the threshold. Then one has crossed *Proserpine's threshold*† and can hear the spiritual world within the gospel. In the *offertory*, we leave behind everything that carries us. In the ancient mysteries this corresponds to the passage through the elements and is reflected in the ritual wording of the offertory: it leads from the motif of burial (as a danger to the

* Steiner, *Esoteric Lessons 1910–1912* (CW 266/2), p. 285.

† Proserpina (Greek: *Persephone*) is goddess of the dead, underworld and fertility, daughter of Zeus and Demeter. With the consent of Zeus Hades abducted Persephone/Proserpina into the underworld to be his wife. Moved by the grief and anger of Demeter, Zeus arranged for Proserpina to return to the upper world for half of the year.

eternal in us) through the elements of the liquid (filling the chalice) and air (smoke from incense) to the fire of love. The *transformation* stage of the ritual, through which *the light of the world*[*] *shines in the darkness* of bread and wine, has its archetype in the mysteries as *seeing the sun at midnight.* And finally, through *Communion* a relationship with God is established, which in the mysteries was called worship of the upper and lower gods *from the closest proximity.*

A Catholic priest once asked Rudolf Steiner for advice on his inner life. In response he gave certain exercises and instructions, including the advice that he should meditate on the four parts of the mass.

"In the course of the day, the soul must be immersed in the four parts of the Mass:

1. Gospel reading, imagining that through the Gospel, for the intellect, God's Word comes to human beings;
2. Offertory, imagining that what one already has of God's essence within oneself is *voluntarily* sacrificed to God;
3. Transubstantiation, whereby one has to imagine that the humanity sacrificed to God is transformed into something truly divine;
4. Communion, whereby one thinks oneself united with God."[†]

Here another aspect is given for the four parts of the mass. The point of view that in the offertory one sacrifices *what one already has of God's essence within oneself* is truly remarkable. We will go into this in the following section. Finally, it should be mentioned that Rudolf Steiner

* "When Jesus spoke to them another time, he said, I am the light of the world. Whoever follows me will not walk in darkness but will have the light of life" (John 8:12).

† *Beiträge zur Rudolf Steiner Gesamtausgabe* (Contributions to the Rudolf Steiner Complete Edition), no. 110, Easter 1993, p. 11.

was asked to translate the Mass by the Old Catholic* priest Hugo Schuster, who "did not want to bring the rituals in a strange translation...in which they are often read today. He prompted me to bring some of the usual Catholic rituals into forms that actually corresponded to their original form. Only then do we see how the spiritual world is revived in these things, and we see what has been distorted since the time of Jerome."† Steiner did not translate the entire Mass, but just the four parts. He gave the first two parts to Schuster in 1919, and the third and fourth parts in 1921.

9.2 The Substance of the Offertory

A frequently asked question is, What is actually sacrificed or offered in the Act of Consecration? Bread and wine are the most frequently occurring wrong answer. This misunderstanding arises because these substances are transformed through the ritual; there is, after all, a connection between what is sacrificed and what passes through transubstantiation.

If we remain strictly with what is shown, spoken, and done (*deiknýmena, legómena, drómena*),‡ however, we would not think that substances are the object of sacrifice. Neither bread nor wine are mentioned in the Offering, nor are they shown; nor are they the object of any ritual action. The chalice is filled in such a way that only the server, and

* Old Catholic Church is a valid form of Catholicism that is independent of the Holy See.

† CW 342, June 14, 1921.

‡ See section 3.2, "Collaboration between the Spirits of Form and the Spirits of Personality." In the ancient mysteries, the trinity of sign, action, and word was known and called *deiknýmena* (the display of what was offered by the priest), *drómena* (the cultic actions), and *legómena* (presentation of religious texts accompanying and explaining the first two).

not the congregation, can actually see which substances are used (unless the pitchers containing the water and wine are made of glass). Thus, the wine is not brought to the consciousness of the community at this point, neither through direct contemplation (*deiknymena*) nor through the word (*legomena*). However, in our time only what happens with complete consciousness in ritual is appropriate. Nothing should take place behind any iconostasis. Steiner attached great importance to this:

> Spiritual reality is present in the ritual on the level of sense perception. And what takes place there in front of the congregation takes place first of all before their conscious observation. Nothing is permitted to take place except what does take place in that way. Otherwise it would not be ritual, not sacrament, but *suggestion*. [italics added]*

Guided by what takes place consciously, the substances in the chalice are, so to speak, not in the picture; they remain essentially removed from our perception and cognition. When the offering is then named with a sacrificial gesture, it is called the "draft of health."

This is different in the Roman Mass (as it existed before the Second Vatican Council), where bread and wine are indeed the offerings. One can follow the emergence of this practice historically: Originally, the bread and wine were simply made available as gifts on the altar in preparation for the prayer of transformation. Then, from the end of the second century onward, the faithful began to associate their voluntary contributions for the maintenance of the clergy with the offertory. This gave rise to the gift procession, the sacrificial procession of the faithful, in which they deposited

* CW 318, *Broken Vessels*, p. 23.

their gifts on the steps of the altar. The bread and wine necessary for later Communion were laid on the altar and then underwent transubstantiation; the rest was for the clergy. Thus, the offertory gradually came into being as the part of the Mass preceding the Canon (the consecration part). From the tenth century onward, the custom of sacrifice gradually began to disappear, but the idea remained that the offertory was the sacrifice of substances (bread and wine).

The first offertory prayer of the Catholic Mass reads accordingly: "Holy Father, Almighty Eternal God, graciously accept this immaculate offering," whereby "immaculate offering" refers to the bread (and the regulation for celebration states: "The priest now raises the paten up to the breast and prays the prayer Holy Father, Almighty Eternal God..."). In the second offertory prayer of the Mass the substances are even directly named: "...let us participate through the mystery of this water and wine." In this sense, bread and wine are therefore the substances sacrificed. But now we must ask: What does it actually mean to sacrifice bread and wine?

The actual sacrifice, the offering of Christ, occurs only in the transubstantiation, where the word offering is repeatedly spoken (both in the Mass and in the Act of Consecration). Actually it is from this offering that the Mass gets its name, the "sacrifice of the Mass." But in contrast to this, what could the sacrifice of bread and wine in the offertory mean? We must see this clearly: In the second century the external gifts of the faithful to the church were conflated with the eucharistic gifts of bread and wine. This powerful after-effect of pagan sacrificial sentiment was still at work even later when the sacrificial offering of the faithful was eradicated from the Mass. The Catholic Church corrected this in the twentieth century. At the Second Vatican Council, the idea that a sacrifice takes place in the offertory was abandoned:

> Some prayers of earlier Mass orders speak of bread and wine as if a ritual sacrifice were already being made at this stage. Sayings such as "accept this immaculate offering graciously" in the offering of the bread, and "we offer the cup of salvation to you, Lord, in the offering of the wine" are premature at this stage.*

The idea of sacrifice has therefore been removed from the relevant prayers in the offertory, which are now called "accompanying prayers for the offertory." The opening prayer now reads:

> Blessed are You, Lord our God, Creator of the world. You give us bread, the fruit of the earth and of human labor. We bring this bread before your face that it may become for us the bread of life.

Accordingly, the third prayer—symmetrical in its form of words—concerns wine. So, clearly there is talk of bread and wine, but not of sacrifice in this part of the current Catholic Mass. This correction, though logical, unfortunately loses the idea of sacrifice; as a result it could be characterized as a correction *downward*.

From its inception The Act of Consecration of Man has had a corrected version of the offertory. It does not continue the idea that substances external to the Mass are being offered. The idea of sacrifice has not been abandoned; it has been purified of any extraneous substances, a correction, so to speak, *upward*.

* Adam: *Grundriss der Liturgie*, p. 145.

What then is the "draft of health" being offered? Our human *willing, feeling and thinking* provide the substance of the offering. It has already been shown that all the sacraments are intended to connect the divine world with the three human soul forces of thinking, feeling and willing. These three soul forces reveal the human being as the image of God as reflected in the Trinity. So, we have the ideal that God the Father should live in our will: "Thy will be done." Where we feel the Christ in us, faith is immediately awakened in us, as with the disciples on the way to Emmaus (Luke 24:32): "And they said one to another, did not our hearts burn in our breasts when he spoke to us along the way, and opened to us the meaning of the Scriptures?" And finally, we strive for truth in the light of thinking that is enlightened by the Holy Spirit: "But when he comes, the spirit of truth, he will lead you into all truth" (John 16:13).

The correlation of the persons of the Trinity to individual soul forces can be seen differently from various points of view, just as is the case with correlating baptismal substances to the Trinity. Approaching this question, we orient ourselves following "The Foundation Stone Verse" of the Anthroposophical Society, which actually originates in the Trinity.* Here, in terms of a human body, God the Father is assigned to the "will expressed in the limbs," God the Son to the "heart–lung rhythm" and God the Spirit to the "reposing head." To the extent that our willing, feeling and thinking become more real with respect to the Trinity, something of God's essence can shine within us.

But our soul forces have been corrupted by the Fall: Ahriman corrupts our will, binding it to the laws of the material

* Various publications, e.g., *Mantric Sayings* (CW 268).

world; Lucifer makes our thinking subjective and therefore capable of error. Steiner summarizes: "Just as Lucifer distorted thinking, Ahriman distorted will."* We are most likely in our *feeling* to still find a direct relationship to the spiritual world, which is why religious life starts from feeling when our *heart is warmed*. Our thinking and willing are then also seized by a strong feeling, brought along, as it were, into the experience of the divine.

The congregation comes to this point in the Offertory. It turns to the divine world in feeling, "which unites with Christ." From this feeling then arises the power of the will, which wants to turn to God the Father. And finally, thinking is also taken hold of and begins to "live in the life of the Holy Spirit." The congregation's feeling can unite with Christ in this way because the hearts of the people *are warmed* after hearing the gospel, even if unconsciously. *Feeling* is awakened, and the offertory can then follow. Christ approaches the church through the reading of the Gospels in a way similar to how he approached the disciples on the way to Emmaus.

Beginning with feeling, human soul forces gradually come to reflect the image of the Trinitarian Godhead. This substance of the Gospel is what *we already have within us of God's being* and can offer to God for sacrifice in the Offertory—*voluntarily*. It is pure human soul substance, in which God's essence has already begun to be present. This soul substance is represented by the contents of the cup as a "draft of health." But we do not cling to it, because we know that in truth it is not our own but Christ's. This is echoed in the meditation verse given by Steiner for the

* *The Michael Mystery*, Jan. 25, 1925, p. 115 (CW 26).

Catholic priest: "Offertory, whereby one must imagine that what one already has of God's essence within oneself is voluntarily offered to God."

9.3 The Essence of Transformation

The word that is used repeatedly—also by Rudolf Steiner—for transformation is *transubstantiation*. It was created in scholasticism. In the two great disputes concerning the Lord's Supper in the ninth (Paschasius Radbertus*) and eleventh centuries (Berengar of Tours†), the concept was developed further until the term *transubstantiation* appeared in the twelfth century, probably first with Gilbert of Poitiers (1154). Thomas Aquinas' deepening of the theory of transubstantiation had the greatest impact. His theory is based on the distinction between *substance* and *accident* or essence and appearance. We always perceive only the appearance of a thing, which can always change. What gives it identity is its essence. The doctrine of transubstantiation now states—put very simply—that the substances (i.e., their essence) of bread and wine are transformed into the body and blood of Christ, while the outward appearance (taste, appearance, etc., which are "accidents") is preserved. The fourth Lateran Council in 1215 elevated this view to dogma. The Christian Community did not adopt this view. The word *transubstantiation* is still used (just as Steiner used the word "Mass" for a long time);

* Paschasius Radbertus (ca.790–856/59), monk and abbot in Corbie, opened the communion controversies of the ninth century with his treatise *De corpore et sanguine Domini*.

† Berengar of Tours (ca.999–1088), born in Saint-Côme (near Tours); director of the school of Tours and archdeacon of Angers, 1040; condemned at several synods for his symbolic Eucharistic teaching (he accepted only the symbolic presence of Christ in bread and wine), ca.1050.

however, our understanding is different* and therefore does not entirely correspond to the traditional meaning.

For Rudolf Steiner, the initial question concerning transubstantiation is fundamental; he dealt with it again and again many years before the foundation of The Christian Community and finally called it "the cardinal question." If science assumes that all natural processes proceed according to strict laws of cause and effect, where does morality fit in? "How can one speak of somehow realizing ethical impulses in a world where everything occurs according to laws which a natural scientist must assume? Where could ethical impulses be inserted if we have universal physical causality?"† In such a world the answer could only be that human responsibility, freedom and morality are illusions, which has already long since been considered inevitable in the fields of natural science.‡ Those who have not forgotten their spiritual dimension, however, cannot be at peace with this idea.

It is generally assumed that those who question the logical applicability of natural law must believe in miracles, but there is another way to break through the power of nature's laws.

> Whoever thinks honestly about the cause-and-effect explanation of nature will find nowhere in the world within the sphere of its applicability that it does not hold. And because it applies everywhere, there *must* be some power that can destroy its applicability. That power is the moral world. The moral world, known to

* Steiner considered transformation (*Wandlung*) to be the proper word appropriate for today's understanding. *Transubstantiation* points to the historical tradition (cf. CW 343, Oct. 10, 1921f).

† CW 342, June 12, 1921.

‡ B. F. Skinner, *Beyond Freedom and Dignity.*

> exist in human nature, contains the power to break the causality of nature, though not by working miracles but through a process of evolutionary development.*

Steiner sees this development contained in the fact that the external world of the senses is coming to an end. According to the logical application of the scientific law of entropy, all energy will eventually be irreversibly transformed into heat, which will at the same time represent the end of all physical processes.† However, our disappearing external world with its natural order is simultaneously accompanied by a rising inner world, a world of moral order. Even though moral impulses do not outwardly break through the laws of nature, the moral world is growing embryonically, so to speak, within outer nature. The moral world will eventually manifest completely when the outer world has come to its end. Thus, through a process of *evolutionary development* the natural, physical world of cause and effect will gradually be dissolved.

This great cosmic future when the earth will one day die is already happening in a small way when a human being dies. Between death and a new birth, we live in a world in which natural causality does not apply; we live in a purely moral world. The deeds and impulses accompanying us during our lives in the world of natural causality have consequences, which become fully apparent in this moral world after death. They then become full reality, and from them

---

* CW 78, Sept. 5, 1921.

† Translator's note: *Entropy* can be summarized in this way: Everything physical inexorably tends toward an increasing state of disorder. Applied to cosmology, the universe is destined for a "heat death," whereby all energy is distributed homogeneously as thermal energy, with every structure or form of any kind reduced to a random distribution of ionized particles. This state is a picture of physical meaninglessness.

we draw impulses for future lives on earth. They become our karma, with which we later re-enter the world of natural laws. Moral impulses that originate *within* the natural-causal world would indeed be an illusion, but not if they *originate outside* the world of the senses.

The karma that we bring with us at birth is a moral substance that actually does its work in the sensory world but without breaking any laws of nature; it is cloaked, so to speak, yet *involved* in the physical world. For example, at the karmically correct moment, an event occurs that appears logically inexplicable, such as a tile actually coming loose on a roof, falling, and hitting me! In the life between death and new birth morality then creates its own reality through *evolution*. In this way we live rhythmically between a natural order and a moral order.

By incarnating, we carry the moral order into the natural order through our karma and our ethical impulses, which work within the laws of nature and yet cannot be derived from nature. One would have to formulate this paradoxically: karma and ethical impulses break through the causality of the physical world—without breaking any such laws. We are then freed from this world and process the results of our life on earth in a world of pure morality. The words of Christ point to this moral order: "My kingdom is not of this world" (John 18:36). But it must be said: *His kingdom does work in this world*. Or, in the words of Rudolf Steiner: "Because of this, [the Kingdom of Christ] *is* of this world! For human beings are here on earth to make the Spirit, which is not present in this world without them, the content of this world."* In this rhythmic oscillation between the suprasensory–moral

* CW 217, Oct. 15, 1922.

and the world of the senses, a new moral order is evolving within the natural one. It will one day appear in its full reality when external nature has come to its end. This lies in Christ's word: "Heaven and earth will pass away, but my words will not pass away" (Matt. 24:35).

The question of how the moral order can work into the natural order also finds a quite self-evident answer in human beings themselves. The actions of human beings are not subject to the causality of nature as long as they do not live merely as beings of nature but as self-determining beings. Although the laws of nature may not be broken within the human organism, we still act guided by a higher order, namely the moral order. Only through this are we also responsible for what we do. Goethe expresses this very memorably: "An animal is instructed by its organs; human beings instruct and control their own organs."* The animal is a pure natural being and is determined by nature, i.e., taught by its organs. Human actions should not be determined by organs, but human beings should determine their nature.

Thus, in the human body there is already a place where the natural and moral order work together in such a way that the moral order (according to the ideal) rules over the natural order without breaking the order of nature (laws of nature). In human deeds, this moral order is transferred into the world. All formations in the world emanating from human deeds are more than just nature. They are true or false, beautiful or ugly, good, or evil. They arise from a realm that is "not of this world," though that realm is actually in this world and transforming it.

Here the question arises of the transformation of bread

* Goethe, *Maxims and Reflections*.

and wine at the altar. Indeed, it is the cardinal question: How do these two orders work together? We have looked at how a rhythmic process is contained in this interplay. Life in an earthly incarnation involves rhythms, as do life between death and a new birth and the formation of karma associated with a new life. If we consider *only* transubstantiation, then the transformed host becomes the decisive factor. It can be seen and worshipped in the monstrance. The transforming process has been lost to our perception. Only through understanding karma can one also understand the transformation of the bread. Up to now in the history of Christianity the idea of karma was prohibited; therefore, the process of transformation could only be conceived in a *static form of transubstantiation*.

Rudolf Steiner describes how "the teaching of karma was taken away from humankind and placed in the midst of teachings about the transubstantiation. But this meant that there was nothing in the external world that was analogous to the teachings concerning transubstantiation, for *it is teaching concerning karma that is analogous to the teachings concerning transubstantiation*. The power through which a person's destiny is 'made' in successive lives on earth is not a power of nature; it is not the power of the Father, it is the power of the Spirit mediated through the Son. This is the power that is also at work on the altar during the transformation of the *sanctissimum*, that is, the host."*

So, we are at the beginning of a new understanding of transformation. We can no longer rely on the scholastic attempt to understand transformation. The distinction between substance and accident is no longer sufficient. What can bring us

* CW 346, Sept. 11, 1924.

further today is the idea of re-embodiment and karma.

> *In the transformed substances of bread and wine, the moral and the natural order rhythmically weave together in the same way as human beings alternate between earthly embodiment and life in the spiritual world. They both represent a process become visible, whose full reality is present only within the unfolding of the activity, the process itself.**

Thus, an understanding of transformation and Communion suggests that grace is also conveyed in these transformed substances, which are the body and blood of Christ. This grace is the power to shape and form karma, that is, "the power of the Spirit mediated through the Son." The power of the Holy Spirit leads us from one incarnation to another; it also works in the third part of the Act of Consecration, the transubstantiation, through epiclesis.† And the power of the Son helps us to bear and order our destiny.

Through transubstantiation (and Communion), therefore, the destiny-forming forces of the moral order are woven into human beings, but also into the external world, as the actual forces of the future. They will one day raise from the perishing world "a new heaven and a new earth" (Rev. 21:1). This also lies in the words of Christ: "Heaven and earth will pass away, but my words will not pass away" (Matt. 24:25). The Act of Consecration with its transforming power contributes to this substantially. The world will one day come to an end, but "if we then look back at the events that took place on this earth as the offering of the Mass, their effects would

* Therefore, viewing of the host in a monstrance outside the Act of Consecration of Man would not be an option for The Christian Community.

† See chapter 4.2, "Mystery." The Greek word *Epiklese* means "calling down," i.e., invoking the Holy Spirit.

always be present. The ritual is more real than nature when it is practiced in the right way."*

In conclusion, we consider again that aspect of evolution in human lives, to which the Lord's Supper corresponds as involution. From the fourteenth year of life we gradually begin to take moral responsibility for our life, to permeate the natural order in this life with the moral order. We have seen that this is a rhythmic process. What happens rhythmically on a large scale between incarnations, happens on a small scale every night. Responsibility for our actions has evolved and morality is inevitably interwoven with the outer course of lives. Thus Rudolf Steiner explains with reference to the process of involution,

> ...as soon as the human being has evolved to the point where the soul–spiritual has entered an intimate relationship with the physical organism—and this is a significant new strength—we enter a rhythmic cycle insofar as we swing back and forth between the soul–spiritual, withdrawing from and re-entering the physical body...the human being needs a process of involution to counterbalance evolution. This involution is receiving Holy Communion.†

We have seen to what extent the new moral order is a process of involution that takes place rhythmically.

* CW 344, Sept. 7, 1922.
† CW 343, Oct. 2, 1921.

Chapter 10
Confession—Sacramental Consultation

The Christian Community has long been searching for a suitable name for this sacrament in German, traditionally called *die Beichte.* The search has been for a name that could express what is new, similar to the Act of Consecration of Man. Various attempts have been made, such as "*sacrament of Christian self-knowledge*" or "*sacrament of conversation*" or "*confessional counselling.*" The pastoral aspect of this sacrament needs to be detached from the juridical aspect accompanying the word *Beichte,* which is usually translated as *confession.* None of these attempts in German have been found satisfactory. In the meantime, in German-speaking countries it was decided to accept the word *Beichte* and to give it a new and unique content for The Christian Community in this modern world without traditions.*

Confession (in Catholicism, the sacrament of Penance) has a complicated history, and we will trace here only a few aspects of its development. A form of public penance gradually developed in the first centuries. Those who had

* Translator's note: In the English-speaking world the word *confession* still carries an unacceptable connotation of judgment, as well as a history of ecclesiastical abuse. Hence, this sacrament has been translated as "Sacramental Consultation." In speaking to the founders, however, Steiner used the traditional German word, *Beichte* (confession). In the following excerpts from his lectures the term has been translated variously as *Confession* or *Sacramental Consultation*, depending on context.

committed serious sins were usually excommunicated, and had to report their sins to the bishop (the sins were not made public). The bishop, through the laying on of hands, then accepted him into the ranks of public penitents of the church, thus initiating a process of reconciliation with the church. The penitents were subject to certain rules and often very drastic prohibitions and injunctions; in any case, they were banned from Communion. After remorse, the penitent was accepted back into the church with Reconciliatory Communion and was again in a state of (baptismal) grace. This was probably the most important aspect of repentance: to restore the lost *state of grace* after Baptism.

Much later, when the church was dealing with the Cathars, it was again stated: "If someone has fallen into sin after receiving Baptism, they can always be healed again through true remorse."* In the Western church, due to the influence of the Irish–Scottish Church, in particular the Columbán missionaries,† private penance gradually became a practice (in the East, monks had already been practicing confession). The penitent as such no longer appeared in public, and reconciliation took place even before the penitential act was completed. In the twelfth century it was counted among the seven sacraments, and through scholasticism it was given a very sophisticated definition. In this form and with the practice of penance (selling indulgences) associated with it later, it became the decisive cause of the eruption of the Reformation. The Council of Trent (1545–1563), with

* Fourth Lateran Council, 1215 (Vorgrimler, p. 235).

† Abbot Columbanus (530–615), born in Leinster, Ireland. He worked from 590 as a missionary in England, France, with the Alemanni (Swabians) around Lake Zürich (Zürisee) and Lake Constance (Bodensee), as well as in northern Italy. He founded several monasteries (including Bobbio Abbey in 614, the oldest in northern Italy). He wrote a strict monastic rule and two penitential books.

its anti-Reformation focus, confirmed the scholastic theology of repentance and defined it "infallible," a designation that still causes headaches among theologians today:

> The Council document devotes remarkably much space to the topic of repentance.... If it were hermeneutically permissible to measure these doctrinal statements against today's knowledge of the biblical theology of conversion, then the conciliar definition of repentance would appear as factually incomplete and unbalanced.*

Other theologians, however, have no problems with it: "Repentance is the soul of the sacrament of Penance." Further:

> In "confession," in the confession of sins, the sinful man as a repentant penitent places himself and his fate into the hands of the mother church, in order to receive from her forgiveness and new life from God.†

Since then, "three acts of penance" have been seen as essential: remorse‡ (combined with intent), confession (confession of sins) and satisfaction (the penitential act, *satisfactio*). An examination of conscience takes place beforehand as the "gateway to the three acts of penance." The goal, the grace of Confession, takes the form of absolution given by the priest; it is an act of judgment (*actus iudicialis*): "I absolve you of your sins in the name of the Father and of the Son and of the Holy Spirit." *Absolvo te a peccatis tuis in nomine Patris et Filii et Spiritus Sancti.*

The Christian Community does not subscribe to these

* Ganoczy, p. 87.

† Auer and Ratzinger, vol. 7, pp. 161, 170.

‡ Scholastically differentiated further into "perfect repentance" (*contritio* = remorse for the sake of the thing) and "imperfect repentance" (*attritio* = remorse because of the fear of punishment); the latter is sufficient for an absolution.

views; in its own theology it does not have a legal, "ascertaining" or judgmental relationship to sin and grace, but rather is interested in its process character. This will be discussed in the following two sections. We will explore the contemporary form of the "gates" to the three acts of penance and the three acts of penance themselves. It should be borne in mind that Rudolf Steiner, when first introducing this sacrament, speaking of its involutional character, continued to use traditional terminology:

> Penance consists of an examination of one's conscience, of repentance, i.e., of the earnest intention to put aside the errors of which one has become aware during Confession...and in what one imposes on oneself or is imposed by a pastor as retribution. This framework includes all that is necessary for repentance; the desire for penance is the involutionary process balancing the evolutionary process of memory and recollection and all that they entail for the human being.*

10.1 Sin and the Sickness of Sin†

Rudolf Steiner does not reject the Catholic formula of absolution on principle. There is a specific context where it is justified. He speaks about it in his lectures on *Christ and the Human Soul,* which he gave in Sweden in 1914 (CW 155). It

* CW 343, Oct. 2, 1921

† The word *sin* sounds outdated today; it is rife with legalistic and or moralizing connotations. Although The Christian Community explores the question of human guilt in new ways, which is also expressed by the new term *sickness of sin*, the word *sin* still plays a role, insofar as it occurs in the ritual wording of the Act of Consecration of Man at two significant locations. Those two occurrences provide a starting place for a new theology of sin. Steiner also frequently uses this word in his lectures. The reader is asked to understand that we use the word *sin* without any judgmental moralizing such as was usual in the Middle Ages and still in some forms of Christianity today.

is necessary to distinguish between two fundamentally different types of sin. On the one hand, there are sins that can and should be put right. If I steal from someone, I can compensate for the damage, but damaged trust is not restored merely through the repair of external damage. Neither is it in my power to restore it; even if the other person is willing to begin to trust again, it will not be possible to restore the original relationship. It has been irrevocably damaged. It is similar to what human beings inflict on the world through actions no longer in harmony with creation because our natural instincts have been corrupted by the Fall. From a purely external point of view, we could think of damage to the environment: Some things can—and must—be put right, while compensation is no longer possible for others (e.g., the extinction of animal and plant species caused by human beings).

However, this is only external; there is an inner aspect to sin for which we cannot compensate. It is a spiritual violation of the world, comparable to the trust destroyed between people. The cosmos, the universe itself, is dragged into the Fall by human deeds. In the words of Paul, "creation has become transitory, not through its own doing, but because of him who, becoming transitory himself, dragged it down with him..." (Rom. 8:20). We would have to add, "and continues to drag it down," for in addition to any personal guilt an individual may incur, one also carries *cosmic* guilt, for which one cannot compensate. Christ's sacrifice consists in taking upon himself this cosmic guilt and carrying it: "The next day John saw Jesus coming to him and said: Behold, the Lamb of God, who takes the sin of the world upon himself!" (John 1:29). But the consequences of this cosmic guilt for our personal destiny are carried by Christ only if we allow it—namely if we open ourselves to the work of Christ.

In this context the formula of absolution is appropriate, Steiner says:

> When in any religious denomination, one of Christ's servants speaks of the forgiveness of sins, it means nothing other than: with his words of forgiveness, he connects with Christ's forgiveness of sins, and says to the soul seeking consolation: Yes, I see that you have developed a living relationship to Christ, you are uniting yourself with objective sin and guilt. This is the objective sin and guilt that is to enter what remains of you on earth, what is the Christ for you. Because I recognize that you have permeated yourself with Christ, I can say, "Your sins are forgiven."*

Just as the consequences of human sinfulness in its cosmic dimension go beyond what we ourselves can carry and answer for, so too is the cause, i.e., original sin. It has come into the world through the Fall of Man, i.e., the temptation of the serpent in Paradise or, expressed in anthroposophical terms, through the Luciferic influence on the human astral body. This fundamental sin is the cause of all further sins, and it is through it that we are capable of personal in the first place. The fundamental sin itself is not yet personal sin. This is why it is called *the sickness of sin* in the Act of Consecration of Man. This brings a therapeutic perspective to the question of sin because the sickness of sin actually belongs to the human constitution and thus to the human bodily nature.† Physicians do not ask questions of morality; their

* CW 155, July 16, 1914.

† The creed of The Christian Community contains the words "...the sickness of sin within the bodily nature of mankind." These words indicate the location of the sickness of sin only and are not to be

professional ethics demand that they be willing to help good and evil people equally, if they ask for help. The term sickness of sin expresses this situation beyond morality better than *original sin*. The idea of washing away original sin, as it has been associated with (originally adult) Baptism since Augustine, is changed to *healing the sickness of sin* through Communion, which is *the healing medicine*. On this point our understanding of Communion follows from Ignatius of Antioch (cf. sect. 4.5, "Medicine"), who called it the "medicine for immortality."

Generally speaking, we are not personally responsible for the sickness of sin, whereas we *are* responsible for our personal sins. Even though they may result from the universal condition of the sickness of sin, we must take responsibility and compensate for them. If a man steals from another person because of a weakness, he cannot excuse his behavior because of that weakness. The world around him will treat the deed pedagogically (the man needs to learn a lesson!), not therapeutically. He is confronted with the consequences of his actions and should learn from his deeds precisely through the work he must do to compensate for them. This happens in smaller episodes in life as well as in the larger arc of karma, which reaches into future incarnations. But here, too, Christ is involved.

Thus, sin is precisely the place where man can meet Christ as a teacher, as in the parables, and as a physician, as in the healings. To overcome the sickness of sin, we need a physician who can help us. For the right compensation of individual sins, we need the teacher who challenges us. Up to now theology has confused these two realms. It also

---

confused with the idea that the human bodily nature is itself sinful, which it is not.

regards individual sins as removable through the grace of God, which in faith can reach out to good and evil people equally. Certainly, we do not wish to portray the grace of God as limited. Nevertheless, we should feel ourselves responsible for contributing to the work of redemption that falls to us. And who would seriously say that we have no responsibility?

10.2 Redemption—Self-redemption—Grace

The word *self-redemption* has frequently called forth an emotional response in conversations between The Christian Community and representatives of other churches. Connected with the idea of karma, the word seems to reflect everything that makes God's grace appear unnecessary.* It seems to favor a kind of *achievement religiosity* that would ultimately question the need for Christ's salvific deed. This objection appeared already during Steiner's lifetime, yet there were several occasions when he responded to this accusation clarifying exactly what was meant.†

On October 5, 1921, Rudolf Steiner said that there can be "no other redemption from original sin than that through Christ Jesus; the other sins are a result of original sin. Individual sins are committed because human beings can be weak and incline toward sin precisely because of original sin. These individual sins find their compensation in what must be achieved through self-redemption; they must be

* For example, in the *Materialdienst* of the Evangelical Central Office for Worldview Issues (no. 4, 2005, p. 135), Werner Thiede writes incorrectly of the matter: "In the opulent Complete Works of Rudolf Steiner, the concept of grace will be largely missed." He was wrong, for there are an extraordinary number of places where Steiner discusses grace.

† Three examples: CW 94, July 3, 1906; CW 131, Oct. 13, 1911; CW 155, July 15, 1914.

compensated for through self-redemption in the course of earthly or supraearthly life."* Self-redemption is therefore necessary in order to compensate *for individual sins.*

But is this a realm where no grace is necessary? The answer is clear: Although it is the realm where we bear individual responsibility for our sins, we are also completely dependent on Christ's help in this realm. In the Act of Consecration of Man it is said: "We can do no works before you," but also that we have the will to "overcome sin, through Christ." Christ's assistance not only refers to the sickness of sin, which must be overcome like any other sickness, but also to the overcoming of individual sin, which has three aspects. The first aspect is: Christ strengthens our will. He does not replace our will; he leaves us completely free, but he supports us. Rudolf Steiner once even called him the "God of the will."† In the Act of Consecration of Man it is also said of him that he "strengthens the will." Therefore, those who are working to compensate for their individual sins will be met by the grace of Christ. He comes to meet them in their efforts and his grace makes up for what their own strength is not yet able to accomplish.

The second aspect is the Christian community itself. Here, as far as possible, a *distribution of burdens* takes place quite inwardly. Paul says: "Bear one another's burdens, and thus you will fulfill the law of Christ" (Gal. 6:2). Although karma may impose a certain task on me, it is possible for another person to help me with my destiny, supporting me in that task, even representing me. This is an essential part of the Christian concept of karma; it would have been unthinkable in pre-Christian times. Steiner describes it: "Just as it does

* CW 353.

† CW 353, March 19, 1924.

not contradict the karma idea when I give something to a poor person, neither does it contradict the karma idea when a community helps a person to carry his or her individual karma. Karma must be fulfilled but another person can support the lot of an individual. Karma can be connected in such a way that a community contributes to the karma of the individual.... Karma must be fulfilled, but another person or community can help to carry it. In this way, entire communities can help someone who has committed an injustice."* There is grace also in this second area of karmic fulfillment and compensation.

Finally, there is a third, well-hidden aspect that Rudolf Steiner refers to as "Christ taking on the office of karmic judge (Lord of Karma)." Within the context of our earthly lives or in the greater context of our karma altogether, compensation for our personal sins can take various forms. We can balance our karmic debt with others through deeds that benefit them, or we might balance that debt so that *many* people benefit—in which case the compensation not only restores an original balance, but something new is created in the world. For example, in Germany part of a traffic fine is allocated to nonprofit organizations. What is at first merely compensation for a misdemeanor can also mean something positive for the world. This, too, can be seen as a kind of grace.

The fact that Christ has taken on the office of karmic judge (from Moses†) means that an individual's personal

* CW 123, Sept. 11, 1910.

† Steiner's description points to a further step in the transition from the Old to the New Covenant. Moses said: "An eye for eye, a tooth for tooth, hand for hand, foot for foot..." (Ex. 21:24). This is the principle by which a lost moral balance was restored, a return to the original state. Through Christ, the possibility is opened up to create something additional, something new for the future, for the world, through the balancing.

karma is no longer merely personal. Our efforts toward "self-redemption" are interwoven with the working of Christ's grace for all humankind. In selfless effort toward self-redemption, individuals can also serve Christ, if they live with the attitude that working on their own karma is at the same time working for all people. This shows how the sins of individual human beings, through the grace of Christ, can be transformed into raw material from which blessings and healing for all humanity can arise. God's grace can work not only in the sphere of objective sin and the sickness of sin, but also in the sphere of individual sin and its compensation. However, without the will to bring about compensation for individual sins, without the will to balance karma, this grace cannot be effective. It must be attached to the will of an individual human being, who thereby receives the possibility to bless and bring salvation to others. This will is, on the one hand, quite individual, and on the other hand, Christ, the "God of will," is also working through it. But only when we allow it.

10.3 The Form of the Sacrament

For the sacraments discussed so far, we have seen certain connections with the first seven-year periods of life. Baptism as the Baptism of infants has its place at the beginning of the first seven-year cycle, even though it can still be performed until Confirmation. Confirmation concludes the second seven-year period that was accompanied and supported by the Sunday Service for Children, and thus creates a transition from the second cycle to the third. The Act of Consecration of Man with Communion has the function (through the astral body that is becoming free) of beginning the third seven-year cycle, which is, qualitatively speaking, also *the beginning of the second half of life*. The significance of Sacramental Consultation begins with the fourth and continues through the following seven-year periods, i.e., throughout the rest of a person's lifetime. Rudolf Steiner calls these sacraments the *earthly* ones. There are seven sacraments, "of which four are especially earthly, namely Baptism, Confirmation, Eucharist, and penance. These four are just as human as the physical body, etheric body, astral body and I."* These four bodily sheaths of a human being are connected to the first four seven-year cycles, during which those sheaths are born, so to speak, or emerge completely, one after another—until the human being has completely "arrived" on earth.

Through the four earthly sacraments, the basic facts of our human earthly incarnations are, so to speak, *Christened*. Baptism establishes our relationship to the earth and to community; Confirmation establishes a relationship to personal responsibility; the Act of Consecration of Man establishes a relationship to the moral order in its rhythmic connection to the natural order; and Sacramental Consultation establishes the relationship to oneself. Now, with the fourth sacrament, we have arrived at the *center of gravity* of our humanity.† Here, too, where it is a matter of consolidating the "I," the very spiritual core of a human

* CW 342, June 14, 1921.

† Furthermore, in the totality of the seven sacraments, which are a developmental organism, the fourth stage is the middle. Every evolution or development takes place in seven stages: the first four unfold the external reality (evolution), then comes the "ebb tide" part of the entire development (involution). It is the same with the sacraments. Up to Sacramental Consultation, the given has value in an evolutionary sense; the sacrament adds the corresponding involutional balance, sanctifying it. Transition takes place here in the fourth step.

being, this occurs rhythmically, as an oscillation in time. This is the ability to remember, which changes in adolescence and becomes the foundation for an earth "I." This is another step forward in the evolution that leads to the fourth seven-year period.

> The corresponding involution process is what has been felt in Christianity as the sacrament of penance. There the process of remembrance is baptized or "Christened." And the process of remembering, by being Christened, is, at the same time, elevated into a moral realm. Here human beings not only consolidate their "I," but also they are...led to the involutional process of penance.*

The process of evolution (here, memory) becomes increasingly inward during these years and approaches involution (here, moral memory, or conscience). In the fourth seven-year period they have become nearly identical.

What does it mean "to Christianize memory"? This becomes clear in a conversation between Herbert Hahn and Rudolf Steiner in 1916, arising from a completely different matter. It concerned Steiner's essay "The Education of the Child from the Perspective of Spiritual Science." Three great pedagogical leitmotifs are given to characterize the first three seven-year periods of life: Imitation, authority, and freedom. Hahn asked Steiner whether there might also be such a guiding star of education or self-education for the fourth seven-year period—for the period after the twenty-first year of life.

> [Rudolf Steiner] replied after some reflection that such a guiding star does indeed exist. The years of apprenticeship, as well as the years of travel, belong to this

* CW 343, Sept. 2, 1921f.

> phase of life, and then it is important for people to look back at the path they have taken. During this retrospection, all of the experiences, insights, and knowledge they have acquired should pass before their inner eye—not fleetingly, but carefully. At the same time, people should ask themselves: How does what I have been permitted to experience relate to the fact of Christ's work in the world? How does my knowledge in its present form hold up in the light of Christ? Here, one should not stop with mere memories but consider again, with strong inner activity, all that has been acquired thus far and relate these memories (down to the details) to the living Christ forces at work in the world.*

Hahn adds, "A very great responsibility to educate oneself was assigned here by Rudolf Steiner is attached to a certain age. There is reason to believe that, at any later stage of life, one could make up for its omission at that age."

Initially, it seems astonishing that Steiner assigns this exercise of recollection to the fourth seven-year period. At this age, the human life situation is naturally future-oriented rather than past-oriented. What role should the retrospective exercise play in this respect? What is meant is obviously something deeper, namely that at this age an inner lifestyle must gradually be added to the outer one if the biography is to be healthy. The simple question "how does what I have been permitted to experience relate to the fact of Christ's work in the world? How does my knowledge in its present form hold up in the light of Christ?" (Steiner)—is the question of conscience par excellence. Am I identical to myself, do I act as I actually want to act? *The Christ question is the "I" question.* This is the beginning of a Christianized memory.

---

* Hahn, *Von den Quellkräften der Seele*, Arlesheim 1959, p. 28f.

This leitmotif for the fourth seven-year period, as well as for the lifetime that follows it, can also be understood as *the* leitmotif for the self-examination of penance, of Sacramental Consultation as a whole.

Let us now look at the individual elements of "complete repentance," which Rudolf Steiner described as an "expression of what should be the process of involution matching the evolutionary process of total memory,"* along with this question: What form do these elements assume in Sacramental Consultation as practiced in The Christian Community in a way appropriate for our time?

The *examination of conscience* as the "gateway to the three acts of penitence," as prescribed by the Council of Trent,† can today have only one form, as it has been handed down by Herbert Hahn as a motto for the fourth seven-year cycle. This motto, we have said, could apply to Sacramental Consultation as a whole; but we want to use it now in particular for the examination of conscience as described by Rudolf Steiner.

The human experience of repentance or remorse, as the first of the three "acts of penance" with which the Trentine council dealt so extensively and which some theologians say is "the soul of the sacrament of Penance," has undergone a tremendous metamorphosis in recent centuries. What does this look like for a contemporary person searching for a way to conduct their inner life? Rudolf Steiner advised people concerning their inner life in his Esoteric School. In different formulations, we find him repeatedly saying: "One should not encourage remorse. It is worthless for one's own

* CW 343, Oct. 2, 1921

† Council of Trent (1545–1563) issued 17 dogmatic decrees covering aspects of the Catholic Church in dispute at the time.

personality as well as for the world. But we should learn every day from our past for our future, and thus make life a lesson."* In a little more detail he says elsewhere:

> One does not cling to worry and remorse concerning what one has done, but one transforms it into a resolution to do everything better in the future. One becomes one's own architect and builder. An architect does not stand in front of, and remorsefully lament, a house he has built, that it is not better, but evaluates the steps he took in building it to make the next one better. In the same way we should evaluate ourselves. In remorse and sorrow our personality dies; through learning it ascends. Remorse and sorrow are of no use; the time we waste on them we should use for evolving higher.†

In summary, we can say: Remorse must be replaced by learning. Steiner's words are in stark contrast to the finely chiseled Scholastic concepts of *contritio* and *attritio*, perfect and imperfect repentance. His words also contradict the view that remorse is the soul of the sacrament of penance for human beings today. Remorse is oriented toward the past; I regret an act and say to myself: If only I had not done this! But I did it, and the past cannot be changed. It is now a fact, and I must learn to affirm it. The past is—*as past!*—not evil. It is a part of the world, and with it also my deed has become a factual part of the world, which I now must continue to work on. The past is not evil, but it is imperfect because of my bad deed. That deed needs to be supplemented so that it can become part of a more perfect wholeness.

In that sense, examining one's individual sins can become an objective starting point for learning. Remorse was (and

* CW 264, Dornach 1966 p. 148.

† Ibid., p. 158.

is) understood to be an indication of inner transformation. However, it is also true that only those who have inwardly transformed themselves can learn from a situation. Learning is an expression of inner transformation appropriate for our time; it is future oriented.*

Confession, as prescribed by the Catholic Council of Trent, the actual Confession, is the second act of penance. It is preceded by an act of remorse. Only if the remorse was genuine will the confession of sin also be genuine—and complete. But when remorse has already been transformed into learning, that learning will no longer precede Confession, but vice versa: what is to be learned will result from the sacrament. It can therefore no longer consist of a *confession of sin*; it is then rather a conversation where the relevant facts are brought to light.† This conversation then leads to an awareness of the realm in which learning must take place; it illuminates that part of one's biography that needs somehow to be supplemented by a change in attitude or perhaps new deeds.

Then, the third act of Trentine penitence consists *in redressing a wrong* or *making amends* in some way. It is what "as retribution one imposes on oneself or what the pastor imposes on one."‡ This, too, has been completely transformed in The Christian Community. Of course, it is also appropriate and necessary today for people to work on their weaknesses. Perhaps it was a specific act that caused them to awaken to this necessity; then they *learned* from

* One can also see in remorse a positive meaning "that the person concerned lifts themselves up to knowledge of how they let their consciousness cloud over in the moment when they performed the bad deed" (CW 166, Feb. 1, 1916).

† For this reason, it is called Sacramental Consultation in the English-speaking world.

‡ CW 343, Oct. 2, 1921.

their actions. What human souls now seek, however, is not repentance, but a path of self-education that will allow them to act more appropriately in the future. To this corresponds the willingness of the priest to accompany—through helping and advising—those who, of their own accord, want to subject themselves to this work according to their own strength and possibilities. Then the priest can support the will to learn. Anything else, such as an imposition of some kind of penitential exercise, is out of the question. Again, learning plays a decisive role, but now it is an expression of the will manifesting as a willingness to work upon oneself. It is thus ultimately about individuals empowering themselves.

Reconciliation, atonement with God, is the goal of Sacramental Consultation. Traditionally it is expressed in the granting of absolution, the washing away of one's sins. The Christian Community does not see it this way. On the contrary: *the consequences of sin* provide the essential raw material for spiritual growth in human beings. Sins belong to a human being's self-identity; they present us with essential learning materials. This understanding of sin must not be misunderstood. Of course, sins are not something already positive in themselves. Whoever takes them too lightly merely show that they have learned nothing from them. Lightly dismissed, they remain unfruitful and weaken us even more. Indeed, if they are taken away from us, something of our identity and our future is also taken away. It requires the grace of Christ's power to transform if those sins are not to become merely an unpaid debt to the world. *Only Christ's grace can transform sin into the raw material necessary to evolve and improve human morality.* This was mentioned in the previous section. Absolution takes on a completely new meaning, in that we are shown a path to gradually open ourselves to the grace of Christ and experience sin as work to be done in the future, work that requires our creative powers. This is how we will come to experience true peace.

In this way we see how the elements of *complete penance* find themselves in a transformed form in Sacramental Consultation in The Christian Community. The outer form for this sacrament is rather simple. The first part is consultation with a priest, which is conducted by the priest without vestments in a suitable but undefined environment. The content of this conversation includes all the above elements in the described contemporary form. Then the individual's life can come into focus and perhaps begin to speak itself.

Life is like a school, and our destiny, or karma, is like an individualized curriculum. When we are able to see the loving teacher behind life's necessities and demands and the wisdom behind the curriculum, we can follow the path of learning more fruitfully; trusting cooperation makes us into better students. *The loving teacher behind destiny is the Lord of Karma, Christ himself. He is the one who then begins to speak to us through the circumstances of our life.*

The second part of Sacramental Consultation then follows the conversation: The priest puts on vestments and speaks the words of the sacrament. A third person, who is always present when two people gather in his name (Matt. 20:18), speaks through the ritual words. Christ appears here as *the Teacher,** so the words begin with "Learn." These words express what is meant to take the place of remorse. It

* In another place, in the Sunday Service for Children, Christ appears as teacher in the wording of the ritual. It is said there that "Christ is the teacher of human love."

is a summary of the previous priestly conversation, in which perhaps one or the other opportunity to learn has already been mentioned. And yet the learning here goes far beyond that; it is much more fundamental. It is the call to follow a path. In our confrontation with individual sin we need to make it possible for Christ's helping grace to enter our lives. This path of learning can lead us to where his grace can find its way into our lives. We have said before: of course, God can exercise his grace wherever he wants. There is also, however, the blessing of human freedom, and grace is not effective against misused freedom; *blasphemy against the spirit* cannot be forgiven.*

The path to Christ stated in the ritual is twofold. Rudolf Steiner once called these two paths *the path of thought and the path of will*. The path of thought refers to the understanding that I bring to my fellow human beings. The question always arises: Do I simply reject their wrong opinions, or do I practice tolerance and try to understand the inner correctness of their thoughts by seeking the starting point that led them to their wrong opinion? There are many different starting points as well as paths leading to truth; Steiner speaks of twelve worldviews, all of which have their justification.† Nevertheless, in general they seem to contradict each other, e.g., the idealistic and the materialistic approach.

A special challenge would be to recognize what is justified in another person's worldview, to continue to think their thoughts as if their starting point were your own. One could even follow the other person's train of thought and continue

* "Therefore I say unto you, 'Every sin and blasphemy shall be forgiven; but blasphemy against the Spirit shall not be forgiven.'" (Matt. 12:31).

† CW 151, Jan. 21, 1914.

it better than the other could have. One then becomes a true interpreter of the other person's reasoning. Steiner did this in an outstanding way for Goethe that even experts of the time recognized and called on him to edit the definitive edition of Goethe's scientific writings. He also did this for Haeckel ("Haeckel's teaching is great, and [yet] Haeckel is the worst commentator on this teaching"*) and for Nietzsche. Later he used this approach when writing his book on the history of philosophy, from ancient Greek thinkers to the present day.† Understanding another person this deeply is a path to Christ, the *path of thought*. Steiner describes it as follows:

> The more we develop genuine interest for another person's opinions, even if we consider them to be errors, the more we illuminate our own thoughts through the opinions of others. The more we place next to our own thoughts, which we perhaps consider to be true, the thoughts which others develop, which we consider to be errors, but are nevertheless interested in, the more we feel, in the innermost part of our soul, the words of Christ, which today must be understood as the new language of Christ, who said: "Whatever you do to one of the least of my brothers, you have done to me" (Matt. 25:40). Christ has not stopped revealing himself to human beings again and again, and he will continue to do so even until the end of earthly time. In this way he speaks today to those who want to hear him: Whatever one of the least of your brothers thinks, you have to regard in such a way that *I am thinking in him*.... This is the path today that must be called the path of thought to Christ."‡

* CW 262, p. 20.

† *The Riddles of Philosophy* (CW 18).

‡ CW 193, Feb. 11, 1919.

Those who wish to follow this path must be able to refrain from their own thoughts, which, like in Steiner's words, they "perhaps consider to be true," in order to make room for very different thoughts. By sacrificing our own thoughts, we are creating the foundation for a mutual understanding of great depth. The path of thought to Christ is also a path into community.

The path of the will is based on ideals. Ideals can hardly flourish in the arctic intellectual and spiritual climate of our time, but they are the shining stars of a spiritual life and need people who can open their hearts to them. In young people, to a certain extent, they are still present naturally—as a gift they have brought from the spiritual world. But they do not endure and cannot sustain people through a whole lifetime. They must be replaced by ideals instilled through education in the course of a person's biographical development. If we embrace an active life of ideas with our will so that an idea can become an ideal for us, then we have learned how to acquire ideals. In describing an inner path of training, Steiner mentioned the law that governs this transition: "Every idea that does not become an ideal for you kills a force in your soul; but every idea that becomes an ideal creates forces of life in you."* What kind of life forces are these? They do not proceed from the ideals that we bring with us at birth but come from the ideas that we have acquired ourselves.

> Acquired idealism—namely self-educated idealism that cannot be lost when we leave youth behind—this is something that opens the way to Christ, because it is something that can be acquired only in life between birth and death.... This is the path of will to the Christ.†

* CW 10, p 28.

† CW 193, Feb. 11, 1919.

The proper relationship to a genuine ideal can only consist in this: that I serve the ideal. Too often, though, idealists who see themselves in the service of an ideal seem to want to rule over others "for their own good"; a tendency to dominate or even tyrannize others with one's ideals can arise. Serving here does not mean asserting one's own will, however, but rather taking an ideal into one's own will as a kind of divine willing: that is, to *receive one's will*. The highest of all ideals is Christ himself, who is the representative of ideal humankind. The Christian Community is united in the service of this ideal. The path of will is also a path into community.

The *third person*, who speaks in the sacrament *as a teacher* also provides the material to be learned: to seek once again the path on which the grace of Christ comes to meet a human being. *It is the path of thought and the path of will to Christ*. This path leads into Christian community—but the reverse is also true: Christian community can also lead us on this path. In this way our connection to Christ and to Christian community can become *peace*, which in the Catholic Church is called reconciliation. With the experience of peace, the process has reached its goal, and we can face our life's task with newly won freedom, i.e., unencumbered. Just as Christ is called the "teacher of human love" in the Sunday Service for Children, so also our greatest learning goal, our central life task on earth is to learn to love. "The seed of love is thus placed into the innermost core of the human being. And from there it should flow into all earthly evolution."*

In the ritual part of Sacramental Consultation, the traditional motifs of Confession in the past—examination of

* CW 13, p. 415.

conscience, the three aspects of remorse, reconciliation—are brought to humanity in a fresh and metamorphosed form by Christ speaking through the ritual.

We should *learn to offer our thoughts and to receive our will.* In this way, we set out on a path toward Christ and at the same time place ourselves in the context of Christian community. The grace that comes to meet us on this path will allow us to feel peace and help us become collaborators in the work of love.

Sacramental Consultation is basically concluded with the words spoken by the priest in the ritual, but it is only truly fulfilled through Communion (generally the following Sunday through Communion within the congregation). Only with the taking of Communion is the entire process really complete. One must bear in mind "what it is that makes Confession combined with Communion into a real sacrament."* Confession is as closely connected to Communion as Confirmation. Confirmation leads to Communion by first looking back at one's previous destiny and the role played by Christ during those years. Along the same lines, Confession also involves looking back by means of a Christianized memory, which results in a new perspective on the future. The point of view of Confirmation is "may Christ be the guide on the child's future paths in life." By contrast, Sacramental Consultation has the point of view: "an individual seeks to follow a path to Christ." They are two sides of the same relationship to Christ.

One could say—with a generalizing overview—that Confirmation carries Communion through the third seven-year period of life. Then, in the fourth seven-year cycle, with

* CW 344, Sept. 20, 1922.

the birth of the "I," a new relationship to individual guilt begins, and Sacramental Consultation becomes a preparation for Communion. With each Sacramental Consultation, in a certain sense, what led to Communion during Confirmation is repeated. The "importance of this moment," which is spoken of in Confirmation, thus comes to consciousness in Sacramental Consultation. In Catholic theology the grace acquired through Baptism is restored through Confession. In The Christian Community, we could say: Sacramental Consultation means reconnecting with the grace of Confirmation, which leads to Communion as the healing medicine. In Sacramental Consultation Christ appears as *the teacher*, whereas we find him as *the physician* in Communion. We learn from our transgressions, but only through Communion does the full essence of Sacramental Consultation become clear as the healing of sin.

Chapter 11
Approaching Death

The rituals of The Christian Community surrounding death form a fourfold organism:

Last Anointing
Funeral Service, First Part
Funeral Service, Public Part
Act of Consecration for the Dead

The *Last Anointing* is performed when the process of dying has begun. Ideally it should take place close to the moment of death, but it also presupposes a fully conscious person and should therefore be early enough. The *Funeral Service, First Part* is performed with the body of the deceased present. The individual features of the departed are still visible. According to the archetype, this would take place in the house where the deceased lived and died.

The *Funeral Service, Public Part* then takes place at the grave or as close to the cremation site as possible. For this second part the mortal sheath of the deceased, and with it all earthly visible traces of his or her individuality, lies in the closed coffin and is therefore no longer visible. However, it is necessary that the body of the deceased be present as a prerequisite for the service. *The Act of Consecration for the Dead* is held in a chapel of The Christian Community, if possible. In place of the coffin, the altar now appears as a symbol for *the grave of the earth*. "The Christ Jesus suffered under Pontius Pilate the death on the cross and was lowered into the grave of the earth."* From this grave he then rose after three days.† One can recognize a process in this sequence of rituals. Step by step, the essence of the earthly personality recedes, while the perspective expands to encompass the universal human. An archetype of a path from the earthly into the spiritual appears. The Last Anointing is the sacrament associated with death. The other rituals are not actually sacraments but rituals attached to the sacrament.

11.1 The Last Anointing

The fifth sacrament also has a complicated history. Like Sacramental Consultation, it has evolved over a thousand years to find its identity and place in the circle of seven sacraments. There are no records documenting an anointing in the first Christian centuries. From the fifth century comes the first written document‡ referring to the already existing practice of anointing the sick. It makes clear that the basis for the practice is the care of the sick as described in the Epistle of James: "If anyone is sick among you, call the elders of the assembly to him. Let them pray over him and anoint him with oil in the name of the Lord. And the prayer of faith will heal the sick person, and the Lord will raise him up, and if he has committed sins, they will be forgiven him."§ At that time, everyone was allowed, in principle, to anoint themselves

* From the Creed of The Christian Community.

† The altar in Catholic churches is also considered to be a symbol of a tomb and must always contain a relic. Steiner characterizes the altar of The Christian Community as "a tomb in the form of a table."

‡ Letter from Pope Innocent I in 416.

§ The Letter of James, 5:14f.

or their relatives with oil that had been consecrated by the bishop.

Besides healing, forgiveness of sins became, according to the Epistle of James, an important second part of this anointing. From the ninth century on, a close connection between anointing the sick and the sacrament of penance was gradually established. This development moved the anointing toward the end of life, together with last Communion (*Viaticum*).* That is how the anointing of the sick, in conjunction with penance and last Communion, became a sacrament associated with death. The sequence of the last sacraments became: *Penance–Anointing–Viaticum*.

In the meantime, the anointing of the sick was gradually reserved for priests to perform. In the twelfth century, the name *Last Anointing* (*extrema unctio*)† was coined, thereby establishing the sacrament's connection with death. The aspect of forgiveness of sins was now in the foreground, and the Last Anointing was understood as a special completion of penance (*consummativum*). The Council of Trent confirmed this development and said of the Last Anointing that this sacrament is a "grace of the Holy Spirit, whose anointing takes away the transgressions, if any, and the remnants of sin, and straightens and strengthens the soul of the sick person." The healing of the sick, which is the first theme in the Letter of James, is still spoken of insofar as it is said of the sick person that "sometimes, if it promotes the salvation of

* At that time, because the conditions imposed on the penitent were often harsh, repentance was usually postponed until the end of life, and thus de facto, occurred only once. The *Viaticum* is the last Communion in Catholicism—the food for life after death. It differs from the usual Communion for the sick in its formula for administration.

† The name is to distinguish it from other anointings performed at Baptism, Confirmation and, in some cases, at Ordination. The *Last* Anointing then comes before death.

the soul, the soul also attains physical recovery."* The Council of Trent established the order of the last sacraments differently: *Penance–Viaticum* (Communion)–*Last Anointing.*

The 2nd Vatican Council breaks with this development and detaches last rites from a connection to death. The new name is *Anointing of the Sick* and is understood roughly as described in the Epistle of James. The reasons for this change are unclear; the stated purpose for it was to return to the original, which, of course, raises the (not easy to answer) question of whether the Epistle of James can even be regarded as the origin of the Last Anointing. Some theologians refer to the "old principle that liturgical prayer is also a criterion for faith and the practice of faith (*lex orandi–lex credendi*)."† But it is peculiar that it was probably popular piety (i.e., the asserted *lex orandi*) that led to the medieval conception of the Last Anointing: "Despite the church's manifold, mostly pastorally justified objections to this concept of the 'sacrament of death,' this meaning was preserved in practice in the faith of the people."‡ This is obviously still the case, despite the last Council. In a *Pastoral Handout* it is lamented that the anointing of the sick is "still widely associated with death today. All too often, it is misinterpreted as a sacrament of death, and an official seal with the obligation to die still clings to it." It is necessary to "overcome a centuries-old misconception and the prejudices that have been based on it. This new orientation naturally requires frequent instruction and persistent effort on the part of those responsible."§ Otherwise one must simply say: "But for those to whom the anointing is strange

* Quote from Ganoczy, p. 92f.

† Adam: *Sinn und Gestalt der Sakramente.* p. 121.

‡ Auer and Ratzinger, vol. 7, p. 202.

§ Adam, p. 132f.

and difficult to impart, it is comforting that the actual sacrament of death is and remains the Eucharist."* So the present situation is that the Catholic Church (like the Orthodox and Protestant churches) no longer knows of any specific sacrament for death.

With regard to the actual use of the Last Anointing, The Christian Community is fully in line with the Council of Trent (against the reform of the Second Vatican Council): the Last Anointing is the Sacrament belonging to the event of death, the *anointing for death*, but with a completely new understanding and justification. Also, the sequence of the three sacraments associated with death, which continue to be understood as forming a wholeness, corresponds to the Tridentine sequence (not the changed Vatican sequence): Sacramental Consultation–Communion for the sick–Last Anointing. For The Christian Community, understanding the Last Anointing as the sacrament for death results from the *evolution and involution* perspective. The sequence of the first four sacraments shows evolution and involution growing closer together; in Sacramental Consultation they are in balance. These *earthly* sacraments serve the process by which we become a human being in the course of our lives. Death, however, no longer serves this process of coming to the earth, that is, *evolution*; on the contrary, it guides it into the completely different process of becoming spirit.

In a human being, therefore, "the processes are exhausted, which have been taking place in us since birth as evolutionary processes, and we then have in a natural way a tendency toward an involutionary process.... We come, by developing this further, to the fifth [sacrament]—which is quite naturally

* Vorgrimler, p. 260.

an involutionary process—we come to death, which concludes the life of an individual."*

Then, the role of a sacrament is reversed, so to speak, *not involution balancing and blessing evolution, but evolution balancing and blessing involution.* An evolutionary process must be added by means of a sacrament to an involutionary process. And so, as hitherto an involutionary blessing was added through an earthly sacrament, to a corresponding outer evolutionary event, now—and this applies to the last three sacraments: Last Anointing, Ordination, Marriage—a corresponding evolution must be found to bless external involution. "*The three last sacraments are like the spiritual world shining into human life.*"†

> [We must therefore] bring something to people...that will stimulate their soul–spiritual life in a way similar to the way their physical–bodily nature is stimulated by natural processes. It should be expressed in rhythm that, at death, the physical–bodily nature will disappear again, and the soul–spiritual should again take shape.‡

The content of the Last Anointing, in this respect, is *the evolution that takes place after death*, the development of our soul–spiritual nature in the world of life after death.

Oil plays a special role in this sacrament. The character of oil, its inner qualities, will be outlined here with some concepts found in anthroposophy. In the parable of the wise and foolish virgins (Matt. 25:1–10), oil is an image for the spirit.§ The olive branch brought to Noah by a dove is a

* CW 343, Oct. 2, 1921.
† CW 342, June 14, 1921.
‡ CW 343, Oct. 2, 1921.
§ CW 96, April 27, 1907.

picture of a *revelation from the spiritual world*.* In oil one can see what leads back to the world of soul and spiritual.† In terms of its original essence, oil likewise has the ability to make beings incline toward love.‡ Finally, during a contemplation of the olive tree, Steiner spoke of the "Oil of the earth. In oil one feels the pulsing of the earth's pervasive influence."§ And through oil one can close oneself off in order to develop everything within oneself, independent of external nature."¶

Thus, oil is deeply related the spiritual, but out of a connection to the earthly. As "oil of the earth" it also conveys a power to close oneself off from the world and thus to be "identical with oneself." Through oil, a soul transitioning to the spiritual world is given buoyancy, which "leads it back to the soul, spiritual world." On the other hand, it helps a soul to close itself off and maintain its sense of self as an "I," instead of being dissolved in the spiritual world. This rhythm between devotion—i.e., giving oneself to the spiritual world, and maintaining a relationship to oneself, is only possible through the power of love. On earth, this is the rhythm between establishing a connection with another person and preserving one's own individuality. In one of Rudolf Steiner's mystery dramas we read: "Love should bind separated beings, but not want to kill what is peculiar to each."**

In preparing for life in the Spirit beyond the material realm, the sacramental process uses oil to make a person "inclined to love." On the one hand, it can be said that oil

---

* CW 266/2, Nov. 5, 1910.
† CW 343, Oct. 2, 1921.
‡ Ibid.
§ CW 149, Dec. 31, 1913.
¶ CW 232, Nov. 24, 1923.
** CW 14, *The Soul's Probation*, scene 3.

in the ritual "carries the spirit up into the heights." At the same time, however, it is a spiritual substance that envelops a person and closes them off from the world, thereby replacing *what the soul otherwise derives from the body, a sense of self.* A person can begin to "feel" oneself "outside one's body." In this way, the Last Anointing stimulates our soul, spiritual life and strengthens us for approaching and crossing the threshold of death. For this last stretch of the way, it brings a spiritual awakening in the *higher consciousness* of a person, an increased spiritual orientation and very often also a bodily calming that can lead to recovery.

Within The Christian Community no other sacrament involves an anointing (except Ordination to the priesthood). Therefore, the name *Last Anointing*, if understood quantitatively, does not make sense. Nevertheless, the sacrament's intention is expressed clearly by its name, which often has a helpful effect in pastoral care, clarifying and awakening consciousness. The name also helps to erase the taboo from death. Rudolf Steiner, too, has consistently spoken of the Last Anointing in his lectures, once even using the expression: *death anointing*. Only once did he speak of a *sacred anointing.*[*]

The sacrament itself is simple: essential passages from Jesus' Farewell Discourse (John 17) are read (as at Confirmation). Christ prayed it on the eve of Good Friday, thereby including the disciples entrusted to him in his death, the death that created a future for humankind. Then three crosses are drawn with consecrated oil on the forehead of the critically ill person, together with simple, yet powerful prayers: above the right and left eye and in the middle of

* CW 318, Sept. 8, 1924.

the forehead. Golgotha, the place of the skull with its three crosses, comes to mind. If the strength of the person who has come close to the threshold of death allows it, the celebration, together with the anointing, includes two other short sacramental acts: Sacramental Consultation and Communion. This combination of three sacraments in sequence (Sacramental Consultation–Communion–Last Anointing) is what the Catholic Church (until the Second Vatican Council) called the *sacraments for death*. In principle the same applies to the renewed sacraments of The Christian Community. The name *sacraments for death* has, however, perhaps wrongly not come into general use. One speaks of the Last Anointing even when the larger sequence of three is intended.

11.2 The Funeral Service, First Part*

Ideally, this part of the funeral concludes a three-day period where the deceased has been lying undisturbed in the house where the death occurred. It is followed by the transfer of the body to a cemetery, crematorium, or public place such as church or funeral home that can provide a large chapel for the second, public part of the funeral. The funeral then takes place immediately afterward. Although Rudolf Steiner spoke of this part of the service taking place "in the house where death occurred," this ideal situation is hardly possible anymore. A three-day presentation in the house where the death occurred is rarely an option. It is a great help when suitable rooms for lying in state are available at other locations, such as is sometimes possible in chapels—or side rooms—of The Christian Community.

* This part of the funeral is usually private, with only the family and closest friends present.

The time of lying in state is a very important part of caring for the deceased. From a spiritual-scientific point of view, the moment of death does not bring with it a complete obliteration of any kind of human consciousness. The radical transformation brought about by death proceeds in stages. The numerous testimonies of near-death experiences available today show that the consciousness of the dead is indeed transformed but is still related and similar to our normal daytime consciousness. The higher members of the human being are detached from the physical body, but because the astral body is not yet separated from the etheric body, as is the case in deep sleep, the deceased does not at first lose all earthly consciousness. The astral body's ability to create images in the life body and thereby bring about consciousness is even increased now that the physical body is no longer present. The human soul is conscious of a colorful-flowing tableau of life. It is a vision of one's past life, a plethora of life's experiences all present simultaneously. The biggest crisis of consciousness for the deceased occurs only when the etheric body also begins to dissolve. That dissolution entails the diminishing of the consciousness made possible because of the astral body's connection to the etheric body. Only with the extinction of that consciousness does death occur in its full reality. If possible, the first part of the funeral is held at this time, for it helps to give the departed an orientation as they pass into this darkness.

The ceremony itself is simple; it takes place with the body present and, in part, visible. The deceased is addressed in prayer, but not with the direct form *you*. The language reflects the fact that those next of kin and close friends present are looking as from a distance upon the soul and spirit of the "dear departed one" even as he or she is looking for the peace and light of the world after death. For the deceased it is a matter of completely reorienting themselves to find their reference point in the realm of the boundless and timeless, because it can no longer be found in the world of the senses. Here the bereaved can support the deceased in this search for orientation and, out of true spirit-consciousness, support the departed, who is now seen as a servant of the spirit.

11.3 The Funeral Service, Second Part

The next act contains two aspects. First, the body is given over to the elements. At a burial they are chiefly earth, water, and air; in cremation they are essentially air and fire. Whether one chooses burial or cremation is of no consequence today. In the future, cremation will increase in importance. In the case of suicide, or if the suspicion of suicide cannot be eliminated, burial in the ground should be chosen rather than cremation. After a true suicide, according to Rudolf Steiner, because it was not their time, the soul lacks orientation in the spiritual world and is granted some small measure of solace if they can look back on the remains as the place they were once located. As the elements now receive the mortal part of a human being and the soul becomes homeless on earth, the funeral ritual supports the soul in awakening on the other side of the threshold. In all parts the funeral is a ritual of resurrection. It is not a one-time deed, but the beginning of a process. Therefore, the funeral is also a summons to the bereaved to continue helping the deceased to awaken in their new existence. They do this by seeking a connection to the deceased in an appropriate fashion.

The ceremony takes place at the grave or as near the cremation site as possible. The deceased is directly addressed at the beginning and at the end of the ritual: the thoughts of the bereaved seek the departed where they are now, at the "dwelling place of your soul." There they must deal with waking up into completely new conditions, which only succeeds if they gradually get distance from themselves and become aware of which parts of their biography are worthy of eternity. In this process of separating the essential from the nonessential, those left behind can be very helpful. The funeral ritual contains an initial blessing to aid with this process. This necessary help in awakening to a new existence is an essential part of the funeral. Looking toward the future, at the end of the service the deceased is addressed directly again as an *eternal soul*, with a prayer that they may find the power of resurrection in life after death through the grace of Christ.

11.4 The Act of Consecration for the Dead

The mystery of the soul's after-death journey is woven into the Act of Consecration of Man itself. Rudolf Steiner describes how birth is the path of a human being—from a heavenly human being to an earthly human being—in four stages:

> The processes that take place through birth are: descent from Communion with the spiritual; if you would like a word for it, you could say "excommunion"; the descent, that is, the coming down. The second consists in entering into a relationship with matter. The third is coming under the sway of forces central to earth, adapting to the earth. And the fourth is the ability to hear and speak, which, however, emerges only to the extent that embryonic activity still takes place in a human being after birth."*

* CW 343, Sept. 30, 1921.

These are the four stages of the Mass, the Act of Consecration of Man, in reversed order: Communion – Transformation – Offering – Gospel.

> Through birth we are led down through four stages into earthly existence to the point of speaking a language, through the process of death we are led upward from language to communion.... But the forces of death are continually at work in us. In every moment we are being born and we are dying. Forces of death are at work.... What is a sacrament in the Mass, which is carried out externally, is a process that continually counteracts the process within us of being born. This is what continuously constitutes the forces of death in us.

According to this, the Act of Consecration of Man is "the ceremony of reversed birth processes that works against the death processes within us." Details of the prayers in the Mass correspond step-by-step to the after-death experience. The path begins with the unveiling of the cup at the beginning of the offertory, presenting us with a picture for the moment of death, and then proceeds step by step through the service to the *farthest point* of the after-death existence (called the "Midnight Hour of the World" by Rudolf Steiner*) in Communion. This aspect of the Act of Consecration of Man has a special significance for the Act of Consecration for the Dead, which reflects the path followed by a human being after death. It throws light on this path for the deceased and conveys *bread for the way* by means of Communion, which those people present in the service receive *with the departed*. The consecration for the dead is generally celebrated on a Saturday after the funeral. The vestments worn for this

* CW 153, April 14, 1914.

service are black, which reflects Passiontide. The significance of resurrection in this service is underscored by a reading of Mark 16, the Easter Sunday gospel reading. A special prayer is inserted at the end of the service, in which the name of the deceased is spoken.

Chapter 12
Ordination of Priests

With the Last Anointing an individual human life is completed. The two sacraments that now follow—Ordination and Marriage—have a different character. They refer to human life in society with others and are received only by a few who are receiving it *for others*. Similar to the Act of Consecration of Man, Ordination to the priesthood has its origin in the mysteries. Rudolf Steiner presented this in detail and then summarized: "Ordination itself thus became, so to speak, an external process for what was formerly brought about in the inner human being through initiation."* We will have more to say on the origin in the mysteries but first we consider important moments in the historical evolution of this sacrament.

12.1 Historical Development

The apostles are archetypes for the Christian priesthood. In the beginning there were *the twelve*. They were called by Christ and walked with him, becoming his followers on earth and continuing his work—but with human powers that were filled with the Holy Spirit: They were taught by the Risen One and received their mission at Pentecost through the Spirit sent by Him, namely, to bring the good news of

* CW 343, Oct. 3, 1921.

Christianity to the people and to heal the sick. Through their ministry churches were formed which they then led—directly through their presence or sometimes from afar through letters. As understood by the Catholic Church their ministry evolved over the centuries into a threefold task.

Christianity has one of its roots in Judaism. In the history of Israel, the decisive roles played by leaders are those of the *priest*, the *king*, and the *prophet*. According to the New Testament, Christ is the fulfillment of these roles.[*] From this, the three offices of the priesthood emerge: *the priestly office, the pastoral office, and the teaching office*. The priestly office refers to ritual. Pastoral ministry is connected with the leadership of a congregation,[†] of which an important part is pastoral care. The teaching office includes the proclamation of the Gospel. The Second Vatican Council of the Catholic Church referred to this trinity of tasks as sanctification, leadership, and teaching. In The Christian Community, we usually speak of three tasks as well, namely the priestly celebration of rituals, pastoral care, and teaching.

The distinction of "apostles and elders" (*Presbyteroi*) has existed already from apostolic times.[‡] The word *priest* is, in fact, derived from *presbyteros*. A further step is found in the seven helpers (*diakone*), of whom Acts of the Apostles reports,[§] and finally, the office of the bishop (*Episkopos* = overseer) is

---

* One example for each from the New Testament can illustrate this: "And the crowd said, This is Jesus, the *prophet* from Nazareth in Galilee" (Matt. 21:11). "Then Pilate asked him, 'So are you nevertheless a *king*? Jesus answered: "You say it, I am a king" (John 18:37). "But Christ came as a high **priest** of the good things yet to come" (Heb. 9:11).

† Thus, it also contains in itself the kingly role, an office of leadership. Both shepherd and king lead, but in a complementary way.

‡ E.g., Acts of the Apostles 15:6.

§ Acts of the Apostles 6:1–7.

also mentioned.* The transfer of these offices—or forms of consecration—took place via the laying on of hands.† Up to the third century, five other offices were gradually introduced, a process which, until the Second Vatican Council, served as stages of priestly Ordination: *Ostiarier* (Doorman), *Lector* (Reader), *Exorcist* (Demon Exorcist), *Acolyth* (Companion) and Subdeacon; together with Deacon and Priest these form a sevenfold group. It was unclear whether the eighth level, the consecration of priests, is an additional degree of ordination or merely a juridical mission with special leadership powers. Catholic theology sees in this the origin of its hierarchy of ministries reflecting different degrees of consecration. The view since the Second Vatican Council has been that bishops are considered successors of the apostles and therefore their consecration as bishops gives them "the fullness of the sacrament of Ordination." Priests are not given this fullness through their Ordination but given a "share" in the three ministries that are entrusted to the bishop alone in the full sense (teaching, governing, and sanctifying). Thus, all priestly authority is derived from the spiritual authority of the bishop. The priests make the bishop in a certain sense *present* in the local church and form with their bishop *a single presbytery*.‡

The historical development, however, initially took a different course. Beginning in the fourth century,§ the question

* "For a bishop must be blameless because he administers the house of God; he must not be arrogant and irascible, not a drinker, not violent or greedy" (Titus 1:7)

† This is witnessed e.g., by Paul: "Do not neglect the grace that is in you and that was given to you when the elders (*Presbyteroi*) laid their hands on you together on the basis of prophetic words" (1 Tim. 4:14). "Therefore, I remind you to rekindle the grace of God that was given to you through the laying on of my hands" (2 Tim. 1:6).

‡ Vorgrimler, p. 290.

§ By the "Ambrosiaster" (Pseudo-Ambrosius, fourth century) and Hieronymus.

arose as to whether the ordination of a bishop led to greater spiritual authority than that of a priest. The fact that the bishop was the only priest who could ordain a person into the priesthood was understood as an expression of his pastoral authority (authority in an area of ecclesiastical jurisdiction, administrative power), not of his spiritual authority to ordain. In scholasticism this idea was deepened by the most important theologians, especially Thomas of Aquinas, and thereby became a generally understood truth in the Middle Ages. The center of theological interest was the Eucharist (the Mass). Since a bishop had no greater *eucharistic power* than a priest, there was no doubt in scholasticism that the ordination of a bishop did not confer any additional spiritual power to consecrate.

With regard to the office of sanctification, therefore, priest and bishop were equal. The difference lay in the offices of leadership and teaching, which appeared to imply greater importance within the church, but merely within the context of ecclesiastical law. The fact that Confirmation and Ordination were reserved for the bishop was not understood as an additional spiritual power to ordain. What was essential was the "distinction between authority over a jurisdiction and spiritual authority to ordain." This, however, is judged very critically by today's Catholic theology, because "then the deeper meaning of priesthood as participation in the apostolic office of Christ disappeared from consciousness."*

Scholasticism also brought an innovation into the ritual of priestly Ordination: the anointing of the hands of a priest and the head of a bishop, as well as a solemn presentation of the instruments of Ordination. The laying on of hands

* Auer and Ratzinger, vol. 7, p 314.

was no longer regarded as the decisive gesture. Thus, in the Decree for Armenians (1439), we read: "Thus priesthood is conferred by handing over the chalice with the wine, and paten with the bread."* All these views of scholasticism were confirmed by the Council of Trent. Actual Ordination is thus Ordination to the priesthood in seven stages (see above). The ordination of a bishop is only a ritual and not a sacrament. Priestly Ordination is accompanied by an anointing. The Ordination's essence (its "matter") is the handing over of the chalice and the paten. It is also possible for ordinations to be performed by "mere" priests (not bishops) who have episcopal authorization; they are valid because every priest does have full power to ordain.

The Second Vatican Council fundamentally changed this—actually "infallible"—doctrinal decision of the Council of Trent. The laying on of hands became (again) the essence of the ritual. Since then bishops alone have the power to ordain.

There are now three degrees of ordination: bishop, priest, and deacon. Thus, in the understanding of Catholic theologians, "the original view of the sacrament of Ordination...could be regained."†

12.2 Priesthood in The Christian Community

Against this background, the fact that there is only *one* priestly consecration in The Christian Community is significant. "The fullness of the sacrament of consecration" is transmitted without reservation. Since the Second Vatican Council this "fullness" is granted only to bishops in the

* Quoted by Vorgrimler, p. 281.

† Auer and Ratzinger, vol. 7, p. 338.

Roman Church. In this, The Christian Community follows the scholastic view—as is also the case with the Last Anointing. The scholastic understanding holds that the ritual a priest undergoes to become a bishop does not bestow any additional spiritual power. It adds nothing to the spiritual authority necessary for celebrating the Eucharist, the Mass.

In The Christian Community, too, celebrating the Act of Consecration of Man—and thus all the sacraments—is the defining mission of the priest. The spiritual authority to do so he or she receives through Ordination, and in this, all priests are equal. This complete authority bestowed by the sacrament of Ordination also carries over to all three offices of the priesthood: sanctification, teaching, and leadership. In the Catholic Church (since the Second Vatican Council), the bishop alone has the full power of Ordination, that is, the complete spiritual authority to perform all seven sacraments. A Catholic priest has only a share in that authority, for he lacks the power to ordain or to confirm. Likewise, a bishop alone has full authority to teach and govern, that is, lead—albeit "only in full unity with the Pope and the entire episcopacy."*

By these standards, Ordination into the priesthood of The Christian Community could be seen as an "ordination of bishops." The priests of The Christian Community have not only unrestricted authority to consecrate, but also unrestricted authority to teach what they see as the truth. They also have authority to lead their congregations (with pastoral care). The transfer of these three powers or ministries takes place during Ordination in various ways, most concretely through the anointing, which is at the center of the

* Vorgrimler, p. 288. *Episcopacy* refers to the church government by bishops.

sacrament. Here again The Christian Community follows the scholastic view and not that of the Second Vatican Council. Through an anointing of the hands—performed on the priest from the Middle Ages on—the power to celebrate the sacraments and other rituals (the office of sanctification) is bestowed: the "deed of Christ" is to become active through priestly deeds. The anointing of the head (performed on bishops from the Middle Ages onward) is twofold. Through the anointing of the forehead, the power of the *Spirit Word* is poured into the priest, forming a foundation for spirit-filled *teaching*. Through the *outpouring* of the anointing oil over the head of the priest (three drops), the *leadership office* (pastoral care) is spiritually transmitted, so that the priest will always relate *his or her own being* to *the being of the community*.

In addition to this spiritually unrestricted authority to fulfill the three priestly tasks, there is also the question of how the earthly administration of this new priesthood actually works. The authority to perform worship does have limits; words and gestures are not open to personal choice. They cannot be altered at will by the celebrating priest. The freedom to teach the truth as one sees fit does have its limits; *the content of one's teaching must not contradict the content of the rituals*. Finally, the authority to lead, the pastorate, becomes real only when connected to a concrete community. This is where it becomes necessary for an *administration to exercise jurisdiction*. With The Christian Community's *ordination of bishops*, this administrative authority belongs to the office of sanctification—that is, perhaps surprisingly, to the realm of ritual. In the Middle Ages these two were separated. The special authority possessed by bishops beyond mere priestly authority was of a purely legal nature. This is also the case in The Christian Community (which again follows the scholastic view).

For Rudolf Steiner, hierarchy is a necessary condition for the proper earthly administration of a church based on ritual. It needs a hierarchy of offices, a leadership "attached to the organization of communities on earth. This must be very carefully distinguished."* Thus, a community with the task of regulating its rituals must have an established order on earth. This is the task of hierarchy in The Christian Community. Hierarchy finds its role where priestly authority, grounded in the spirit, is limited by earthly facts; it must deal with responsibilities of a legal nature, i.e., administration and jurisdiction. Such matters do, however, have a direct effect on the realm of rituals. For example, celebrating Confirmations is usually reserved for Lenkers,† but this is not because a Lenker has received an additional Ordination bestowing special spiritual authority. It derives from an agreed upon arrangement within the circle of priests and reflects a rank within The Christian Community's constitution. For this reason, a Lenker can appoint any other priest to celebrate a Confirmation. The same applies to the Ordination of priests, which is usually reserved for the Erzoberlenker.‡ In this way,

* CW 344, Sept. 11, 1922.

† The German word *Lenker* means *guide* or *leader* and is used in German-speaking countries to designate the priest responsible for overseeing and guiding the work within a particular geographical region. The term is frequently used in English-speaking countries since there is no generally agreed upon English translation for *Lenker.* Other terms often employed are Regional Administrator or Regional Overseer.

‡ The leadership of The Christian Community is carried out by *Lenkers*, seven of whom constitute a *Circle of Seven,* which guides the church's work worldwide. This *Circle of Seven* includes three *Oberlenkers*, one of whom is designated as the *Erzoberlenker. Oberlenker* could be translated as *over-guide or leader*, that is, someone who oversees and guides the work over the entire globe. *Erzoberlenker* could be

Lenkers, Oberlenkers, and the Erzoberlenker fulfill leadership responsibilities of an overarching character.

According to Catholic understanding, bishops are successors of the original apostles. Priests of The Christian Community are also called upon by Rudolf Steiner *to become* successors to the apostles. He did not say that Ordination already makes them so. Priestly ministry is intended to be apostolic, insofar as priests should be able to hear the apostles "speaking" to them. However, the inner soul condition necessary to perceive and understand the original apostles must always be created anew. The task is "to bring to the language of the apostles a proper understanding."*

In Catholic theology, the question of what Ordination means for an individual has led to the concept of the essential feature or the character of an individual, in Latin, *character indelebilis*. An essential aspect of character is indelibly imprinted on the individual. The idea that Ordination changes an individual in a specific way is deeply rooted, not only within Catholicism. It overlooks the fact that a priestly deed is never merely the act of a single individual. It is always carried out on behalf of and with authority derived from a community. An awareness of this is beginning to awaken in the Catholic Church, albeit at first quite outwardly, by emphasizing the aspect "that a priest is seen primarily as belonging to the presbyterial college. This college contains many possibilities for mutual help and flexibility, which are not present when a priest is completely dependent on (and at the mercy of) a community."† From the outset, Steiner

---

translated as *First over-guide or leader*. His or her task is to make the final decision on matters the other *Oberlenkers* and *Circle of Seven* cannot otherwise decide upon.

* CW 344, Sept. 19, 1922.

† Vorgrimler, p. 297, fn. 49.

regarded the community of priests as the necessary foundation of the priesthood. This community must even have a special quality, which he calls *esoteric*. What this means is not easy to describe—the term esoteric today can mean many things. Probably the earliest description that Steiner gave for this term is from 1897 and reads:

> A concept is esoteric if it is seen in direct connection with the phenomenon which gave rise to it (the concept). It is exoteric when it is seen as an abstraction by itself separated from the phenomenon.*

With esotericism, then, everything depends upon the context, the concrete reference. If we want to apply this to the physical world, we must say: those who can behold this world in which we live "in direct connection with the phenomenon which gave rise to it" are actually seeing its spiritual origin. The spiritual world is the most important and critical context in which the sensory world exists. Seeing this is to recognize the (physical) world esoterically. The same is true of a community, which, through the will of its members, seeks a connection to the spiritual world, and from this connection wants to work spiritually in the earthly world: one can call this community *esoteric*. From this perspective the intention of those who want to live a contemporary priesthood is not simply to "do what the church does," but to work on earth out of a sought connection with the spiritual world through the power of community. This is the seed of the new church.

The community of priests is called by Rudolf Steiner the "proto-congregation" (*Urgemeinde*).† It is thus the proto-cell

* CW 1e, p. 377.

† CW 344, Sept. 1922 and Sept. 19, 1922.

or basic unit for all the congregations which come into existence through it. They constitute the other context in which the community of priests exists. Are these communities also designed to be *esoteric*? Steiner gives a key to the answer in his book *Christianity as Mystical Fact*, in which he describes how secret pre-Christian mysteries, which were designed to initiate only a few, actually went public with the appearance of Christ. From then onward everyone has been able to share in the blessings of the mysteries, not alone—for this would still require a strict training in the mysteries—but in community, in the context of a Christian community. "Thus, after the 'Mystery of Golgotha' what had been poured into the mysteries within the Temple was now poured into Christian community."* This means that a Christian congregation, in carrying out the Christian act of consecration (the Mass)—the outward form of which itself comes from the Mysteries—experiences as a community the type of initiation that an individual pupil of the mystery religions would have undergone before the death on Golgotha. The congregation as a whole is consecrated. Individual members participate in this consecration, even if they are not yet awakened to the process. "Christianity should be a means by which everyone can find a way to the spirit. Even if they are not mature enough for it, at least they are not cut off from the possibility that they may become part of the mystery stream if only unconsciously.... From now on, those not yet able to participate in initiation should be able to enjoy some of the blessings of the mysteries."†

As individuals become aware of their connection to the spiritual world, as that connection comes into existence

* CW 8, p. 109.

† Ibid., p. 118.

through their congregational experience of ritual, they begin to awaken to the esoteric aspect of community. Thus, the priesthood of individual pastors in The Christian Community is grounded in the congregation of priests. However, this proto-congregation does not exist for itself but rather it exists for, and functions with, an intimate relationship to its congregations with their unseen esotericism.

12.3 The Ordination of Priests in The Christian Community

"The last three sacraments are like light shining in from the spiritual world."* With the sixth sacrament, Ordination into the priesthood, we are again dealing with an *involutionary event*, to which a corresponding *evolutionary event* is added. The involutionary experience belonging to the Last Anointing lies in death itself, through which an individual earthly incarnation, which has unfolded through four evolutionary stages, now collapses into itself completely. We must seek the involutionary experience, which belongs to ordination on the other side of the threshold. However, since there are no private spheres in the spiritual world, its significance is no longer merely individual, but is common to and concerns all human beings. It is a hidden and completely unconscious involutionary experience that concerns all people, in whatever stage of life or consciousness they find themselves. It amounts to a kind of anchoring in the spiritual world. No matter how much we may live on this side of the threshold, in this world of evolutionary experiences, a deeply unconscious connection to the spiritual world remains. We may

* CW 342, June 14, 1921

feel ourselves separated from that world or—perhaps as professing materialists—even think we are separated. Nevertheless, we are still connected even though the "umbilical cord to the spiritual-soul world has been cut."*

This is a far-reaching principle. Already in 1894 Rudolf Steiner expressed it in a completely different way in his book, *The Philosophy of Freedom:*

> We do not want to speculate about the interaction of nature and spirit, but we want to descend into the depths of our own being in order to find there those elements which we have saved in our escape from nature.†

Now what we can find "in the depths of our own being" is not our separation from the spiritual world, but rather our "escape from nature," and our unconscious connection to the spiritual world, which has been rescued from nature. With respect to Ordination to the priesthood, Steiner describes this involutionary experience as follows:

> If we were *completely* cut off from the spiritual, soul world, we could never find our way back. But it is an involutionary process of great depth, which is always present within us, a completely hidden process, even more hidden than what happens within us when we go through death with our physical organism; therefore it is a process that does not come to consciousness at all in the course of an individual's life.‡

The associated evolutionary process is, first of all—as with the Last Anointing—the sacrament itself. However, the sacrament does not by itself finish the process; all further

---

* CW 343, Oct. 2, 1921.
† CW 4, p. 34.
‡ CW 343, Oct. 2, 1921.

actions and deeds resulting from Ordination belong to it. Everything that an ordained person will do thereafter *as a priest* is an unfolding of their invisible relationship to the spiritual world. For this reason, the ancient name *bridge builder* (*pontifex*) is appropriate. However, a modern priest will not simply connect two separate worlds, for the connection today must be an active making-conscious of an existing relationship that lives deeply within our unconscious. It is the connection that we have "saved," that is, carried over into our earthly being.

For a contemporary church, however, the congregation must also be included at this point. It can be said that a congregation is only created through the work of a priest, but the reverse is also true: A priest can only work where a congregation *is already present*—on whatever level of reality. If, therefore, through Ordination to the priesthood and the stream of celebrated sacraments that results from it, an evolutionary process is created that corresponds to an involutionary process present through a subconscious connection with the spiritual world, then this is true not only for the priest. The congregation, in praying and co-celebrating with the priest, also creates and builds on this evolutionary process, adding an involutionary process to it. In this we are "not dealing with something individual; we are dealing with an interrelationship with the heavenly–spiritual. This is something that is present in every human being, although unconsciously."* "In every human being," means here also with every member of the church. Ordination to the priesthood can be understood as a modern initiation, as a beginning (*initium*), that starts with an individual person, but which then takes hold of the

* Ibid.

whole community. *Ordination adds the evolutionary process of the ritual stream to the involutionary process that is present both in the priest and in the community.*

This congregational involvement, which applies to every sacrament, has a special meaning in Ordination because *the inner structure of The Christian Community as a church* emerges in this sacrament. One moment in particular makes clear how the congregation helps to bring the priesthood into being—when the celebrant reads the ritual words from the pulpit that state that *the spirit of your community* has *acknowledged* these people as now having been ordained into the priesthood. It is still necessary, however, for the individual members of the community, each for themselves, to follow in this recognition. Without this recognition, priestly activity is not possible; it is altogether a prerequisite for the priesthood to be effective in the world.

It may seem unusual that the community should contribute so directly to the process of bringing the priesthood to life. While conscientiously preserving the spiritually essential elements of Ordination, this sacrament also brings to expression the role that a modern Christian must play in ritual. Yet there still remains the essential task of finding a social form appropriate for the spiritual structure of The Christian Community as a church.

Chapter 13
Sacrament of Marriage

13.1 Initial questions

The institution of marriage in Western societies today is in crisis, as seen in the ever-increasing divorce rate.* As a result, it is less and less common for children to grow up in an intact family. So many failed marriages lead to the question: What is this institution really based upon? What is its foundation in reality?

The superficial answer is simple, even banal. Because human beings incarnate in a one-sided way, either as male or female, they seek balance in members of the opposite sex. These personal inclinations are supplemented by an objective necessity that weaves together with personal longing: caring for offspring and for humanity's continued existence on earth. Throughout history, various forms of marriage have evolved around these two facts. Important questions have been answered in differing ways by various cultures: Is divorce possible? Is marriage for life or is it determined by external situations and therefore limited in time? Is marriage polygamous or monogamous? This was already the case when Christianity appeared with a new question: Is there something like a Christian marriage? Does it have a

* Compare Wolfgang Gaedeke, *Ehe, Sehnsucht–Idee–Wirklichkeit.*

specific form and its own content that would distinguish it from pagan—i.e., pre-Christian marriage?

From today's point of view the reality that gave rise to the development of marriage has changed. In the modern world (again one must say: in Western societies) the conviction that men and women have equal rights is firmly anchored. Of course, the path to the full reality of this idea has a very long way to go still. This represents great progress on the path to full liberation of individuals from the constraints of society. This has also led to the loss of almost all forms of mutual interaction between men and women that were previously customary and sustaining. This includes what was thought to be natural distinctions between masculine and feminine activities or professions. By and large, it is a principle of daily life that there be no distinction between masculine and feminine.

In recent decades we have seen an apparent contradiction to this fact in the vast flood of *psychological* literature dealing with the theme of what is specifically feminine and increasingly what is specifically masculine. These books are characterized by a treatment of what is specific to each sex, usually not in relation to the other sex, but centering on just one. Recognizing these specific traits serves the beneficial purpose of *self*-discovery.

A third fundamental change in modern consciousness refers to offspring. In today's biographies, especially those of women, children play only a subordinated role—at least statistically. At the same time, we see an archetypal experience fading away: the once almost universal experience that the man/woman relationship of *two people* implicitly contains a tendency toward a relationship between *three people* with the arrival of a child. The spiritual archetype of three can be described very well with Goethe's concept of "polarity and enhancement"* (we will go into this in more detail later).

The consequence of these transformations is an altered regard for opposite-sex relationships, which were previously possible almost exclusively within marriage. The aforementioned non-distinction between men and women in daily contact makes it more difficult to form a relationship with another person as a "you" experienced in the "I–you" polarity. Of course, there are many other possible ways to create an "I–you" relationship. Accordingly, the names for these relationships have changed from the traditional term *common law marriage* to simply "partnership" or "life partnership," which have the advantage of leaving open whether the two life partners are gender polar or not. Sexuality is still the least affected by this levelling of gender relations.† For this reason, its significance as a motive for partnership is often in the foreground and then often becomes the source of painful illusions. A relationship already grounded in itself can be strengthened by the power of sexuality, but a relationship based *merely* on sexuality can never endure in the long term.

So, it must be said that for modern people *the reality from which marriage once emerged* is beginning to retreat in all its essential elements and has in part already withdrawn. If marriage is to have any future at all, a reality from which it can emerge must first be found. In the following sections we will pursue this question. We cannot build on the *theology of marriage* as it has developed in the two previous

* In a letter of May 24, 1828, to the chancellor von Muller.

† One could ask the question, whether perhaps sexuality has nevertheless also been affected by it. In any case, the number of people who profess an ambivalent sexual orientation is increasing.

Christian millennia; there is too much discontinuity. However, in the area of *sacramental liturgy* we do find a bridge to the marriage ritual of The Christian Community. Here we find continuity.

13.2 The Emergence of Church Weddings

Early Christianity did not at first change anything essential in existing forms of marriage; they were simply continued, cleansed of their pagan elements (sacrifices to house gods, oracle questioning, etc.). There is no evidence in early Christianity for the existence of any marriage ceremony performed by priests or bishops. It limited itself to advice that the couple should not marry without the consent of the bishop and without their community's knowledge. The church invited the newlyweds to strengthen their marriage (*confirmare*) by offering sacrifices and celebrating Mass together; within the service the congregation asked for God's blessing for the couple. *The mutual consent (consensus) of bride and groom was regarded as the foundation of the marriage.* Until the Middle Ages, the declaration of consensus was carried out in the bride's house in the presence of the closest family members. It was an event that concerned the two families. Afterward they moved to the church, where the already concluded marriage was blessed. The actual marriage was not performed in public.

The development of a marriage ceremony performed by a priest in the name of the church was hindered by canon law. It recognized only marriage by consensual agreement. According to medieval sacramental doctrine, the spouses administered the sacrament to each other. A public church blessing was not necessary for a marriage to be valid. Thus, in the Middle Ages, so-called clandestine (secret) marriages appeared. Although unknown they were nevertheless valid according to canon law. As a result, the church soon demanded a *church wedding* and thus a public form of marriage. The declaration of consensus was no longer allowed to take place in the bride's house, but rather in view of the house of God (*in facie ecclesiae*) just outside the church door. It had to be delivered before an authorized priest and two or three witnesses. The Council of Trent* eventually made this form of marriage compulsory and created the *ecclesiastical wedding* in the strict sense.†

The form of a wedding ceremony is divided into two completely separate parts. The first part contains the consensus, the mutual yes-word, by which the marriage contract is concluded as a legal act and a marriage is established. This was a matter for the bride and groom (of course, at one time in the past, it was essentially a matter for the families). No church was necessary. Moving this act from the bride's house to the church door changed nothing about this in principle, except that the marriage was guaranteed the necessary publicity. The word of consent was now publicized *in the face of the church*. This event was an external fact but also constituted an inner truth. The second part of the ceremony takes place inside the church and adds the blessing (*benedictio nuptiarum intra missam*, bridal Mass). From the sixteenth century onward, however, the declaration of

* Council of Trent (Concilium Tridentinum), held between 1545 and 1563 in Trent (Trento in northern Italy), issued 17 dogmatic decrees covering then-disputed aspects of the Catholic Church.

† Today it is relatively easy for a bishop to dispense with this form of marriage if circumstances require—e.g., in the case of marriages involving two different religions, because the consensus of the spouses alone—not church ritual—is still considered the essential element for the creation of a marriage.

consensus was brought into the church, whereby these two parts come together to form an act performed before the altar—usually in conjunction with a Mass.

13.3 Reasons to Marry

At the beginning of every marriage emerges the question: Why are we marrying? In past centuries, the reasons for marriage were not usually personal and did not even involve individual affection. Instead, perspectives asserted by parents and a wider social circle determined who married whom. This was true not only for the nobility, but held also for wide swaths of society. Marriage was, at the same time, *marriage politics*. The story of Romeo and Juliet at the beginning of the modern era symbolizes a turning point in a couple's personal decision for each other. The decision was theirs, if necessary even against the interests of the families. Today (in Western cultures) this is normal; marriage has emancipated itself from family and other social influences.

However, very serious problems come with this very recently established freedom of choice. When the decision to marry was not only a personal matter then the reason for marrying was experienced as something objectively given—like a destiny coming from outside oneself. At the start of the marriage, although there may have been no personal affection, there was a kind of objective affection manifesting as the will to live together and work on a common task. For this reason, the couple could feel supported and carried by this for the rest of their lives. Personal affection usually, or at least often, arose and their will to live together could carry them even through personal difficulties, which of course also existed. Furthermore, the community in which they lived supported the marriage because it was jointly responsible for its coming into existence.

The question of why we should marry is completely different when the couple itself carries all the responsibility for the decision. What are my reasons for wanting to marry this particular person? Let us consider how a hypothetical case might unfold today. Let's say that Don and Mary wish to marry. Don's course of reasoning might sound like this*: I am looking for honesty and complete trust. I feel challenged and touched by this woman. There are many points where our worldviews and habits match, and we complement each other so well in our common need for domestic community, education, style and much more. What is important is that Mary is also outwardly an attractive woman to me. But of course, Mary's enormous ability to grasp and evaluate a situation correctly is a characteristic that makes her so fascinating to me as an individual. I experience her ability as an enormous enrichment of my life.

How might Mary look at Don? There are many things I like or even admire about Don. One small thing, but still important for me: I like how sensitively he plays the piano. I like his humor; I like the way he deals with other people. He is extremely helpful, he is not moody…there are always topics that Don is enthusiastic about. He can hold up and persevere through difficult times, and on the other hand, he can also let go when something is done or cannot be changed. This is a quality that I admire and that often helps me insofar as I often can't do this on my own.

Who could have produced so many varied thoughts concerning the basis for their marriage five hundred years ago?

* From notes written for the author by an engaged couple. *Names have been changed.*

In this sort of rationale, there is no sense of destiny at work—everything has become entirely personal; and yet only in this way can a couple take complete responsibility for their marriage decision today. In the past the reasons for marriage that came from outside the couple were reliable and stable. How will the feelings and observations described here develop in five, ten, twenty years? What will still apply then? And if they no longer apply, will the foundation of marriage have fallen away?

If we are consistent on this point, we must probably answer the question in the affirmative. By taking complete responsibility for our marriage, we must also be able to check after a certain period of time whether the reasons for the marriage are still valid; they may have ceased to apply in the meantime. For marriage to be regarded as a lifelong institution, we need completely objective reasons that go beyond our own personal desire to be married. Experience has so often shown personal reasons alone to be unreliable over time. But this is not a widely accepted truth today.

Thus, the question arises whether perhaps lifelong marriage has been superseded due to the evolution of cultural norms. Rudolf Steiner was once asked to comment on this question. His response was printed in an anthology together with those of other famous personalities.* In his reply, he rejected the view that the difficulties of marriage in his day were because marriage itself was no longer appropriate in the modern age. "The situation is more like this: in many areas the present age places people in a conflict between their individual, personal experience and the entire context in which they live. This conflict affects many relationships,

* Paungarten (Hrsg.), "Das Eheproblem im Spiegel unserer Zeit. Äußerungen bekannter Persönlichkeiten zu dieser Frage."

only one of which is the institution of marriage. The consequence for many marriages *does not depend upon the nature of the marriage* but upon many things that are external to this nature."

The entire social context is, however, the most important factor for marriage, because "through marriage, people place themselves into two of humanity's social contexts, different from each other yet each a wholeness unto itself. For this reason, in no way can people assume the right to make demands on marriage merely from a personal point of view."

This touches on a crucial point: In the modern era certain soul forces have helped us to become outwardly autonomous beings. Those forces have enabled us to free ourselves from the destiny-determining pressures of society. However, unless those same soul forces are developed further, they will never enable us to create communities, certainly not any community of life. A marriage simply cannot be conducted through the force of individualism alone. As a consequence, people will either withdraw inwardly and sacrifice a portion of their individuality for the sake of the marriage or they will feel the need to escape the *prison of marriage*.

This brings us to a new kind of community, in which the interests of an individual no longer need be sacrificed, a community compatible with human freedom. It is based on people who do not cease to strive for freedom even after they have attained external social autonomy. This new kind of community can only be created by people who are *on a path toward internal freedom and independence*; it is a freedom toward which no one can be enticed. The kind of marriage that emerged from the old form of community, and functioned as a part of that community, is no longer viable in a modern culture that does not support such marriages. Marriage of the future, which is found in, and based on, the qualities of *communities of the future* stands only at the beginning of its development. Today our day-to-day lives are a mixture of these elements. We continue to depend on the sustaining power of traditional communities and so we seek them out. We currently experience the external freedom and autonomy that is granted to us by modern society, and yet we know that this autonomy has yet to be transformed through hard inner work into inner freedom and autonomy. And then, in nascent seed form, there is the future "community of 'free spirits' of which we dream."* Marriage today is also a mixture of these elements. Its very nature is future oriented. *It is a community of free spirits that must constantly be grasped anew out of the future.* But it unfolds into present reality out of the future only if it is *wanted, i.e., consciously willed.* Then it can also become a sustaining community in the traditional sense, as well as a buttress, from which the spouses must (and should) again and again wrest their personal freedom anew.

So, what could be the reasons to marry today? There can actually be only the one ideal: to bring into reality something of this marriage of the future, if only in a very nascent form. In any case, the path to this ideal must first find its way through layers of personal feelings, intuitions, and desires. As in the preceding example, a couple must first try to explain to themselves how they account for their very personal motives, if possible, often and anew. Then the personal aspects recede and create space for marriage to be taken up as a supra-personal task.

* In a letter by Rudolf Steiner to Rosa Mayreder, Nov. 4, 1884 (CW 39).

What is marriage? What distinguishes a *marital* community from other two-person relationships such as friendship, professional partnership, life partnership, joint parenthood, etc.? The marriage liturgy of The Christian Community can serve as an essential source of theology to help us answer this question. Three elements can be identified in the marriage ritual, which together constitute the essence of a marriage. If one of these elements is missing, an important, perhaps even historic communal relationship can of course still exist, but we would not speak of a *marriage*.

13.4 Community of Life

The first element is called *community of life*. In European languages and probably in most languages of the world, the word for life has a double meaning. On the one hand, it means the temporal event between birth and death, the course of life. One can have a long or short life. On the other hand, one can be exhausted or refreshed, have more or less vitality, be *full of life* or not. These are two very different meanings of the word *life*. *Community of life* is probably most often understood from a biographical perspective. Two people live together, they walk a common path together through life. This is the external side of a community of life, visible to everyone.

The second meaning of *life* is the hidden side, but it is also the bedrock of marriage: the *etheric body* (also called *life body*) consists of the spiritual forces sustaining human life that become intimately interwoven when two people live together. The physical body is sharply delineated and enables us to be separate from our surroundings. The *life body*, made up of spiritual life forces, is not isolated in that way. These forces not only shape and sustain human life, they can also interweave and unite with those of another person. The fact of two people living together over the course of time creates a kind of *common etheric body, a third entity.*

Physically, two human beings are always distinct from each other. Therefore, the *bodily* reality of a marriage is found in this union of two life bodies that creates a fabric of interwoven etheric forces. The words from the Bible, "Therefore a man shall leave father and mother, and shall cleave to his wife, and they shall be one flesh" (Gen. 2:24) does not refer to the physical *flesh* but to a body of spiritual etheric forces. Thus, in marriage we have not only the etheric bodies of a man and a woman, but also the etheric body the two weave together, which is constantly growing and getting stronger. It could be called the *marital body.* If a marriage succeeds—in the sense that living together succeeds—one can occasionally perceive traces of this common marital body manifesting in their physical appearance. Some characteristics of their handwriting may become similar; in some ways they may even begin to look like one another. And if one of the spouses dies after decades of marriage, it is not uncommon for the other to die soon thereafter because he or she now lacks some of their common life forces.

With concepts provided by anthroposophy, we can describe what serves to create and develop this marital-body, what promotes its growth, and what burdens it. The experiences of day to day life are intimately connected with the flow of a person's life forces. This includes, for example, rhythm, habits, and the experiences inscribed in memory. Similarities in these areas strengthen common etheric forces. A further and important area is sexuality. It unfolds its deepest activity also in the area of etheric forces.* Its contribution to the common marital body is great, independently of the arrival of children. But here, too, everything depends upon a sense of community.† The couple should have a common view toward the *third*—i.e., an experience of the *we*, not just the *you* or *me*. Inasmuch as a common marital body can be strengthened, it is also vulnerable. If there are too few common experiences or if the rhythms of life are very different, this is a strain on a marriage, on the common etheric. And a correspondingly even greater injury can be caused by actions related to sexuality.

One can find the etheric realm of marriage appropriately symbolized by a plant. The laws of the etheric are visible in a special way in the plant kingdom. A plant is always subject to the laws of growth, even if there are pauses, or periods of no growth, and even if trees do not grow all the way to the sky. The same holds true in marriage (when, as we have said before, living together succeeds): it has a life-foundation that continues to grow—in different phases. There is no cause to say: this is enough, nothing is growing anymore. It is always growing—perhaps in an unexpected place and in a different form. Even an old tree continues to grow, but perhaps no longer adds to its height. In a similar way, this growth of the

* That today sexuality also—and apparently above all—appears in connection with the astral aspect of the human being, i.e., in the area of "drives, desires, passions" (Steiner, e.g., CW 11, p. 215), can be understood as a consequence of the luciferic intervention (the Fall into Sin).

† One might think that in the field of *sensual* love, common ground is a matter of course. But in reality, the opposite is the case. Sexuality may bring people together externally, but *by itself* it cannot lead them out of their inner alienation. It can even intensify a sense of estrangement if the other person is, in truth, an unloved object. It therefore needs the protective, nurturing context of a soul-filled community in order to unfold the forces that create and sustain a common marital-body.

common etheric body never comes to an end in marriage; it gains its strength from faithfully living together. Thus, the interweaving of life forces in marriage is not intended to end prematurely. From this perspective, lifelong marriage is still appropriate today. In Rudolf Steiner's words concerning marriage,* this idea is expressed in a different way, insofar as *Steiner does not mention time spans, such as "lifelong."* This expresses a temporal quantity that easily becomes an abstraction and may no longer be appropriate in concrete situations. It is simply impossible to account for every situation that might arise in human lives. He uses the word *stable* to express what he means in a more qualitative way. The society surrounding a marriage will have to "have an interest in the fact that a marriage...can be considered a stable relationship that can be counted on once it comes into existence." With an objective view of marriage, we almost feel compelled to "acknowledge the importance of stability, no matter how our personal interests may incline to other things."†

13.5 The Decision or Resolve

Many people form a community of life with another person without being married. For a marriage to exist, a second essential element must be added to community of life: *an actual resolve or decision to be married.* We move now from the bodily sphere of marriage, to the *"I"-sphere* where individual, personal resolve is essential. There is something very satisfying about every decision we make. It is as though, for a moment, we connect ourselves with the future as if we

* From a letter by Rudolf Steiner to Rosa Mayreder, Nov. 4, 1884 (CW 39).

† Ibid.

had already reached our goal. This is a typical activity of the *"I"*; from the present we can relate ourselves to the past (mentioned in our discussion of Sacramental Consultation), and, at the same time, establish a direct connection to the future. Only a being possessing an "I" can make a decision. But then, of course, the path into this future must actually be followed. The future, which shines into the decision, does not come toward us of its own accord; with our willing we must deliberately bring it about. The decision that leads us into the future through our will brings us to ourselves. For this reason, our will is weakened if we abandon the decision. But the will, as an expression of the power of the "I," is strengthened if we remain true to the decision. On a path of inner development, as Rudolf Steiner described it, there are conditions for esoteric training.

The fifth of these conditions is *steadfastness in following a decision once made*. Steiner says the following about this:

> Nothing should induce students to deviate from a resolution they may have made, save only the admission that they were in error. Every resolution is a force, and if this force does not produce an immediate effect at the point to which it was applied, nevertheless it works on in its own way. Success is only decisive when an action arises from desire. But all actions arising from desire are worthless in relation to higher worlds. It is only love for an action that is decisive. Everything that drives esoteric students to a particular action should be grounded in this love.... They will learn to sacrifice their actions, indeed their whole being, to the world, regardless of how the world may accept their sacrifice.*

* CW 10, p. 109.

Three motifs are important to us from Steiner's description: first, the caveat for later recognized errors of judgment in making a resolution, then the insignificance of outward success (such success is significant only with "actions arising from desire"), and finally the substance of love, in which the decision comes to expression and becomes a sacrifice. We can apply this directly to an understanding of the essence of marriage. In the sphere of the "I" we find love, sacrifice, and the willingness to forego the desire for external success to be the bedrock on which marriage rests. Love, therefore, does not belong primarily to the bodily sphere of marriage (community of life), but to the "I"-sphere, where decisions and resolves originate.

But what does the caveat for later recognized errors mean here? When marriages fail, those involved very often focus on the thought: I was mistaken. But Rudolf Steiner does not think that a subjective awareness of error is sufficient to abandon a decision. The fact alone that a resolve did not lead to obvious success does not mean that the decision was a mistake. Perhaps precisely then "steadfastness in following a decision once made" is called for. In any case, the decision refers to a specifically chosen future which connects a marriage beyond personal desire to a community. Any conclusion that an error was made could only come from such a supra-personal perspective. Otherwise, we are judging whether an error was made at the outset merely from a subjective perspective that belongs to actions arising from desire.

An important question for many people is whether a marriage is the result of karma. If that were the case we would not be free in our decision and would merely be fulfilling a destiny. There is even an old saying that *marriages are made in heaven*. If everything that comes to us from outside is seen as fate, then marriages in former times were indeed always destiny. Inasmuch as such marriages were subordinate to family or political influences, they certainly did have the character of fate. This changed, however, as the decision to marry gradually became more personal. Concerning human encounters, Rudolf Steiner spoke in a lecture* about karma coming from the past, which works within our subconscious, and future karma, which is created by our conscious actions. Karma we bring with us from the past is necessarily fulfilled precisely because it works entirely in the unconscious. We take our steps on earth blindly guided to where we meet our destiny. Generally speaking, if we were not blind in this regard, we would not be mature enough to voluntarily continue on a path leading to a difficult fate that we might see coming toward us. However, in actions guided by a full waking consciousness we are free. We can then create seeds of future destiny through our actions.

When two people meet, they have been led unawares to this meeting. But the moment they become aware that they are facing each other, this unconscious guidance comes to an end. What happens now is—as far as it happens consciously—a seed for future karma. But in everything that unconsciously continues to unfold between them, where they are not yet acting as free individuals, karma from the past continues to work. When two people meet, they are free in the moment but are then responsible for what grows out of that encounter. Marriage is only one of many possibilities. The sacrament of Marriage builds on this freedom. The

---

* CW 240, Jan. 25, 1924.

unconscious karmic forces that remain must then be processed. We do this by awakening step by step, a process that is nearly always painful. But through this inner work the experience of freedom in the relationship grows. With time the *yes* spoken in the sacrament becomes increasingly conscious. It can never be disappointed.

In concrete reality *nothing is truly either-or*. The *yes* is always a mixture of both elements, and this mixture is different in every human being. Perhaps the degree to which the *yes* is spoken in freedom is very small. Such a marriage is then entered into largely with forces from the past, that is, karma. The difficulties that arise and must be worked through are then also mostly from the past. Perhaps the opposite is the case: there is no unconscious necessity for two people to enter into a union. The marriage is then carried by a greater degree of freedom. In any case, the sacramental Marriage ceremony refers only to that part of the *yes* spoken in freedom. The unconscious part—even if it is much larger—is not taken into account.

The resolve expressed by the yes-word is only complete if it is made public. This follows from the fact that marriage is not a private matter. It is intimately connected to the essence of what community should be in the deepest sense. This fact justifies the Tridentine* demand that the declaration of consent between a bride and groom† should not take place in the private home of the bride, but publicly *in the face of the church*. What does that mean today? What is a *published decision*?

---

* Council of Trent (1545–1563) issued such dogmatic decrees covering disputed aspects of the Catholic Church.

† At that time, of course, consent did not yet have the significance attached to it here with the words *decision* or *resolve*.

In terms of the outside world, we could certainly imagine many ways of publishing it—through newspaper announcements, by proclamation in a public square, etc. Those who read or hear the message might consider it a truly imaginative approach, but it would not be understood as a reality. The publication must take place in a language understood by society, by the community in which it occurs, otherwise it would have no effect. The language understood by society will vary in different cultures. In Germany, this function is fulfilled by the registry office.* This is where the marriage decision is published in a form understandable to everyone *horizontally*, so to speak. Thus, it becomes a social and at the same time spiritual reality. A second, additional spiritual factor of marriage gives it a *vertical* dimension. This is the publication that occurs during the church ceremony when the couple stand before a priest who is celebrating the sacrament as a representative of Christ and the participating congregation. Thus, the formula of the Tridentine Council with its demand *in the face of the church* can be understood and affirmed today with a double meaning: *horizontal, worldly* (registry office) and *vertical, spiritual* (sacrament).

13.6 Man and Woman

The third element required to constitute a marriage is the fact that it is not just two people in general who marry, but a man and a woman. This may seem so obvious that we overlook the unusual nature of this fact.† Usually when

* In America, this function is most likely carried out by the county clerk's office and involve a marriage license.

† Even those who do not take it for granted that *marriage* refers to man and woman, but who would like to see it applied to same-sex

two people decide to marry today the actual personality of the other person plays a superficial role compared to the generic element, which so often proves to be the decisive factor. That is, the overriding factor is not necessarily the actual individual but the gender, i.e., the sex of the other person. Before a typical young man knows whom he will marry one day, he already knows that it will be a woman. And when he has found her, he sees first a *woman,* and then an individual human being. Is a human encounter of this kind, in which a generic aspect is most important, really appropriate for someone inclined toward freedom? Marriage is the only sacrament in which the tension between individual and typically generic aspects of a human being has become the content of the sacrament. After all, the generic aspects of a human being appear not only in one's sex, but also in everything that characterizes a person in a broader context, including language, people, ethnicity, life experiences (e.g., military veterans), professional contexts, church, and so on.

In his book *The Philosophy of Freedom,* Rudolf Steiner also dealt with this question of whether individuality is possible at all so long as the generic plays such an undeniable role in human relationships. His answer is unequivocal:

> If we experience it properly, what is humanly generic does not limit our freedom, nor should it be made to do so artificially. As human beings, we develop qualities and functions of our own, whose source can only be sought within ourselves. What is generic about us serves only as a medium through which we can

---

relationships as well, have a union in mind with regard to "marriage," in which the respective sex of the participants plays a decisive role and not the universal human.

> express our own distinct being. We use the characteristics nature gives us as a basis, and we give these the form that corresponds to our own being. We look in vain to the laws of the genus for an explanation of that being's actions. We are dealing with an individual, and individuals can be explained only individually. If a human being has achieved such emancipation from the generic, and we still want to explain everything about that person in generic terms, then we have no sense for what is individual.
>
> It is impossible to understand a human being fully if one bases one's judgment on a generic concept. We are most obstinate in judging according to type when it is a question of a person's sex. Man almost always sees in woman, and woman in man, too much of the general character of the other sex and too little of what is individual.[*]

According to this view, generic features form a foundation for individuality. Generic aspects even receive a unique imprint through the stamp given them by the individual. In any case, this is true for someone who has "achieved this emancipation from all that is generic." It is therefore not a matter of denying what is generic, but of freeing oneself from it so that it serves as a means to "a form appropriate to their own nature." To what extent the generic still dominates someone, or to what extent it serves them, will vary with every individual, for everyone is entitled to follow their own path. "No human is all genus; none is all individuality."[†]

Thus, it can be helpful for a married couple's mutual understanding for them to appreciate what is *typically masculine* and *typically feminine*. It can occasionally help in daily

---

* CW 4, *Intuitive Thinking as a Spiritual Path*, p. 226.

† Ibid., p. 229.

life to better distinguish the essential from the nonessential. However, we must bear in mind that it can be dangerous to psychologize a relationship using masculine/feminine distinctions. A relationship is only alive if the partners see each other in light of their future and not merely in view of what has already come to pass. Going into the future we should gradually free ourselves from the dominance of generic stereotypes by learning to perceive what extends beyond the generic and is individual in every person. Only in this way can we really do other people justice.

While the masculine/feminine duality can tempt us to abide by generic characteristics and neglect to perceive concrete individuals, it is also true that there *is* an archetypal masculine/feminine spiritual polarity. Beyond the personal this archetype leads us to a supra-personal objectivity. Paul was the first to speak of this supra-personal masculine/feminine dynamic. He described it as a central Christian mystery, even using the ancient Greek word *mysterion*, which is associated with ancient Greek mystery religions. In the earthly realm it can only be reflected at best. "Therefore man shall leave father and mother, and turn to his wife, and be joined to her. This mystery is great; but I say this with Christ and the church in view" (Eph. 5:31f). Paul sees in marriage something extending far beyond the earthly awareness of the couple. *It is a picture for the way in which Christ works in and with the church.* This picture reflects the archetype of the masculine initiating and leading, which is completed by the feminine reflecting and understanding.*

With this polarity in mind, a married couple can strive

* For a full discussion of the masculine/feminine archetypal polarity, see Michael Debus, *Mary and Sophia: The Feminine Element in the Spiritual Evolution of Humanity.*

over time to embody in their marriage the dynamic expressed by this objective archetype of Christ as the leader or, as Paul says, as the head of the congregation.* However, in modern human beings the archetype of masculine behavior is not inexorably attached to the husband, nor does the archetype of the feminine need to be continuously embodied by the woman, though they do frequently align with tradition. The legitimate demand for individual, autonomous growth today often calls for these archetypes to reside in the two sexes counterintuitively, perhaps for mere minutes, or for entire lifetimes. In any case, this archetypal polarity presides spiritually over all marriages.

In Steiner's discussion of the sacraments he refers to this masculine–feminine polarity from the point of view of evolution and involution. As we saw in our previous discussion, the Last Anointing was the first sacrament that brought an evolutionary rather than an involutionary contribution to the corresponding fact of life. The first four *earthly* sacraments were involutionary blessings. But with the Last Anointing, dying, as a fact of life, is itself a process of involution. We could say: all involutionary processes refer to the threshold between the living and the dead. Death is the vanishing point at the threshold, where all lines of life meet. When dying, everyone crosses the threshold individually. Strength to do so is given us by the Last Anointing as an added evolutionary blessing. Life beyond the threshold is possible most especially through the power of the Holy Spirit. Ordination to the priesthood is also associated with a process of involution, *a completely hidden process* beyond the threshold. This deeply unconscious connection links everyone to the spiritual world.

* Eph. 5:22.

The evolution associated with this connection becomes conscious in ritual actions as the ongoing Ordination into the priesthood. It is a movement from the spiritual world to the world of the senses and from the world of the senses into the spiritual world, just as Christ says of himself: "I went forth from the Father and came into the world; again I leave the world and go to the Father" (John 16:28).

In marriage the underlying involutionary gesture can only be found at an even deeper level of the spiritual world—we could even say at an even higher level—than in Ordination. The latter concerns our connection to the spiritual world. However, in an even higher world, opposites within the earthly world are superseded,* united, as it were. At that level, the physical world of the senses also appears very differently. It is no longer seen as completely *other* than and estranged from the spirit; it appears as an aspect, as a different manifestation of the spiritual world. This is the world of the Father God, who in the creed of The Christian Community is described as "an almighty divine being, physical, spiritual." He encompasses the world of opposites. The last three sacraments are "like light shining in from the spiritual world"—i.e., from the world of the Holy Spirit, the Son, and the Father.

The relationship between the spiritual and the physical world can appear within the world of the Father. It has an "image in the earthly" and "is naturally given in the relationship between man and woman.... When we refer to the masculine and feminine, we are pointing to a deeply hidden involutionary process."† Rudolf Steiner characterizes the dif-

* Nicolaus Cusanus (1401–1464) coined the term *coincidentia oppositorum,* the collapse of opposites, for the realm of the Father God.

† CW 343, Oct. 4, 1921.

ference between man and woman in such a way that both have an imperfection in the way they incarnate in their bodies: man too deeply, woman not deeply enough. But "what is only imperfectly present in man and woman" can be supplemented through the addition of an "external sacramental deed, which provides a corresponding evolutionary impulse."

The deeply hidden involutionary process—which corresponds in the world of God the Father to the relationship of the spiritual to the physical world—is reflected as the image of man/woman through the sacrament of Marriage. Through the wedding ceremony, the masculine and the feminine become archetypes of the most elevated kind, reaching far beyond the individual and pointing to a distant future when this polarity will once again be united into a higher unity. Thus, *in marriage, man and woman take on a task on behalf of all of humanity that is just as objective as the task of the priesthood.*

Such far-reaching perspectives give weight to the idea that marriage is not merely a personal matter but serves the world in an objective way. However, it would seem that those perspectives are a poor fit with the realities of daily married life. Actually, it is appropriate that the tension between the ideas expressed in a sacrament and the reality on earth is greatest in marriage. This aspect of marriage can also make it easier to understand why the marriage sacrament is the seventh and last of the sacraments. Of course, it is not necessary for the daily life of marriage to be burdened by such points of view; but they are a part of marriage's ever-present spiritual background and its accompanying social task.

We now have before us the three elements that constitute marriage: community of life; the decision or resolve is published (in a socially understandable language); a man and a woman. Thus, marriage appears as a reality of its own, as a spiritual entity that has its bodily nature in community of life and its I or ego in the resolve. It is the culmination of the man/woman polarity into a unity, which is continuously being born. This third element finds an earthly image in the child that is born out of the marriage. And like a child, this third element needs attention and care. Where the three constitutive elements come together, marriage is born. The sacramental ceremony does not directly create marriages; it is rather like the Baptism of a marriage connecting it with Christ, the source of all power to transform.

13.7 The Form of the Marriage Sacrament

One of the reasons why scholasticism already counted the wedding ceremony as last of the seven sacraments was the view that it was the *least spiritual* sacrament.* However, we have seen that it reaches farthest into the spiritual world, right into the sphere of the Father God. At one end of the sevenfold spectrum of sacraments is Baptism. Here the responsibility still lies entirely with the congregation, within which the child is borne. Step by step, the congregation's responsibility for initiating a sacrament recedes until, in the seventh, the Sacrament of Marriage, it is merely a witness to the event.† The responsibility clearly lies with those who

* Rudolf Frieling, *Die sieben Sakramente in der Geschichte der Christenheit*, Stuttgart 2001.

† *Witness* here is not meant to imply a passive role. By always maintaining a wakeful awareness of what they have perceived and therefore know for certain (namely, that each of the two spouses has actually spoken an unqualified yes), the Witnesses give them an important spiritual support to carry out their decision. However, they bear no responsibility for the realization of the decision.

are to be married, whose *yes* response *seals* and *blesses* community of life.

In the sacrament of Marriage as practiced in The Christian Community, the word *yes* spoken by the couple occurs at the beginning of the service. This location parallels the historical development of the wedding ceremony. The bridal couple's declaration of consent was formerly made *in the face of the church*, i.e., in front of and before entering the church. In The Christian Community, the word of consent is not spoken in front of the church but *before Christ*. In each of the sacraments Christ appears in a special way. In Sacramental Consultation he is the teacher, in Communion he is the physician. And at the very beginning of the marriage ceremony he is the one who *transforms earthly work into spiritual work through his own deed of sacrifice*. Thus a basic theme of marriage is heard; marriage is earthly work entirely. But it should not remain that way. What is done and suffered in marriage should be transformed so that it becomes an earthly image for a spiritual reality. Marriage should be a place of transformation; therefore, it is based on a willingness to make sacrifices. Thus, the first act of the marriage sees the priest speaking *in the name of Christ,* who always stands behind the *transformation of work of earth into work of spirit.*

The second act contains the question and yes-answer of the man and woman. The priest's question does not echo any traditional formulation of this essential question.* It

* One of the three possible forms of consent in today's Catholic rite is: [*Groom's name*] do you accept your bride [*name*] as your wife and do you promise to be faithful to her in good days and in bad, in health and in sickness, and to love, respect and honor her until death do you part? *Yes* is the answer of the bridegroom. Then he puts the ring on the bride with the words, "Wear this ring as a sign of love and faithfulness. In the name of the Father, the Son and the Holy Spirit." The bride then does the same.

addresses the bridal couple's entire fabric of destiny. The karma we bring with us from the past should be understood as something we have acknowledged and accepted while still in the spiritual world. In that world we understand it and have united, even to the point that it becomes our own decision, our own resolve. Karmic events that then befall us in the course of our lives are simply the earthly actualization of our prenatal resolutions.

In the depths of our soul we are always affirming our karma; we know that it benefits us and that we need it. We know there is no such thing as bad karma; all karma is good for us—though some karmic events may be more painful than others. Unaware, we always carry these prenatal resolves within us. We *walk* by means of them *in the world of spirit*. In any case, these unconscious decisions representing our past karma will necessarily become earthly reality. But it is important to know that marriage today is not one them; *marriage is no longer a fate that inexorably befalls us*; marriages are no longer made in heaven.

However, we can imagine that an earthly resolve is intended with such intensity and so deeply that it is taken up by the spiritual world *retroactively*, so to speak. Then it would have the same weight of necessity as a prenatal resolve; it becomes true destiny. This is what actually happens at a wedding ceremony in The Christian Community. The question asked of the bride and groom individually refers to these decisions that constitute karma ("Do you intend to take into those resolves with which you walk in the world of spirit..."). Their *yes* response indicates their willingness to adopt another such resolve, as if it had also been made before birth: the intention and decision to enter into a community of life with the other. In traditional language this means *to live together as husband and wife. Their yes response—spoken before Christ—transforms destiny.* From now on marriage *is* karma. However, in this moment they are not unconscious of their karma and, hence, are able to assume some control over it; awareness of the significance of their resolve means they have overcome the inevitability of karma. The karma of marriage is indeed still necessary, but we are not, as we are otherwise, unfree in following it. In the past, marriages were a portion of the necessary destiny we brought with us. Today they should consciously be transformed into an objective reality. One of the effects of the sacrament of marriage is this: marriage becomes a karmic fact created in full consciousness.

Then there is the question of divorce. What happens when a marriage that was begun with a sacrament ends in divorce? Is a second marriage possible? There is no simple answer, no spiritual law that provides answers to these questions. However, there are points of view allowing us to evaluate a situation. First of all, the intention and decision to live together in *community of life* as man and wife is absolute with no conditions attached; it has the character of an *only once* decision. A resolve of this nature cannot be made a second time. The only objective reason why a marriage cannot find its earthly realization—that is, that the *third element, the very being of the marriage,* has become impossible—would be that it has withdrawn. But that is impossible because *community of life* is based on the *intention of the decision.*

The forms available for a community of life encompass a wide spectrum. Deficits in one area of life can often be compensated for in another areas, at least for a time. However, an ongoing spatial separation made necessary by forces external to the marriage (e.g., because a spouse has been permanently institutionalized) would certainly make it just about impossible for most married people. Reasons leading to a marital separation are rarely as objective as such circumstances; they are nearly always of a personal nature. The spectrum of such reasons is diverse; there is rarely only one reason. At one end of the spectrum we find capitulation after a long struggle for the marriage and a feeling that one's strength is completely exhausted; at the other end we find rash superficiality and people simply not taking the marriage decision seriously. In any case, after divorce there will remain a residue of destiny that will have to be processed at some future time. How this residue manifests in life, what it entails, can vary enormously, but it remains attached to those involved.

When—after a divorce—a second marriage is in the offing, the question sometimes arises whether it is appropriate to celebrate the sacrament a second time. In such cases it is occasionally said that the sacrament should be *waived*. Just as one wishes that every newborn child be baptized, it certainly seems appropriate to wish that every marriage, once it becomes a reality (in the sense of the previously mentioned elements, i.e., after the civil marriage), be blessed by the sacrament. After all, we would never refuse to baptize a child simply because of circumstances leading to its birth.

Nevertheless, there is an aspect to be considered that comes with the ability to make resolves. Those who repeatedly report their resolves to others and then fail to live up to them lose their credibility. This loss of credibility begins with their first unrealized decision. As Rudolf Steiner once said: "A center for the strength of the 'I' is established through marriage. For this reason, what is supposed to flow into and strengthen the 'I' is weakened in those who destroy marriage."* Therefore, when people marry again, all those involved must consider carefully to what extent they still have the strength to make such a life-changing resolution. This kind of strength can also grow and manifest itself over the years in various ways. There is simply no universally applicable standard for evaluating such situations. Regardless of how one may approach a second sacramental Marriage, it is important to bear in mind that some kind of karmic remnant from a previous marriage remains as a task.

We now come to the third act of the marriage ceremony, which strikes a different note. The crucial question that requires *yes* as an answer is exactly the same for the man and woman. Each expresses his or her intention to take *community of life* into the resolves with which they advance in the spirit. Intentions can only come from an intender, that is, an "I." The human "I" is the deepest, most spiritual center of a human being; it is neither male nor female. It is a human being, an individuality speaking, completely independent of sex. Next, the two witnesses are addressed; their concern is that the resolve also finds its way into life. The marrying couple are seeking *the gate of community of life*. Here they appear differentiated as man and woman; the *spirit-will* of the man and the *soul–spirit* of the woman have joined together to form community of life. The witnesses to the marriage are given the task to always keep this alive in their hearts, to never lose awareness of the wedding couple's words. They are witnesses that the couple said *yes* and they reinforce and support the decision, especially in those moments when the

* CW 107, Nov. 16, 1908.

couple begins to lose sight of the fact that they did say *yes* to the union as it is actually lived in reality.

With the fourth act we have arrived at the center of the wedding ceremony, where the rings are exchanged. In the Middle Ages, there was only one ring. The groom put it on the bride's finger, thus obliging her to be faithful (not the other way around). The ring, worn on her hand, made it visible to all that she already belonged to someone. At the same time, however, the union implied that she was always acting *in his name* and her actions represented him. This ancient, originally pagan, custom of one-sided ring wearing was initially also used in Christian wedding ceremonies, even in some German dioceses until 1950, in Roman Catholic rituals even until the Second Vatican Council. At the same time, however, beginning in the eleventh century, a mutual exchange of rings became established in the Byzantine engagement rite, as well as in the *Mozarabic* (Spanish) wedding rite.* In Germany, it was not until the thirteenth century that a mutual obligation to remain faithful applied to both men and women. The first evidence of a mutual ring exchange dates back to the fourteenth century.

A further step is taken in the marriage ceremony of The Christian Community. Imagine the mutual exchange of rings in such a way that the ring is connected with *both the "I" and the life forces.* Then the symbol means that the spouses are offering these forces to each other and at the same time, receiving them. It sometimes happens that a woman, who has relinquished her own professional career for her husband's sake, exclaims bitterly, *I have sacrificed the best years of my life to you…*, and then points to the disappointing

* Adolf Adam, *Sinn und Gestalt der Sakramente*, p. 174f.

result. Perhaps such an arrangement led to a positive result, in which case the man says, *Everything I have become, I owe to you.* When two people are involved, these are negative and positive examples of sacrifice and receiving sacrifice, which are symbolized in the mutual exchange of rings.

The reality is quite different when marriage involves three elements. In the examples mentioned, we must ask the question: who can accept the burden of another person sacrificing the best years of their life for them? And as beautiful as gratitude is, what is actually being expressed when a person owes everything he or she has become to another? What dependencies are revealed here? In the wedding ceremony of The Christian Community the ring exchange does not involve the bride and groom putting their ring on each other's finger. *As a third party the priest places the rings.* The man and the woman give their rings to the priest. The rings are then blessed, whereupon the priest places the man's ring on the woman's ring finger and the woman's ring on the man's ring finger. This conveys the idea that sacrifices necessary in marriage should not be thought of as directly linked to the other, but to a third party. Of course, the third party in not the priest but the one in whose name he or she acts. One can also say that the third party is *the being of the marriage.* In this way, it would be more correct to say: *I have sacrificed the best years of my life to our marriage....* Although this sentence is only slightly different from the first, its quality, mood and feel are completely different.

A sacrifice given to an unworthy person can be pointless (in the New Testament this is referred to as throwing pearls before swine*), but it always makes sense to make a sacrifice

* "Do not give what is holy to dogs, and do not throw your pearls before swine, for they may trample them with feet and turn on you to tear you

for the marriage. The same applies to indebtedness; one could owe a great deal to one's marriage. The sacrifices marriage requires should be thought of as an offering directed toward the sphere of Christ. A spouse need not be burdened with this. This is the devotional aspect of the ring. The sacrifice is then transformed in the sphere of the Christ and can benefit the spouse in a manner appropriate for him or her; this means that the ring is received. This whole sequence is like a subtle process of sacrifice, transformation, and communion, which takes place in the *holy of holies* of marriage. Here male/female does not play a role—just human individuals at their highest level as we saw in the question addressing their resolve. Man and woman are again addressed equally at this point in the words of the sacrament.

The fifth act of the marriage ceremony leads again into the realm of life, where man and woman are differentiated and addressed accordingly. In a certain way, the wedding ceremony reaches its peak here. God is now mentioned for the first time in the service. Everything up to that point was merely human action. *A spirit of God* looks at what is happening in the wedding ceremony. The duality now definitely becomes a trinity. The substance of love is implanted in the marriage at this point in the ceremony, indeed, without even being named. Actually the word *love* is not mentioned anywhere in the ceremony.

In his mystery dramas, Rudolf Steiner characterized the essence of love: "Love should bind separated beings, / But should not want to kill their peculiarities." What follows in the ritual speaks of binding together now what had been apart. At the same time, a symbol is held aloft for all to

---

apart" (Matt. 7:6).

see: two sticks tied together in a flat cross*; they are not in parallel, a symbol which would mean the loss of peculiarities. Each stick has its own direction—but at the point of intersection are they bound together. This binding does not create a new static condition, but rather a process: the parts that were separate are not simply brought together; *they are united in their uniting,* showing that *marriage is a process and not merely a state of being.* How the spouses relate to one another as man and woman is illuminated here by the substance of love.

The spiritual level is even higher here than in the third act of marriage, where the witnesses receive their task to support in a living way the bride and groom who, as man and woman, seek the gate of community of life. We have said above: through the marriage ceremony, the masculine and the feminine become sublime spiritual archetypes, reaching far beyond the individuals involved. They point to a distant future when this polarity will once again be brought together into a higher unity. Thus, in marriage, man and woman assume a task on behalf of all of humanity; an objective task extending beyond their personal lives. We have arrived at the point where marriage itself becomes the archetype and the task is expressed. The words of the ceremony do not refer to how the couple chooses to conduct their life together. They convey "in the earthly an archetypal image that displays in the earthly the relationship between the spiritual-soul world and the physical world of the body."† This relationship is a very hidden process of involution. It would be wrong to

* This is also known as the Andreas Cross; it is used as a symbol for warning signs at railroad crossings.

† CW 343, Oct. 2, 1921.

attempt to derive any behavioral norms from it.* Words are now spoken telling the man to *shine before* the woman in the light of Christ, and the woman is told to *follow*...the man in the light of Christ. *But these words use the man as a symbol for the spiritual world and the woman as a symbol for the earthly world of the senses, the physical world.* Here an archetype is shining through the ritual. The words are *in no way intended to prescribe* the proper behavior of a married couple; they say nothing concerning what the personal relationship between the spouses should be. From the spiritual world into the physical, the Redeemer *follows* fallen humanity. Accordingly, John the Baptist, who represents fallen humanity, *goes before* and prepares the way for the Redeemer.† With time this archetype reflecting the relationship between the spiritual world and earthly world can shine down onto earthly marriages. As couples live in the light of the resurrected one, the Christ, this archetype will find its earthly image as well as a future in which these two worlds will shine forth reunited.

---

* TRANSLATOR'S ADDITION: The masculine and feminine characteristics that are archetypal and not merely artefacts of culture reside in both men and women interchangeably. Men may well display feminine behavior and women can certainly display masculine behavior as occasion may require it—in life altogether and especially in a marriage. Naturally, when the ritual words express the archetypal feminine gesture, the woman is addressed; and likewise, the priest turns to the man when speaking about the archetypal masculine gesture. It is important to bear in mind, however, that the words *"shine before her*...and *follow him"* as they appear in this sacrament are not prescribing marital conduct but reflecting the overarching dynamic of the masculine–feminine polarity, which will constantly be at play in a marriage, regardless of which spouse embodies the masculine or feminine.

† As Rudolf Steiner explains, Michael the Archangel and Christ also stand in a relationship of *going before and following after.* "In a sense, Michael *goes ahead* carrying the light of spiritual knowledge, while Christ *follows* behind him carrying the demand for general human love (CW 218, Nov. 19, 1922).

The sixth and the seventh acts of the marriage ceremony are retrospective and prospective. They contain a blessing that flows from the trinitarian God and is meant to fill the couple's earthly thinking, earthly feeling and earthly willing. It is essentially a prayer that the destiny created in and by the resolve to marry be fulfilled. Like the priesthood, marriage, if understood correctly, is also a ministry. The priesthood refers to the church of Christ, the marriage ministry refers to humanity.

After twenty-five years and again after fifty, the marriage ceremony can be repeated. This silver or golden wedding ceremony is not thought of as a renewal—as if the power of the marriage ceremony lasted only twenty-five years—but is in fact a repetition. After having been spoken daily, privately, over nine thousand times in twenty-five years, the same yes-word is spoken again publicly. It sounds different now, like water enriched with mineral salts while flowing underground before coming to the surface as a healing spring. The daily *yes* in marriage can thus be heard publicly three times in the course of fifty years.

PART IV:
RENEWED SACRAMENTALISM

Chapter 14
Sacramental Theology for a Modern and Future World

14.1 Summary

After our detailed discussion of the seven sacraments, we now once again consider the question of sacraments altogether.

Augustine ascertained two crucial aspects of a sacrament, which also applies to sacraments in The Christian Community. They are *visible signs of an invisible grace* and they are *signs whose fulfillment brings about what is designated.*

Ignatius of Antioch calls Communion the *medicine of immortality*. In The Christian Community it is accordingly called the *medicine that makes whole* (for the sickness of sin).

We have discussed the *intention* with which a sacrament is celebrated. Today, a priest should not, as in the Middle Ages, have the intention to "do what the church does," but should have a *personal* intention, albeit not an arbitrary one. In an age when the Spirits of Personality are the guiding force at work in human beings, it is necessary for the celebration of sacraments to be carried out by priests whose personal intentions stand behind their prayers.

Finally, we have brought forth a point of view that sees

the sacraments as part of a *sevenfold organism*. This sevenfold aspect seems to have come about in the Middle Ages more as a result of chance than from a satisfactory theological explication (apart from the attempt made by Thomas Aquinas). As we have seen, the most significant events in human life can be seen as processes of *evolution and involution*, and by thus using an all-encompassing understanding of evolution, it proved possible to account for the sevenfold nature of the sacraments.

14.2 The Act of Consecration of Man in Relation to the Other Sacraments

In Scholasticism the essence of the sacraments was seen as having three aspects (see section 5.2): the actions of the ritual, its objective effect, and its fruitfulness in life (the actual grace). The objective effect, the middle aspect, was called *res et sacramentum*. It is to be found in the person receiving a sacrament. In the three sacraments that cannot be repeated—Baptism, Confirmation, and Ordination—Catholic theology speaks of a seal (*character indelebilis*) that is indelibly imprinted on the human soul. There is no corresponding description of an indelible objective effect in the other sacraments (Confession, Anointing the sick, Marriage), which are not inherently once in a lifetime. All six of these sacraments are called *casual services* (*casualies*), because they take place only from case to case (*casus*), connected to individual destinies.

Already in Scholasticism the objective effects of the Mass were described quite differently: "In the Eucharist *res et sacramentum* is the real presence of the Body and Blood of Christ" (see section 5.2.2, Sacramental Reality). What represents transformation of the human being (as an *objective effect*) in the six casual services is seen as the transformation of bread and wine in the Act of Consecration of Man. However, in the six casual services the substance that is transformed is the human being. In the Act of Consecration of Man this substance is bread and wine at the altar, where what is otherwise hidden in human beings becomes visible. "Through transubstantiation, what actually takes place in the deepest human interior is brought forth into the external world."*

On this basis, we can say that in terms of the inner process (not necessarily in its external form), there is a certain parallelism between casual services and the two parts of the Act of Consecration of Man preceding the transubstantiation. In the Act of Consecration of Man, the Gospel Reading and the Offering precede the transformation. These elements can also be found in the casual services, which would require a separate discussion. Just as one can say at the end of the consecration: in the bread the body of Christ *is* present and in the wine his blood, so one can say at the end of the other sacraments, e.g., Baptism: Clara *is* baptized. An objective reality has been created. Through her actions in the course of her life Clara must *show* herself to have been baptized; only then is the sacrament complete. It is not enough to leave the church baptized (or confirmed, etc.)—*the life that follows is an integral part of the sacrament.*

In the Act of Consecration of Man, the life that follows corresponds to the fourth part, to Communion. Here the book is on the right side of the altar, now signifying that the service is carried by the congregation's inner activity. Then the moment comes when the congregation rises, comes forward and receives Communion at the altar. This is also a profound

* CW 343, Sept. 27, 1921f.

image for the "fourth part" of casual services, which must no longer take place in the church, but in life itself. The full grace of the sacrament is received then as Communion in the midst of life through an individual's activity of continuously lifting oneself to a higher level. A sacrament cannot develop its full effectiveness without this continuous inner activity. Then the altar, the place where we raise ourselves to a higher level in daily life, is the true center of our being, our *sanctum sanctorum*, the inner holy of holies: "It is very telling that Jean Paul describes becoming aware of his 'I' as 'an incident…veiled in [the] human holiest of holies,' because we are each totally alone with our own 'I.' This 'I' is the self of each human being."*

In this inner Holy of Holies, Communion can take place, the union of our essential being with Christ. In the mysticism of Paul this means: "I live, but not I, but Christ lives in me" (Gal. 2:20). In this innermost center we can find our true goals in life as *communion*. Conversely, in the Act of Consecration of Man, Communion can serve as an inner stimulus to carry the fourth part of the sacraments (Baptism, Confirmation, Marriage, etc.) in daily life. We strive toward the moment when we begin to prove ourselves baptized, confirmed, married, and so on.

An ordering of the seven sacraments results from this perspective that is comparable to the heliocentric picture of the planetary system. The sun is in the center while all the planets receive their light from it. In this way the six sacraments are also illuminated as casual services. They are brought into a whole by the Act of Consecration of Man, our Mass, which stands at its center as the proto-sacrament.

* CW 9, *Theosophy*, p. 49.

This is an entirely different sequential ordering of the sacraments, although already established in Scholasticism. And it makes sense, seen from the crucial perspective of evolutionary development. There are numbers and numerical relationships, which seem to hold sway over earthly events. Cycles of development are structured according to the number seven. This applies to the largest evolutionary cycle, the cosmic evolution of the earth in seven planetary stages—as well as to the small cycle of the week with its seven days. Thus, the sevenfold nature of the sacraments also represents such a cycle of development encompassing earthly and cosmic human biography: four sacraments are *earthly*, three sacraments are *like the spiritual world shining in (on life)*.*

One could also say: Four sacraments refer to what has already become (evolution) and three to what the flow of time is bringing us from the future (involution). We would now also expect the overarching laws of evolution to be reflected in the seven sacraments. That would mean that the stages of cosmic evolution described by Rudolf Steiner are to be found in the individual sacraments. The first stage (*old Saturn*) would correspond to Baptism, the second stage (*old Sun*) to the Sunday Service for Children and Confirmation, the third stage (*old Moon*) to the Act of Consecration of Man, and so forth.

Rudolf Steiner described in a lecture† how these cosmic stages of development are also reflected in human lives—the Saturn stage in the first seven-year period, the Sun stage in the second seven-year period, and so forth. In discussing individual sacraments, we have already connected the four *earthly* sacraments to the first four seven-year periods of

* CW 342, June 14, 1921.

† CW 96, March 4, 1907.

human biography. Now we can point out that cosmic evolution is also reflected in them. We can deepen this essential perspective with a discussion of one particular detail.

In the lecture on biography mentioned, Steiner says that during the third seven-year period (14 to 21), corresponding to the Moon-stage development, an individual's astral body is released and soul-forces appear. These forces need to be purified, or they must be discarded. "Something emerges that sometimes must really be treated like the slag or dross from the Moon; indeed, some things must be cast out, as it happened with the Moon." If this does not happen or is unsuccessful, disturbances can occur, even illnesses (e.g., *dementia praecox*), because the astral body's relationship to the etheric body is not as it should be. "The astral body is sometimes very clever, but the way the astral body should relate to the etheric body is in disorder."

Rudolf Steiner says something similar concerning the relationship of an individual's soul and spiritual nature to the physical, bodily nature when discussing the third sacrament, albeit from a different angle. Here, too, we are dealing with the delicate relationship between astral and etheric bodies. This is connected to the fact that, during the third seven-year cycle, "human beings... are continuously in a kind of state of vibration, returning to the spiritual soul, then re-immersing in the physical body, so that they are in a rhythm, whereby they are threatened either to lose themselves ecstatically in their spiritual soul nature or to sink into their animalistic nature, completely down into the body. Individuals need something that opposes this evolutionary process as an involutionary process, and this involutionary process consists of receiving Holy Communion."*

* CW 343, Oct. 2, 1921f.

Thus we can say: The third universal evolutionary stage corresponds to the following three events: one, *old Moon* development in the cosmos; two, the third seven-year stage in human biography; and three, the Lord's Supper in the succession of the sacraments, Holy Communion helps to overcome the soul, psychological challenges that begin in the third seven-year period and continue throughout life.

In this sequential order of the seven sacraments, the Act of Consecration of Man is not in the center (the fourth stage), but is the sacrament of Consultation, which belongs in the center as the "I" sacrament. This sequential ordering has provided the foundation for our discussion of the individual sacraments. One must employ this order to understand the sacraments in their relationship *to human individuals*. However, the experience of the sacraments *in the life of a congregation* is based on the other ordering (that of the solar system), in which the Act of Consecration is like the Sun at the center of the sacraments.

14.3 The Effects of the Sacraments

Scholasticism saw many theologians attempting to understand the effects of the sacraments. We will now examine this question from the perspective of the anthroposophical understanding of the human being. A fruitful starting point is the threefold structure of the sacrament described in Scholasticism. The first aspect (*sacramentum tantum*) is the act of worship as such, as performed by the priest. It is a visual deed consisting of what is shown, spoken, and actually done (*Deiknymena, Legomena, Dromena*). Pictures, also imagined images, always have a stimulating effect on the etheric body, described often by Steiner.* They follow the path from consciousness into life, from the astral body into the etheric body. This is intensified when religious images are involved, because religious themes also have a direct effect on the etheric body.† In ritual itself, the religious and the pictorial aspects are the underlying elements, whereby the etheric body is powerfully influenced. This influence works to bring about a transformation, a spiritualization of a human being's Life Spirit,‡ which otherwise happens only on an esoteric path of individual training. We can therefore say that the act of worship itself, the first aspect of the sacrament, has an effect on the etheric body of the person and thereby stimulates a process of transformation, which leads to the spiritual world.

The third aspect (the second aspect will be discussed later) of the sacrament (*res tantum*), is the actual grace ("Clara shows herself to have been baptized"). It refers primarily to another, different, aspect of a human being. The Luciferian infection that caused the Fall of Man took place in the astral body. In the Garden of Eden this part of the human being was still very pure, mirroring the world in its objective truth, but it became self-oriented and self-referential through Lucifer's

---

* "We are to think as much as possible in pictures. This affects the etheric body" (CW 266/3, Nov. 6, 1905).

† "...his religious experiences and many other experiences imprint themselves on the etheric body and transform it into life spirit" (CW 13, p. 75). "But nothing can replace religious education. The images of the supernatural imprint themselves deeply into the etheric body.... All religious conceptions must become pictorial conceptions" (CW 97, Jan. 12,1907).

‡ "But with symbols, with sacramentalism, the act of worship, one works more deeply into a human being, right into the etheric body" (CW 167, May 9, 1916). This remark, however, is found in a context by which Rudolf Steiner deals with the abuse of symbols and so on. Concerning *Life Spirit,* see Steiner's account in his book *Theosophy* (CW 9), chap. 1, "The Essential Nature of the Human Being."

temptation. The astral body became covetous, always wanting more, which made it vulnerable to error. This covetousness shows itself in the story of the woman who is open to the Luciferian temptation in the Garden: "Then the woman saw that it would be delicious to eat from the tree, that the tree was a feast for the eyes and the tree was desirable for gaining wisdom" (Gen. 3:6). This selfishness separated the astral body from its surroundings, thereby initiating the Fall into sin. The human being was sundered from paradise, from a direct perception of truth.*

The Fall has been an ongoing process also affecting the other "bodies" (etheric, physical, and "I") of the human being. Its last stage, the *intellectual Fall*, is especially evident in today's materialist, scientific way of thinking.† In paradise, the human being had not yet fully arrived at selfhood. Humans already had the lower members of their being, the physical, etheric, and astral bodies, but did not yet truly possess an "I." Only "I"-beings, however, can take full responsibility for their actions.

We have already quoted Lessing, who expressed the thought that before the fall of man, he was not yet master of his actions and therefore could not follow moral laws.‡ Rudolf Steiner extends this thought by including the bodily members of the human being:

> The seduction of Lucifer, this temptation of Lucifer falls precisely at the time when the human being was just about to receive his "I," i.e., his ego. It is, then, a human form of behavior that lies before our present stage of

* Although the words sin and sunder are not etymologically connected, they are in their meaning nevertheless very closely related.

† Cf. Steiner *Awake! For the Sake of the Future* (CW 220).

‡ *The Education of the Human Race,* no. 74.

> "I"-development. However, it has cast its shadow onto humanity's entire ego-development. Who, then, has actually become a sinner? Insofar as the human being does not yet possess an "I," we cannot say he has become a sinner—at least not fully. Through Lucifer the human being became a sinner with that part of his nature, with which he can basically no longer become a sinner today—for today he does possess his "I." At that time, then, man became a sinner *with his astral body*.... It is therefore a deed of pre-ego development. It is a quite different deed from all the deeds that man has been able to do, once his ego had even just barely begun to enter his being.*

Thus, through the Fall, we have become guilty in a sense—innocently guilty, but we nevertheless must bear the consequences. It is not a guilt for which we can atone and balance our debt by our own efforts; we need help that can only come to us as grace, through Christ. Steiner expresses this:

> Through Christ's presence on earth, strength comes to us to ascend again, even without merit, just as the sickness of sin came to us without our guilt. For neither involve the personal element of a human being, in which the "I" lives, but with what precedes and follows the "I".... The human being made his astral body worse through original sin, and likewise can make it better again through the Christ impulse. This is the equivalent; this is what is truly called grace."†

Thus, grace makes it possible to transform the astral body, even though it has become worse due to the Fall. Transforming the astral body means to acquire discipline and master *oneself*. The fact that we with our weak ego forces have any

* CW 127, May 3, 1911.

† Ibid.

prospect at all of making progress is due to the grace of Christ, who, in words from the Act of Consecration, "strengthens human wills." *He strengthens the will but does not replace it; he builds on our efforts.*[*] As the work of transformation takes place in our astral body, the first seed of our higher self, Spirit-Self, gradually emerges.

Although we must constantly live under the influence of our untransformed astral body, which has the tendency to separate us from the world through selfishness, we nevertheless gain through Spirit-Self the spiritual strength to connect with other people without losing our individuality. We can create new communities of the kind discussed in section 7.1 on Infant Baptism. The apostles, filled with the Holy Spirit, created the first such community on the morning of Pentecost. It is fair to say that the Pentecostal flames *resting*[†] upon the heads of the apostles were not only a sign of the Holy Spirit's presence, but also a sign that the power of the Spirit-Self was beginning to work in the apostles. In this way they also received the strength to perform entirely new deeds in the name of Christ. In this, we have an image of the third aspect of the sacrament, the actual sacramental grace (*res tantum*). When it begins to take effect, when we begin to *show* ourselves to be those who have received a sacrament, a Pentecostal moment enters into our lives: sacramental grace shows itself to be a gift of the Holy Spirit.[‡] It does not come on its own—it comes to meet our striving, yet we cannot predict

---

* It should be superfluous to emphasize here once again that this concept has nothing to do with self-redemption. It is not *we* who redeem ourselves, but through our efforts we contribute to the work of redemption that has become possible through Christ.

† "And there appeared to them tongues as of fire, resting above the head of every one of them" (Acts 2:3).

‡ In the Eastern Church, the seven sacraments are understood as the seven gifts of the Holy Spirit; cf. sect. 5.1, "Why Seven Sacraments."

when and how it will manifest. Likewise, Pentecostal flames were experienced only by those disciples who were prepared, and yet it was undoubtedly an unforeseeable event for them.

How can we understand the second aspect of the sacrament, the objective effect (*res et sacramentum*) of sacramental action (Clara *is* baptized)? What we have described for the wedding ceremony applies to all sacraments: the actual objective effect lies in a transformation of destiny. The sacraments add something to the karma already at work in our lives. They have consequences in our present life, not only in the future, as is the case for other deeds. St. Augustine called this effect of a sacrament a *seal* and attempted to understand it using the concept of a sacramental mark (*character*). The image of a *seal* was taken from the military world of Roman times: a soldier was branded with a *seal* and thus became a *member* of the military and, at the same time, incurred an obligation to serve. This suggests that sacraments bring both new karmic possibilities as well as new tasks. In section 9.3 we have seen that the power at work in the Act of Consecration during the transformation is also at work in transforming and shaping karma. All the other sacraments proceed, so to speak, to a point corresponding to the third part of the Act of Consecration of Man—i.e., the transubstantiation, where the karma-transforming and karma-forming forces unfold. However, the tasks resulting from these forces must then be faced and fulfilled in life. At the end of each sacrament these tasks are spoken. When taken hold of, they are the path on which sacramental grace comes to meet us; we are then not only baptized (confirmed, married, etc.), but also begin to *show* that we have been baptized (confirmed, married, etc.).

A sacrament's objective effects are, therefore, spiritual,

and yet manifest on earth in the realm of our personal karma. They correspond to subtle effects in the human constitution. When a sacrament is performed with conscious intent the resulting blessing can manifest as a new task in life. This happens because the conscious prayer occurring in the sacrament is taking place in our astral body, the vehicle of consciousness. The objective spiritual effects of our conscious prayer imprint and transform the etheric body, i.e., our *life* body and therefore *life itself*. The essence of this process is the transition from consciousness into life. At this point freedom and necessity coincide. What first arose in human consciousness in the sacrament and should now pass over into life itself does not remain an abstract task but becomes an element of our human constitution. We could paradoxically say that a task has been woven into our individual human constitution having the character of *a necessity that leaves us free*. This is the nature of Christ, who, in order to leave us completely free, shields our "I," while at the same time sternly directing his gaze at cosmic necessities. This is the Christ of the Apocalypse, the Christ of consequences. It may not be surprising, therefore, that Rudolf Steiner connects this critical location in human beings, where the astral body interacts with the etheric, where the transition from consciousness to life occurs, with our experience of Christ. Anthroposophy "approaches the Christ problem by bringing to life the concept of the etheric body and the astral body, and in turn what results from their interaction. You see, by discovering, as it were, the Christ experience at the boundary between the astral and etheric bodies, you must consider the Christ experience in a positive way." Appropriate Christian worship can lead to this experience, for it is to be understood out of an "insight into the interaction taking place between what is experienced in the astral body and what is experienced in the etheric body."* We can therefore imagine that at this point the objective effect of the sacrament delicately touches the composition of the human being's bodily nature.

This becomes clear at a certain place within the Ordination. The objective aspect of priestly work is expressed when it is said that what the priest performs *in sign is to be done in spirit*, i.e., what is visibly taking place is also occurring in spirit. This *priestly* work can be spoken of because at that moment the candidate is given the stole as a symbol or sign of his or her priestly dignity. The stole plays an important role in the array of priestly garments, signifying that the person wearing it is a priest. *It is worn between the white Alba symbolizing the etheric body, and the chasuble (in the color of the festival), which symbolizes the astral body.* Steiner said: "the stole indicates the link between the astral and etheric bodies."† Rituals carried out by a priest thus emanate from this *in between place* within the human being. In sacraments, Christ connects with this place in human beings in an objective way and thus places them within "a necessity that leaves them free." This new situation thus created can perhaps be best characterized by the word *disposition*.‡ The objective effect of a sacrament is seen in the presence of an inner disposition, which nevertheless leaves us free to take up the task connected to the sacrament. We can then follow the path on which grace comes to meet us. It is the grace that God has planned for

* CW 343, Sept. 28, 1921, morning.

† CW 343, Oct. 6, 1921 morning.

‡ In Scholastic theology the term *exigitive disposition* was coined—i.e., a "favorable" disposition.

us as a gift of the Holy Spirit, and which we experience as the beginning of the Spirit Self's awakening.

Perspectives for the threefold effect of a sacrament have thus emerged: The conscious act of worship itself has a strong beneficial effect on the etheric body and stimulates its transformation. A second—objective and lasting—effect of the sacrament takes place in human karma and finds its expression in the human constitution. Our bodily nature is altered at the border between the astral and etheric bodies, where an experience of Christ is to be sought. A third effect is connected with the activity of those who receive the sacrament. It is seen when we take up our tasks and receive a gift from the Holy Spirit connected with the transformation—or redemption—of the astral body. The Trinity holds sway in these three effects of the sacrament.

14.4 Church and Community

Finally, we have yet to discuss a concept from scholasticism that many contemporary Catholic theologians would rather do without, and therefore relativize as much as possible. It is the term *ex opere operato*, the idea that a sacrament is effective "by virtue of its execution." This means that if the matter, form, and intention are right then the sacrament actually "works"—conveying blessings—regardless of the external or moral condition of the priest or of the person receiving the sacrament. The crucial question behind this concerns the objectivity of the sacraments. This is also a central question for The Christian Community.

After Baptism in The Christian Community, if one could not be sure that a child is actually baptized or, after a marriage ceremony, that the marriage is actually sacramentally blessed, or whether the Act of Consecration of Man actually blessed anyone, then a healthy congregation could not come into existence. Does the spiritual reality of the sacraments always depend on the celebrating priest? If so, then people would only flock around priests whom they trusted to perform the sacraments in a valid manner, while others might disagree with that assessment for merely personal reasons. And although today the personal gifts of individual priests do play a legitimate role, the *church* which is to represent the Kingdom of Christ can only be founded on the suprapersonal. But we must not let this fact lead us into *ex opere operato*, the notion that the validity of a priest's sacramental celebration is completely *impersonal*.

In The Christian Community, everything that concerns ritual celebrations is grounded in the community. The covenant with God, from which the rituals of The Christian Community also originate, does not refer to an individual person, as in the time of Noah (Gen. 6:18) or Abraham (Gen. 17:2ff), but rather to a community that Steiner called the proto-community or proto-congregation. The spiritual justification for carrying these new sacraments and rituals into the world (or carrying them into congregations where they can influence society) does not derive from an individual but from the community of priests. From this proto-community individuals are commissioned and sent forth to their congregations. In our time such a community cannot obligate its members to a specific world view.* Modern human beings cannot be required to adhere to a certain dogma; they must be free to pursue the truth. We must be free to recognize as truth only what we can understand or (in faith) experience.

* Of course, this also holds true for anthroposophy.

The same is not true with respect to the will. People may want very different things. It must therefore be clear that those who found such a proto-community are wanting (are willing) the same thing—a community that sustains the life of ritual. The archetype for this proto-community is the circle of apostles.

There are essentially three elements of will that matter here: In their deeds, the apostles brought the kingdom of Christ, which is not of this world (John 18:36), effectively into the world. Similarly, today's servants of ritual cannot derive their impulses for action from the earthly; ultimately their initiative must come from the spiritual world. Secondly, the apostles sought to understand what they had experienced during the three years with Christ. This happened during the forty days from Easter Sunday to Ascension when the Risen One taught them, as with the disciples on the way to Emmaus (Luke 24:13ff).* At Pentecost came the great influx of knowledge. Today's priests will also strive for this goal: to also understand more and more deeply what they believe because they have *experienced* Christ in their hearts. This is a very individual path of knowledge. It differs from the anthroposophic path of knowledge in that it is not without assumptions, for the goal of knowledge is already given *in faith*, as inner experience. The third element of will is the willingness to work continuously on oneself and to follow an inner path. This applies today in a special way even more so than during apostolic times. The apostles could still feel themselves carried day by day by the reality of the spirit. We find a reference to training, for example, in what Paul wrote to his disciple Timothy, who was a bishop in Ephesus.

* Rudolf Steiner also spoke concerning the teachings of the Resurrected One: CW 211, April 13, 1922.

Timothy was not to abandon himself to the outer life but should build an inner life: "But you, a man of God, flee from that danger. Strive tirelessly on the path that leads to justice, to greater devotion, to faith, to love, to patience, to steadfastness, and gentleness. Fight the good fight in the battle for faith, take hold of eternal life, to which you have been called and for which you have made a good confession before many witnesses" (1 Tim. 6:11f).

In this way, the proto-congregation of priests is continually re-founding The Christian Community. Because of the clear alignment of their united willing, this community of priests can serve as a vessel for the substance of the sacraments. Thus we can rely on the spiritual objectivity of the sacraments, i.e., they do bless, as they are brought into the world of earth following the will of the spiritual world. It is not the individual priest who guarantees this because of some ostensible *sacred authority*, but the community. Therein lies the secret of community, that weaknesses of individual members can be compensated through it. As long as the community of priests sustains an individual priest, he or she will be able to effectively administer the sacraments. However, this community also has the responsibility to determine the moment when an individual can no longer be sustained because they have in fact detached themselves from the community, even if they themselves interpret their situation differently. There can be no transition between *inside* and *outside*, between belonging to the community and standing outside it, but only a clear either/or. It follows that as long as The Christian Community is truly alive and the proto-community supervises those who celebrate the sacraments to confirm that they are really within the community, we can trust in the spiritual objectivity of the sacraments. The strength of the community is then greater than the weakness of individuals. The same can also be said of individual congregations. Here too, the congregation carries the weaknesses of an individual and—as a congregation—contributes to the objectivity of the sacraments. For with the renewed sacraments as celebrated in The Christian Community the priest is not the only member possessing agency. In an essential way, the congregation itself also bears responsibility for initiating and sustaining through its inner activity the sacramental stream of blessing.

The objectivity of the sacraments is grounded in the Catholic church through its understanding of sacramental authority based on *ex opere operato.* Objectivity, however, can also be based on a community process if that community is constituted in such a way that it can be a source of supra-personal spiritual action. If those involved truly want community as it is described above, *in a threefold way*, the community will be able to transform the personal willing of individuals into supra-personal spiritual action.

This presents us with a picture of a new church with a new form of community. We have already spoken of old and new communities in the section on infant Baptism. The proto-congregation and all other congregations of The Christian Community are constituted in this way where the *interests of the individual* are *not* to be sacrificed to the community, but conversely, the community is formed out of the individually willed intentions of its members. However, in order to survey the historical development leading to this new form of community, it is not enough merely to look back at the ancient forms and then look from there to the new communities.

The actual origin of earthly human beings precedes the

most ancient communities as imagined in nature or, speaking biblically, in the garden of Eden. The greatest wisdom can be found in the processes of nature: just as animals can leave themselves entirely to the wise guidance of their instincts, the human being was also originally guided by wisdom in every manifestation of life, albeit not an individualized type of wisdom. This paradisiacal original state was ended by Lucifer's intervention, whereby humans lost the quality of a *natural being*. One must see this clearly: of course, we still participate, to some extent, in nature. We still have *natural* needs, like eating, sleeping, moving, etc. Nevertheless, in our essential being we no longer feel that the natural world is our true home; *we must form our own human realm*. The thought that we could return to nature is an illusion and not a possibility for us anyway. If we cannot maintain our position above nature, we actually sink below it; when we simply surrender ourselves to nature, there are no good outcomes. Goethe expressed this thought in *Faust* when, in the Prologue in Heaven, he had Mephisto say about the human being:

> He would live a little better,
> If you had not given him heavenly light
> to shine upon him
> He calls it reason and needs it alone,
> Only to be more animal than any animal. (283–86)

If we wish to return to nature while employing our reason, then reason allows us to refine our pleasures without bound and causes us to become "more animal than the animals."

The first form of the human kingdom Rudolf Steiner characterized with his "Fundamental Social Law": As human culture begins, humanity strives to create social associations."

Outside the "garden," culture begins, bringing with it those "social associations" that give rise to the first forms of morality. These laws—both social and legal—lead human beings from the outside. In the end, we will free ourselves from these communities in a way that is spiritually legitimate. We will then have to add to this outer liberation, which will come of itself, true inner freedom, which can only arise through our own activity. Only then can we really become free individuals. In *The Philosophy of Freedom*, Steiner summarized these three phases of development:

> Nature makes human beings merely natural creatures; society makes them law-abiding actors; but only they can make themselves into free beings. At a certain stage of their development, nature releases human beings from her chains; society carries this development up to a further point; but human beings must give themselves the final polish."*

At the transition from nature to society we find the work of Lucifer. The transition from the old forms of community to true human autonomy succeeds only when isolation is not the only result of this lawful development, but when the human being gives himself *the finishing touch* in this process of becoming a free being. But it would be an illusion to believe that we alone would have the strength for this final touch. Just as the figure of Lucifer stands at the transition from nature to society, so Christ accompanies the transition to free individuality. He helps us, but not from the outside, which would mean taking our agency away from us. As we discussed in the last section, he does not act other than to strengthen human wills and therefore, protect our freedom.

* Steiner, CW 4, *Intuitive Thinking as a Spiritual Path*, p. 159.

At this third stage, then, there are human beings who appear as individuals who have been *liberated from external constraints*. And then there are people who additionally have gained *inner freedom and autonomy* through the help of Christ Jesus. These are the "true Christians" spoken of in the Offertory in the Act of Consecration. This freedom is only gradually becoming accessible to human beings of the present; we are still at the beginning. Nevertheless, it must be said that this epoch of freedom was already heralded two thousand years ago with the Resurrection of Jesus Christ.

And then we behold two further epochs ahead of us: a time in which communities of a completely new kind will again be formed, beyond the isolation of individuals. We have called them Christian communities. Finally, from these communities there will emanate a power to bring forth a completely new natural world, a *human* natural world. One could also call it a natural world transformed by humanity—nature that has gone through a process similar to that undergone by bread and wine at the altar during the transubstantiation. Paul speaks of Nature's longing for transformation: "All around us creation waits with great longing for the sons of God to begin shining forth in humankind. Creation has become transitory, not through its own doing, but because of him who has dragged it down with him, and so everything in it is filled with a longing for the future. For the breath of freedom is to pass through creation too; the tyranny of transience is to cease" (Rom. 8:19ff). (This was discussed in section 2.3 concerning sacramentals.)

We can point to five great epochs of human development. The first three occurred without our active engagement; over time we have become individuals and active agents. From now on, however, these future epochs will become a reality only through conscious human activity. This is the Christian era. It begins in the third epoch, as we begin to become free by providing *the finishing touch* ourselves—but the future is present already now in sacramental deeds.*

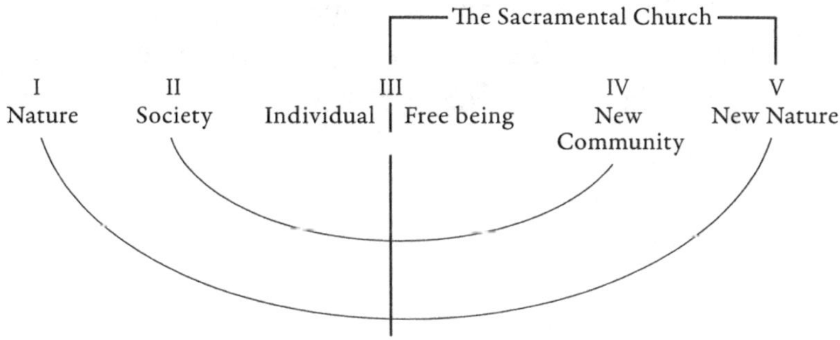

Congregations that arise through the sacraments are an image of future communities shining into the present. And the substance that arises through transubstantiation at the altar is the reality of future earth already working into the present. The sacraments, through which the future is already at work in the present, exist in their own layer of reality.

Ordinarily, we are aware of only two realities: the *physical world of the senses* and the *spiritual world* (matter and spirit). In sense reality we experience the present. The reality that will be given to us by our senses in the future can be found already now in the spiritual world, as pure spirit—as an intention, so to speak. Sacramental reality, however, lies in between. It brings the future into the present, not merely as spirit, but as reality given to us through our senses. It

* The path outlined here also applies, in a corresponding form, to the path of anthroposophy. See chapter 2.4, "Ritual and Sacrament in Anthroposophy."

works in the sense world, but purely spiritually. Between the sense world and the spiritual world there is therefore still the sacramental world as a separate, third layer of reality. Through it, we who live in the world of the senses are already connected to the future. The place where this reality appears is the Christian church with its sacraments. Already now, spiritually autonomous human beings, as well as the new communities of the future, as well as renewed nature, are all becoming reality through its sacraments.

Chronology

384–322 BC: Aristotle

AD?–110/117: Ignatius of Antioch

100–165: Justin Martyr

160–220: Tertullian

ca. 170–235: Hippolytus of Rome

200–258: Cyprian

205–270: Plotinus

?–355: Donatus of Carthage

354–430: Aurelius Augustine

5th–6th centuries: Dionysius Areopagita (Pseudo-Dionysius)

530–615: Columban the Younger

790–856/59: Paschasius Radbertus

810–877: John Scotus Eriugena

1000–1088: Berengar of Tours

1080–1154: Gilbert of Poitiers

1100–1160: Peter Lombard

1130–1205: Peter of Poitiers

1198–1216: Pope Innocent III (pontificate)

1170–1245: Alexander of Hales

1190–1263: Hugh of St. Cher

1225–1274: Thomas Aquinas

1270–1308: John Duns Scotus

1274: Council of Union of Lyon

1311/12: Council of Vienne

1439: Doctrinal Decree for the Armenians

1483–1546: Martin Luther

1493–1541: Theophrastus Paracelsus

1545–1563: Council of Trent

1646–1716: Gottfried Wilhelm Leibniz

1729–1781: Gotthold Ephraim Lessing

1749–1832: Johann Wolfgang von Goethe

1861–1925: Rudolf Steiner

1872–1938: Friedrich Rittelmeyer

1886–1948: Odo Casel

1895–1959: Emil Bock

1900–1972: Gottfried Husemann

1901–1986: Rudolf Frieling

1922: Foundation of The Christian Community

1962–1965: Second Vatican Council (Vatican II)

Bibliography

Michael Debus references numerous volumes in The Collected Works of Rudolf Steiner by "CW number." Efforts to translate the collected works are ongoing. A list of those titles follows this bibliography, as well as titles for available English translations.

Adam, Adolf. *Sinn und Gestalt der Sakramente*. Würzburg 1975.

———. *Grundriss der Liturgie*. Freiburg 1992.

Auer, Johann, and Joseph Ratzinger. *Kleine Katholische Dogmatik*, Band VI (1974) und VII (1979). Regensburg.

Barfield, Owen. History in English Words. Hudson, NY: Lindisfarne Books, 2002.

———. *Saving the Appearances: A Study in Idolatry*. Middletown, CT: Wesleyan University Press, 1988.

Beckh, Hermann. *Alchymie. Vom Geheimnis der Stoffeswelt*. Dornach 1987.

Birnbaum, Walter. *Das Kultusproblem und die liturgischen Bewegungen des 20. Jahrhunderts*. Tübingen 1970.

Bock, Emil. *Das Neue Testament in der Übersetzung von Emil Bock* (cf. epilogue). Stuttgart 1983.

Arie Boogert. *Der Weg der Seele nach dem Tod*. Stuttgart 2005

Daems, Willem F. *Denn der Himmel ist der Mensch und der Mensch ist der Himmel. Paracelsia*, Dornach 1993.

Dausend, Hugo. *Die Sakramentalien*. Düsseldorf 1930.

Debus, Michael. *Anthroposophie und die Erneuerung der christlichen Kirche*. Stuttgart 1989.

———. *Mary and Sophia: The Feminine Element in the Spiritual Evolution of Humanity*. Edinburgh: Floris Books, 2013.

Debus, Michael / G. Kačer. *Das Handeln im Umkreis des Todes*. Hrsg. Anthroposophische Gesellschaft Stuttgart 1999.

Dogmatic Constitution on Divine Revelation. Nov. 18, 1965.

Evangelischer Oberkirchenrat Stuttgart (Hrsg.). *Zur Frage der Christlichkeit der Christengemeinschaft*. Filderstadt 2004.

Finkenzeller, J. *Lexikon für Theologie und Kirche*. Freiburg 1958, 1965.

Fischer, Engelbert. *Die Menschenweihehandlung—was ist das?* Stuttgart 2002.

Frieling, Rudolf. *Die sieben Sakramente in der Geschichte der Christenheit.* Stuttgart 2001.

Gädeke, Rudolf. *Die Gründer der Christengemeinschaft.* Dornach 1992.

Gädeke, Wolfgang. *Ehe, Sehnsucht–Idee–Wirklichkeit.* Stuttgart 2006.

Ganoczy, Alexandre. *Einführung in die katholische Sakramentenlehre.* Darmstadt 1979.

Goebel, Robert. *Schelling, Künder einer neuen Epoche des Christentums.* Stuttgart 1975.

Goethe, Johann Wolfgang von. *Aus meinem Leben: Dichtung und Wahrheit* (From my life: Poetry and truth), 1811–1833.

Hahn, Herbert. *Von den Quellkräften der Seele.* Arlesheim 1959.

Handbuch der Kirchengeschichte. Freiburg/Br. 1985.

Harlan, Volker. *Das Bild der Pflanze in Wissenschaft und Kunst.* Stuttgart 2001.

Harrison, C. G. *The Transcendental Universe: Six Lectures on Occult Science, Theosophy, and the Catholic Faith.* Hudson, NY: Lindisfarne Books, 1993.

Hotz, Robert. *Sakramente im Wechselspiel zwischen Ost und West.* Zürich-Köln 1979.

Kaiser, Günther. "Jugend als gesellschaftliches Massenphänomen." In H. Schäfer (Hrsg.). *Gewaltkriminalität Minderjähriger.* Bd. 1. Heidelberg 1979.

Kurras, Eberhard. *Christus-Erfahrungen. Petrus—Paulus Johannes.* Stuttgart 1975.

Lenz, Johannes. *Das Ereignis des Todes.* Stuttgart 1997.

———. *Der Gottesdienst für die Kinder.* Stuttgart 1999.

———. *Die Konfirmation.* Stuttgart 2000.

———. *Lebensgemeinschaft und Trauung.* Stuttgart 1993.

———. *Die Menschenweihehandlung.* Stuttgart 1999.

———. *Die neue Beichte.* Stuttgart 1983.

———. *Priestertum im 20. Jahrhundert.* Stuttgart 1988.

———. *Die Taufe.* Stuttgart 1995.

Lexikon für Theologie und Kirche (LThK²). Freiburg/Br. 1986.

Lexikon für Theologie und Kirche (LThK³). Freiburg/Br. 1995.

Lin, Jean-Claude. *Wirken im Zeichen von Kunst. Wissenschaft und Religion.* Stuttgart 1999.

Lorenz, Rudolf. *Die Religion in Geschichte und Gegenwart,* vol. 1. Tübingen 1968.

Maas, Wilhelm. *Menschenweihehandlung und römische Messe. Rudolf Frielings "Messe-Studien" im Gespräch mit der katholischen Liturgiewissenschaft.* Stuttgart 1999 (unpublished).

Meyer, Rudolf. *Zur Erlösung der Tierwelt.* Stuttgart 1970.

Mirbt, Carl. *Quellen zur Geschichte des Papsttums und des Römischen Katholizismus*. Tübingen 1924.

Neuner, Josef, and Heinrich Roos. *Der Glaube der Kirche in den Urkunden der Lehrverkündigung*. Regensburg 1971.

Paungarten, Ferdinand von (ed.). *Das Eheproblem im Spiegel unserer Zeit. Äußerungen bekannter Persönlichkeiten zu dieser Frage*. Munich 1913.

Piault, Bernard. *Was ist ein Sakrament*? Aschaffenburg 1964.

Rau, Christoph (ed.). *Vom Kultuserleben*. Stuttgart 1983.

Reitzenstein, Richard. Hellenistic Mystery-Religions: Their Basic Ideas and Significance. Eugene, OR: Wipf and Stock, 1978.

Religion in Geschichte und Gegenwart (RGG[3]). Tübingen 1956, 1965.

Rittelmeyer, Friedrich. *Rudolf Steiner Enters My Life*. Edinburgh: Floris Books, 2013.

Sam, Martina Maria. *Im Ringen um eine neue Sprache*. Dornach 2004; in English: *The Challenge of Spiritual Language: Rudolf Steiner's Linguistic Style*. Forest Row, UK: Rudolf Steiner Press, 2020.

Scheffler, Armin. *Die Alchemie der Jahreszeiten. Betrachtung zu den Jahreszeiten-Imaginationen Rudolf Steiners*. Stuttgart 1998.

Schmaus, Michael. *Katholische Dogmatik*, Bd. III/2. Munich 1941.

Schroeder, Hans-Werner. *Die Christengemeinschaft. Entstehung–Entwicklung–Zielsetzung*. Stuttgart 2001.

———. *Vom Erleben der Menschenweihehandlung*. Stuttgart 1997.

———. *Der kosmische Christus*. Stuttgart 1995; in English: The Cosmic Christ. Edinburgh: Floris Books, 1997.

Schühle, Erwin. *Entscheidung für das Christentum der Zukunft*. Stuttgart 1969.

Skinner, Frederic (B. F.). *Jenseits von Freiheit und Würde*. Hamburg 1973 (in English: *Beyond Freedom and Dignity*. Indianapolis: Hackett, 1971.

Sloan, Douglas. *The Redemption of the Animals: Their Evolution, Their Inner Life, and Our Future Together*. Great Barrington, MA: Lindisfarne Books, 2015.

Stählin, Wilhelm. *Berneuchen antwortet*. Kassel-Wilhelmshöhe, Germany: Johannes Stauda-Verlag, 1939.

Teichmann, Frank. "Die Entstehung des Entwicklungsgedankens in der Goethezeit." In Wolfgang H. Arnold (ed.). *Entwicklung. Interdisziplinäre Aspekte zur Evolutionsfrage*. Stuttgart 1989.

Thiede, Werner. *Wer ist der kosmische Christus?* Göttingen 2001.

Vorgrimler, Herbert. *Sakramententheologie*. Düsseldorf 1987.

Wenz, Gunther. *Einführung in die evangelische Sakramentenlehre*. Darmstadt 1988.

Cited Titles from The Collected Works of Rudolf Steiner

Works not available in English translations are identified by their original German titles.

CW 1 *Nature's Open Secret: Introductions to Goethe's Scientific Writings* (Anthroposophic Press, 2000).

CW 2 *Goethe's Theory of Knowledge: An Outline of the Epistemology of His Worldview* (SteinerBooks, 2008).

CW 4 *Intuitive Thinking as a Spiritual Path: A Philosophy of Freedom* (Anthroposophic Press, 1995).

CW 6 *Goethe's World View* (Mercury Press, 1985).

CW 8 *Christianity as Mystical Fact: And the Mysteries of Antiquity* (SteinerBooks, 2006).

CW 9 *Theosophy: An Introduction to the Spiritual Processes in Human Life and in the Cosmos* (Anthroposophic Press, 1994).

CW 10 *How to Know Higher Worlds: A Modern Path of Initiation* (Anthroposophic Press, 1994).

CW 11 *Cosmic Memory: The Story of Atlantis, Lemuria, and the Division of the Sexes* (SteinerBooks, 2020).

CW 13 *An Outline of Esoteric Science* (Anthroposophic Press, 1997).

CW 14 *Four Mystery Dramas* (SteinerBooks, 2014).

CW 15 *The Spiritual Guidance of the Individual and Humanity: Some Results of Spiritual-Scientific Research into Human History and Development* (Anthroposophic Press, 1992).

CW 18 *The Riddles of Philosophy: Presented in an Outline of Its History* (SteinerBooks, 2009).

CW 23 *Towards Social Renewal* (Rudolf Steiner Press, 2000).

CW 26 *The Michael Mystery* (SteinerBooks, 1984).

CW 28 *Autobiography: Chapters in the Course of My Life, 1861–1907* (SteinerBooks, 2000).

CW 31 *Gesammelte Aufsätze zur Kultur- und Zeitgeschichte 1887–1901* (Collected essays on culture and current events 1887–1901).

CW 34 *Lucifer–Gnosis; Grundlegende Aufsätze zur Anthroposophie und Berichte aus den Zeitschriften «Luzifer» und «Lucifer–Gnosis» 1903–1908* (Lucifer-Gnosis: Foundational essays on anthroposophy and reports from the periodicals *Lucifer* and *Lucifer–Gnosis*, 1903–1908).

CW 38 *Briefe Band I: 1881–1890* (Letters, vol. 1: 1881–1890).

CW 39 *Briefe Band II: 1890–1925* (Letters, vol. 2: 1890–1925).

CW 53 *Ursprung und Ziel des Menschen* (The origin and goal of humanity).

CW 56 *Die Erkenntnis der Seele und des Geistes* (Knowledge of the soul and spirit).

CW 59 *Transforming the Soul*, vol. 2 (Rudolf Steiner Press, 2006).

CW 60 *Antworten der Geisteswissenschaft auf die großen Fragen des Daseins* (Answers of spiritual science to the greatest questions of existence).

CW 64 *Aus schicksaltragender Zeit* (From a destiny-burdened time).

CW 67 *Das Ewige in der Menschenseele. Unsterblichkeit und Freiheit* (The eternal in the human soul. Immortality and freedom).

CW 72 *Freiheit – Unsterblichkeit – Soziales* Leben (Freedom – Immortality – Social Life).

CW 77b *Kunst und Anthroposophie. Der Goetheanum-Impuls* (Art and Anthroposophy. The Goetheanum impulse).

CW 78 *Anthroposophie, ihre Erkenntnis Wurzeln und Lebensfrüchte* (Anthroposophy, its knowledge of roots and the fruits of life).

CW 79 *Die Wirklichkeit der höheren Welten* (The reality of the higher worlds).

CW 92 *Die okkulten Wahrheiten alter Mythen und Sagen* (The esoteric truths of ancient myths and legends).

CW 93a *Foundations of Esotericism* (Rudolf Steiner Press, 2019).

CW 94 *An Esoteric Cosmology: Evolution, Christ, and Modern Spirituality* (SteinerBooks, 2008).

CW 96 *Original Impulses for the Science of the Spirit: Christian Esotericism in the Light of New Spiritual Insights* (Completion Press, 2005).

CW 97 *Das christliche Mysterium* (The Christian mystery).

CW 98 *Natur- und Geistwesen - ihr Wirken in unserer sichtbaren Welt* (Nature and spirit beings: Their work in our visible world).

CW 104 *The Apocalypse of St. John: Lectures on the Book of Revelation* (Anthroposophic Press, 1985).

CW 107 *Disease, Karma, and Healing: Spiritual-Scientific Enquiries into the Nature of the Human Being* (Rudolf Steiner Press, 2013).

CW 112 *The Gospel of St. John and Its Relation to the Other Gospels* (Anthroposophic Press, 1994).

CW 123 *According to Matthew: The Gospel of Christ's Humanity* (SteinerBooks, 2002).

CW 127 *The Mission of the New Spirit of Revelation: The Pivotal Nature of the Christ Event in Earth Evolution* (Rudolf Steiner Press, 2021).

CW 131 *From Jesus to Christ* (Rudolf Steiner Press, 1991).

CW 144 *The Mysteries of Initiation: From Isis to the Holy Grail* (Rudolf Steiner Press, 2021).

CW 145 *The Effects of Esoteric Development* (Anthroposophic Press, 1997).

CW 149 *Christ and the Spiritual World: And the Search for the Holy Grail* (Rudolf Steiner Press, 2008).

CW 151 *Human and Cosmic Thought* (Rudolf Steiner Press, 1961).

CW 153 *The Inner Nature of Man: And Our Life between Death and Rebirth* (Rudolf Steiner Press, 2013).

CW 155 *The Spiritual Foundation of Morality: Francis of Assisi and the Christ Impulse* (Anthroposophic Press, 1995).

CW 162 *Kunst- und Lebensfragen im Lichte der Geisteswissenschaft* (Art and life questions in the light of spiritual science).

CW 166 *Necessity and Freedom* (Anthroposophic Press, 1989).

CW 167 *The Human Spirit: Past and Present – Occult Fraternities and the Mystery of Golgotha* (Rudolf Steiner Press, 2016).

CW 175 *Building Stones for an Understanding of the Mystery of Golgotha: Human Life in a Cosmic Context* (Rudolf Steiner Press, 2015).

CW 182 *Death as Metamorphosis of Life: Including "What Does the Angel Do in Our Astral Body?" and "How Do I Find Christ?"* (SteinerBooks, 2008).

CW 186 *The Challenge of the Times* (Anthroposophic Press, 1979).

CW 187 *How Can Mankind Find the Christ Again? The Threefold Shadow-Existence of Our Time and the New Light of Christ* (Anthroposophic Press, 1984).

CW 193 *The Esoteric Aspect of the Social Question: The Individual and Society* (Rudolf Steiner Press, 2001).

CW 196 *What Is Necessary in these Urgent Times* (SteinerBooks, 2010).

CW 211 *The Sun Mystery and the Mystery of Death and Resurrection: Exoteric and Esoteric Christianity* (SteinerBooks, 2006).

CW 216 *Die Grundimpulse des weltgeschichtlichen Werdens der Menschheit* (The basic impulses of the world-historical development of humanity).

CW 217 *Becoming the Archangel Michael's Companions: Rudolf Steiner's Challenge to the Younger Generation* (SteinerBooks, 2006).

CW 218 *Waldorf Education and Anthroposophy 2* (Anthroposophic Press, 1996).

CW 219 *Man and the World of the Stars: The Spiritual Communion of Mankind* (Anthroposophic Press, 1982).

CW 220 *Awake! For the Sake of the Future* (SteinerBooks, 2014).

CW 222 *The Driving Force of Spiritual Powers in World History* (Steiner Book Centre, 1972).

CW 224 *Die menschliche Seele in ihrem Zusammenhang mit göttlich-geistigen Individualitäten. Die Verinnerlichung der Jahresfeste* (The human soul in its connection with divine spiritual individualities. The internalization of the annual festivals).

CW 229 *Das Miterleben des Jahreslaufes in vier kosmischen Imaginationen* (Experiencing the course of the year in four cosmic imaginations).

CW 237 *Karmic Relationships 3: Esoteric Studies* (Rudolf Steiner Press, 1977).

CW 240 *Karmic Relationships 2: Esoteric Studies* (Rudolf Steiner Press, 1974).

CW 254 *The Occult Movement in the Nineteenth Century and Its Relation to Modern Culture* (Rudolf Steiner Press, 1973).

CW 257 *Awakening to Community* (Anthroposophic Press, 1975).

CW 262 *Correspondence and Documents 1901–1925* (Anthroposophic Press, 1988).

CW 264 *From the History and Contents of the First Section of the Esoteric School: Letters, Documents, and Lectures: 1904–1914* (SteinerBooks, 2010).

CW 266/2 *Esoteric Lessons 1910–1912: From the Esoteric School* (SteinerBooks, 2012).

CW 268 *Mantric Sayings: Meditations 1903–1925* (SteinerBooks, 2015).

CW 269 *Ritualtexte für die Feiern des freien christlichen Religionsunterrichts. Das Sprachgut für Lehrer und Schüler der Waldorfschule* (Ritual texts for the celebrations of free

Christian religious instruction. Collected verses for teachers and pupils of the Waldorf school).

CW 318 *Broken Vessels: The Spiritual Structure of Human Frailty* (SteinerBooks, 2002).

CW 333 *Freedom of Thought and Societal Forces: Implementing the Demands of Modern Society* (SteinerBooks, 2008).

CW 342 *First Steps in Christian Religious Renewal: Preparing the Ground for The Christian Community* (SteinerBooks, 2010).

CW 343 *Vorträge und Kurse über christlich-religiöses Wirken, Bd.2 Spirituelles Erkennen–Religiöses Empfinden–Kultisches Handeln* (Lectures and courses on Christian religious work, vol. 2: Spiritual knowledge–religious feeling–cultic action).

CW 344 *Vorträge und Kurse über christlich-religiöses Wirken, Bd.3, Vorträge bei der Begründung der Christengemeinschaft* (Lectures and courses on Christian religious work, vol. 3: Lectures on establishing The Christian Community [to be published in English in 2022]).

CW 345 *Vorträge und Kurse über christlich-religiöses Wirken, Bd.4, Vom Wesen des wirkenden Wortes* (Lectures and courses on Christian religious work, vol. 4: On the essence of the active word).

CW 346 *The Book of Revelation: And the Work of the Priest* (Rudolf Steiner Press, 1999).

CW 353 *From Beetroot to Buddhism… Answers to Questions* (Rudolf Steiner Press, 1999).